TESTIMONY TO ISRAEL

CHAIM YEDIDIAH POLLAK
(A.K.A. THEOPHILUS LUCKY)

MESSIANIC
LUMINARIES
SERIES

TESTIMONY TO ISRAEL

CHAIM YEDIDIAH POLLAK
(A.K.A. THEOPHILUS LUCKY)

Excerpts from *Edut LeYisra'el*
Translated from the Hebrew by Jordan Gayle Levy

VINE OF DAVID

VINE OF DAVID

Testimony to Israel: Chaim Yedidiah Pollak (Theophilus Lucky)
Published 2016 by Vine of David, a publishing ministry of
First Fruits of Zion, Inc.

Design, editing, and compiling: Jerusalem, Israel
Printing and distribution: USA

Comments and questions may be sent to: feedback@vineofdavid.org

Vine of David is a publishing arm of the ministry of First Fruits of Zion dedicated to providing liturgical resources for the Messianic Jewish movement and to resurrecting the voices of Messianic pioneers and luminaries. If you would like to assist in the publication of these voices from the past, you can sponsor the translation and publication of their important works by visiting www.vineofdavid.org for needs and opportunities.

The Bram Center for Messianic Jewish Learning is in the heart of Jerusalem. Short term learning, day tours, or to visit The Bram Center please write to: info@thebramcenter.org.

Vine of David
Israel / United States / Canada

US Distribution: PO Box 649, Marshfield, Missouri 65706-0649 USA
Phone (417) 468-2741, www.ffoz.org

ISBN: 978-1-941534-18-2

Also available from Vine of David:
The Siege of Jerusalem
Window on Mount Zion
The Delitzsch Hebrew Gospels: A Hebrew / English Translation
Love and the Messianic Age
Love and the Messianic Age: Study Guide and Commentary
The Everlasting Jew

First Fruits of Zion: www.ffoz.org
Vine of David: www.vineofdavid.org

CONTENTS

שֶׁשָׁם עָלוּ שְׁבָטִים, שִׁבְטֵי־יָהּ,
עֵדוּת לְיִשְׂרָאֵל, לְהֹדוֹת לְשֵׁם ה׳

For there the tribes, the tribes
of HaShem—*a testimony to Israel*—go up
to give thanks to the name of HaShem.

—Psalm 122:4

CHAIM YEDIDIAH POLLAK
(A.K.A. THEOPHILUS LUCKY)

ACKNOWLEDGEMENTS

Numerous people have contributed toward the creation of this book. Thanks to Raymond Lillevik for composing the biography of Lucky that appears in this book. We are also grateful for his thorough research into nineteenth-century Jewish believers and into the life and teaching of Theophilus Lucky. See his book *Apostates, Hybrids, or True Jews: Jewish Christians and Jewish Identity in Eastern Europe 1860–1914* (Eugene, OR: Pickwick Publications, 2014).

Thanks to Jordan Gayle Levy, for whom the long hours translating Lucky's nineteenth-century Hebrew has been an act of love. Your dedication to this project has kept it going. May the merit of your labor be a blessing.

Thanks to D.T. Lancaster and Sheldon Wilson for their insightful input, suggestions, and clarifications on Lucky's material.

Thanks to Hilary Le Cornu for sharing her translations.

Thanks to the team at Caspari Center and Israelsmissionen for helping us find the photographs.

Thanks to Boaz Michael and the whole team at Vine of David and First Fruits of Zion.

Finally, thanks to all of our *FFOZ Friends*. Without your generous support, this project, and others like it, would not be possible at all.

A FRIEND OF HASHEM

TRANSLATOR'S FOREWORD BY JORDAN GAYLE LEVY

In Hebrew, the name Yedidiah means "friend of HaShem" or "beloved of HaShem." A truly intimate friend is someone who is very close, someone privy to intimate secrets, privileged information, and one to whom everything is explained in clear detail. Such was God's apparent relationship with Chaim Yedidiah Pollak (Yedidiah ben Aharon), also called Theophilus Lucky, whose name aptly described his connection with HaShem. Yedidiah's writings speak to us of deep, complex, theological and soteriological topics with simple clarity and sure authority as someone who received these words whispered into his ears and heart by HaShem himself, his beloved friend.

Pollak, popularly known as Lucky, did not shy away from difficult topics or strong pronouncements in his divinely imparted confidence. His wording is specific, as was the audience whom he addressed. He speaks to us, the Jewish people, whether we are disciples of Yeshua or not, with firm words of warning, stern rebukes, and deep, affectionate love. His heart for Israel pulsates in his words, and his love for the Jewish people saturates every page of his writings. He wants us—Israel—to behold our Messiah, Yeshua of Nazareth, and allow him to spur us to greater passion for our religion, calling, and covenant responsibility. He wants us to see the destruction that our disobedience to the Torah and our rejection of the one whom HaShem sent to us has incurred. He wants us to return to the former glory of bygone days: dwelling securely in the land, the head of the nations, serving HaShem in love. These things will surely come, according to Lucky, once the entire Jewish nation accepts her Messiah.

As a Messianic Jew, I could not help but feel new-found inspiration when reading and translating Lucky's words. His conviction is unwavering, his allegiance to the Messiah is indisputable and unmistakable. Amidst his unbridled passion for Messiah, he retains his Jewish observance, teaching us how to do so while keeping Messiah as the absolute focal point, mediator, and cause of that observance. He stands out as a wise father of Messianic Judaism, illuminating a path of observance to the Torah of Moses and the Testimony of Yeshua, a path that was most certainly unpopular among both Jews and Christians in his day. Even today, more than a century later, we find this path scarcely trodden. Yet we can look to Yedidiah as our spirited guide and forerunner.

RESURRECTING THE TESTIMONY TO ISRAEL

This anthology is comprised of articles that originally appeared in the nineteenth-century Messianic Jewish periodical *Edut LeYisra'el*. Lucky wrote, edited, and published the journal over the course of approximately ten years. The majority of the original articles featured in the periodical were his own, some written under his own name, others under pseudonyms.

We have chosen to name this anthology after the title that Lucky gave to his journal: "Testimony to Israel" (*Edut LeYisra'el*). It seemed only natural since all the articles came directly from this journal and because the core message in every article testifies to Israel that Yeshua is the long-awaited Jewish Messiah. There could be no better title for the anthology than the one Lucky himself chose. This title is more than just name, rather it is a vocation and commission.

Almost all of his major articles have been translated and represented in this anthology. Lucky wrote entirely in Hebrew, which in itself was a great innovative feat for the time, considering that the Jewish *lingua franca* of the day was Yiddish, as Hebrew had not yet fully undergone its modern revival.

Characteristic of nineteenth-century rhetorical flourish, Yedidiah is very dramatic in his wording, and he uses everything in his power to articulate both his passionate love for his Jewish brothers and his absolute conviction that Israel must recognize Yeshua as the promised Messiah. His voice almost jumps off the page. My translation will occasionally employ archaic, dramatic English phrasing in an attempt to convey the authentic sound of Lucky's vibrant Hebrew voice.

Lucky also wrote poetry, and his strongest pieces appear in this work. Translating poetry literally, word for word and thought for thought, is very difficult and nearly impossible when trying to convey the ornamentation of the original rhythmic flow and rhyming couplets. My translation takes creative license in order to retain a sense of the lyrical quality in English. All poems appear in the Hebrew as they were originally written, with the exception of the lengthiest poem, "Words of Peace and Truth," which was edited down slightly.

All translations of the Old and New Testament passages cited by Lucky are my own, although I consulted various translations such as the Jewish Publication Society (JPS), Artscroll Stone Edition Tanach, Delitzsch Hebrew Gospels (DHE), English Standard Version (ESV), and the New American Standard Bible (NASB). In addition, all translations of Jewish literature quotations are also my own, also consulting common English translations such as Artscroll or Soncino. I chose to offer my own translations of biblical passages to facilitate the discussion. The specific ideas and nuances that Lucky attempts to convey are not always captured by conventional English Bible translations. Also, many of the passages he cites include his own embellished paraphrases of the biblical text. He will even add or change words in these verses, either as modes of clarification or as a method of manipulating the text—as is customary amongst Jewish expositors—to offer his own interpretation.

The footnotes are Lucky's own, and they are just as vibrant and informative as the main body of the text. However, Vine of David has supplied footnotes that appear in square brackets [like this], most of them consisting of my translation notes or additional explanations. Some of the documentation merely provides references to passages of Scripture, Jewish literature, or liturgy, which Lucky alludes to but neglects to cite. In other notes I attempt to show the reader the Hebrew word, phrase, or pun that Lucky specifically uses to make a particular point, a point that would be entirely lost in the English translation. I also provided clarifications for the reader to assist in understanding Lucky's commentary, theological stances, as well as descriptions of people, places, things, or events that Lucky offhandedly mentions in the assumption that his audience consists of religiously experienced, well-educated Jews of the late 1800s.

A SAGE IN ISRAEL

When translating Yedidiah's articles, his work astonished me with their layered depth. I loved his descriptions of difficult theological paradigms and problems, which are still relevant for the Messianic Jewish movement today. For example, he creatively handled the subject of the divine nature of the Messiah using the Torah, Jewish literature, and his version of common sense to better communicate a concept that has typically been misunderstood and deemed heretical (even idolatrous) in Jewish camps for millennia. Lucky shows us a perspective that helps answer the objections.

The words of the Nazarene have often been difficult pills for Jewish readers to swallow, especially as they have been so often misinterpreted by both Jewish and Christian commentary. Lucky attempts to clarify the teachings of Yeshua in their original context by drawing from the broader world of Jewish thought. He explains such passages as the Sermon on the Mount with sharp precision, introducing ideas and perspectives on Yeshua's core teachings at which Messianic Judaism is only now beginning to arrive more than a hundred years later. Reading Lucky's interpretations and paraphrases is exciting, as if a floodlight has been turned on in a dimly lit room, dispelling confusion.

Also remarkable for such an early period in the development of Messianic Judaism, Lucky seems to grasp the spiritual inclusion of Gentiles, whom he dubs "uncircumcised proselytes." Granted, his perspective on the Gentile inclusion is different than the perspectives we discuss today, for institutional Messianic Judaism as we know it did not yet exist. Nevertheless, he has a high view of his Gentile Christian co-religionists and their historical emergence within the Jewish monotheistic faith. He values their inclusion and distinction as decreed in the Jerusalem Council, and he recognizes the unprecedented work of God in bringing the nations near to himself through the Messiah. While Lucky never speaks directly to Gentile believers (his assumed readership was entirely and exclusively Jewish), he does eagerly invoke the Gentile believers by name as a sign and testament proving to his Jewish readers that Yeshua is indeed Israel's Messiah.

Yedidiah was ahead of his time. He started down the path of Torah-observant, Messianic Judaism before such a thing was even deemed possible for a disciple of Yeshua. He blazed a trail along which we are still stumbling. He claimed allegiance to both Judaism and to the good news of Yeshua. Today's modern Messianic Jewish movement is just beginning to cautiously explore a path that Lucky and his disciples walked over a century ago. We are still processing the idea and defending the concept that these two identities need not be mutually exclusive. Yedidiah was truly a sage in Israel, and he stands as an illustrious teacher, elucidating many concepts and clarifying arguments that are still relevant in the Messianic Jewish conversation today.

Even recent Jewish scholarship will concur with Lucky on many points. Many scholars agree that there is nothing truly idolatrous or inherently "un-Jewish" in the New Testament's notion of a divine-like Messiah, or that Yeshua was indeed Torah observant, as were all his followers in the first century, or that Christianity began as a sect of Judaism that was almost exclusively Jewish at its inception. In the generation since World War II, both secular and religious Jewish scholars have conceded many of the arguments that Lucky championed before the turn of the last century. Ideas that at the time must have seemed radical are now mainstream among Jewish academia. That is not to say that Lucky has nothing new to contribute to the conversation today. Even though many of his views have been accepted by present day scholarship, he still lays claim to a few views that remain radical and compelling even today.

TRANSFIXED BY THE SAVIOR

However, we must not take Lucky out of his context and treat him merely as a scholar. The main thrust of his life was to call his Jewish brothers to a radical faith in the Galilean rabbi. In his view, therein lies the solution to every pain and suffering in Israel. Believing in the Messiah would not only revitalize the individual Jewish soul, but it would resurrect the glory of the Jewish nation and reestablish the Jewish land. Messiah is the focus of every word he writes. Messiah is all. Lucky never loses his sense of wonder and amazement over him. He remains perpetually transfixed by the Savior. To Lucky, belief in Yeshua and discipleship in him are matters of paramount importance for every Jew. Lucky's writings are not mere academics; they are rabbinic, pastoral, and devotional in nature. He called for radical reformation of Israel and every heart.

I am honored to contribute to his mission by giving Lucky his voice once again, and I am excited that Yedidiah ben Aharon's words will not fall into complete oblivion, only accessible to a Hebrew reader familiar with Biblical and Mishnaic Hebrew on the faded pages of century-old journals. God willing his words will be an encouragement and a challenge to us all: to Jewish readers—disciples of Yeshua or not—and Gentile believers in the Jewish Messiah. May the words of this intimate friend of HaShem endure as an important literary and theological addition to our Jewish heritage, and may they be a light to us for generations to come.

A LAMED-VAVNIK

HENRY EINSPRUCH[1]

Chaim Yedidiah Pollak was one of the most remarkable men I have ever known. Born in 1854 in a little village near Stanislau, Galicia, his father intended for him to become a rabbi, but, being left an orphan in childhood, he was reared by a relative.

Pollak enjoyed excellent educational advantages. He attended the University of Berlin, as well as Abraham Geiger's *Hochschule*, an academy for Jewish studies, and, before he reached the age of twenty-two, had received the degree of doctor of philosophy. He was a thorough Hebrew and Greek scholar; read Latin and French; spoke Polish, German, Yiddish, and English with ease. In his old age he mastered the Holland Dutch language to such an extent that he could preach and also write in it for the press. His linguistic versatility was little short of phenomenal. If he was not literally able to speak all languages it was only because he had never had occasion to use them all! He was also learned in most departments of knowledge: history, philosophy, theology, and literature.

While pursuing his studies Pollak became acquainted with the New Testament. He was struck by the pure Jewish character of the evangelist Matthew, and also felt himself attracted by the mysticism of John. In the course of his studies at Geiger's *Hochschule*, he discussed these

---

1   [Jewish believer best known for translating the New Testament into Yiddish.]

things with one of his teachers, Israel Levi. There was a heated discussion between them with the result that Pollak was dismissed from the school. Israel Levi is quoted as predicting, "Nothing good will come out of Pollak, and in the end he will be a most *unlucky* man."

Pollak never forgot that Levi had called him an "unlucky" man, and after he accepted Jesus as his Messiah, he changed his name from Chaim Yedidiah Pollak to Christian Theophilus Lucky—lucky, the fortunate one.

After completing his studies at the University of Berlin, he came to America and entered Union Theological Seminary in New York. On the voyage from London he met a man who had lost his coat. Lucky gave him eight dollars to buy a new one, which left him bankrupt in a strange land. This incident illustrates his characteristic generosity.

Upon graduation from Seminary with honors, Lucky was ordained to the Gospel ministry, and was associated with the Seventh Day Baptist Church. He felt the weight of the responsibility that lay upon his shoulders to carry the message of the Messiah to his brethren, but preferred to follow the method of St. Paul, which was to urge Jews to accept Jesus as Savior, and then allow them to observe their honored customs if they so desired.

Lucky had an ardent love for Israel and a deep regard for the laws of his fathers. He believed that a Jewish Christian should not forsake the holy Sabbath, the observance of the Jewish festivals, and the dietary laws. His diet was strictly kosher.

On Friday evenings he would always attend synagogue and heartily join in all the prayers. On Yom Kippur, the Day of Atonement, Lucky stayed in the synagogue all day and fasted. He also observed Tisha B'Av, the day on which the Temple was destroyed.

Lucky began the publication of a Hebrew paper entitled *Edut LeYisra'el*, "Testimony to Israel," mainly for educated Jews. His writings were in the purest Biblical and post-Biblical Hebrew, and his own thoughts were expressed with elegance, copiousness, and perspicuity. The renowned Hebrew scholar, Professor Franz Delitzsch, praised his knowledge of the Hebrew language and the genuine Christian spirit that permeated his writings. Some of his articles seemed to be suffused with a soul-enkindling spirituality. In everything he wrote, Christ was all.

There was scarcely a country in Europe where Lucky had not been. He labored in his native Galicia, as well as in Russia, Romania, Serbia, Germany, England, and Holland. He was acquainted with leading people in these countries, and had an extraordinary memory. His friends were his friends in a very personal way, and included Hebrew scholars and other Jews of note throughout Europe and America. Numbered among them were the late Dr. Solomon Schechter, the giant of Jewish scholars, down to many an obscure rabbi.

I first heard of Lucky in 1911 when I came upon his Hebrew journal, *Edut LeYisra'el*. The make-up of the paper greatly intrigued me, and a letter to the editor resulted in correspondence between us, which I still have among my prized possessions. I finally went to Stanislau and met Lucky face to face.

I shall never forget my meeting with him. He was intensely human and a brilliant conversationalist. While he was modest, he was not cringing or fawning. He had shapely hands, long artist's fingers, scrupulous personal cleanliness and neatness. Lucky was then about sixty years of age, and his gentle eyes, high forehead, and silvery white beard reminded me of a prophet of old. His instinctive refinement and aristocratic bearing and presence made an impression on me that I shall never forget.

Lucky was a man of simple life and utterly unselfish. He was a devoted follower of Christ, a man of gracious spirit, understood by few, loved by many. I soon realized that he was a learned man, equally at home in the Talmud and Bible, as well as in the whole range of Jewish literature. Scholars consulted him as an expert in Hebraica, and commanded his enthusiastic attention.

During our meeting I remarked that on my way to Stanislau I spoke with a Christian about the ideas propounded in *Edut LeYisra'el*. "How do you know he was a Christian?" Lucky asked. "The fact that one is a Gentile does not mean that he is a Christian."

When I questioned how he, a Jew, could believe in Jesus, a smile came over his face. "I have been asked this many times," he began, "and it is because I am a Jew, who conscientiously tries to live according to the Law of Moses and the prophets, that I believe the Messianic hope of Israel has been fulfilled in Jesus. Many call me a convert, a proselyte.

That is not true. I have not gone *over* to the Gentiles—Jesus is flesh of our flesh and bone of our bone."

"Are there many who hold your ideas?" I asked. Thoughtfully he replied, "There are quite a few." This was an understatement, for Lucky was the focal point of an active movement made up of rabbis, writers, and others who sought to restore Jesus into the Jewish framework.

He was a true and loyal son of Abraham. In early life he had committed to memory the Old Testament in Hebrew. A friend opened the Hebrew Old Testament to one of the prophets and challenged him, but Lucky said, "Start it for me." After a few words, he continued the chapter and repeated it to the end.

Lucky passed away at the beginning of World War I. His followers, though accepting the Messiahship of Jesus, never severed their connection with the Jewish community, and many perished in the Hitler Holocaust.

A critical Jewish writer, Samuel Freuder, makes the following comment: "Lucky was a Jewish missionary and an honest man; a strange creature indeed... Yet, as the Talmud has it, 'A myrtle among weeds remains a myrtle.' Lucky was absolutely truthful and honest... The townspeople did not look upon him with the usual feeling of hatred shown an apostate. Love begets love, and they knew how intense was his love for the Jewish people."

Professor M. Weisberg, author of *The History of Neo-Hebrew Literature,* who knew Lucky personally for fifteen years, refers to him as "a most interesting personality, and an idealist whom both Jews and Christians respected and loved. His manner of life was like that of a *Lamed-vavnik*"[2] (one of the thirty-six righteous men to whose piety, according to Jewish tradition, the world owes its continued existence).

Lucky died in 1916, at the age of sixty-two, and was buried in the Jewish cemetery at Plau, in Mecklenburg. To the many who knew him, his name will long be a fragrant benediction.

---

2   [Pronounced lah-med vahv-nick. The Hebrew letters *lamed* (ל) and *vav* (ו) have the numerical value of 36.]

CHRISTIAN THEOPHILUS
(CHAIM YEDIDIAH) LUCKY
IN THE LAST YEARS OF HIS LIFE (CIRCA 1915)

POLLAK-LUCKY, CHAIM ZEEV

YEDIDIAH TEOFIL (THEOPHILUS)[3]

פּוֹלַאק־לוקי חיים־זאב – ידידיה טעאָפיל

Born in Tysmienica 11 September 1854, died 25 November 1916.

Pollak Lucky was born to and raised by religious parents. He studied Torah in yeshivot and with rabbis in Hungary. In the year 1872 he traveled to Berlin. He studied at A. Geiger's seminary (*Hochschule*) and simultaneously studied in high school (*gymnasium*). In Berlin he changed his religion to Christianity according to his own outlook, which he described with the name "Assembly of the Messiah," a sect to which Torah-observant Jews who also believed in Jesus of Nazareth belonged. He secretly conducted missionary work and at the same time published articles in Hebrew periodicals that existed during that time. After he left Berlin he took up permanent residence in a town near Tysmenytsya, and from there he made a connection with the intellectuals of Tysmenytsya, and he even turned up there from time to time. Much later he became close with the authors of *Ha-Emet* (The Truth) belonging to Aaron Samuel Liberman. He also assisted in publishing *HaKol* (The

---

3 Shlomo Blond, *Tismenitz: Sefer Yizkor* (Tel Aviv, Israel: Hamenora Publishing House, 1974). Translated from the Yiddish and Hebrew. This book is a memorial to all notable Jews of Tysmenytsya, Galicia.

Voice) in Yiddish. In the end, he was known for his missionary work. He went to America in 1882, opened a Christian theological institution (1885), and changed his name to Lucky. He began to publish a monthly journal called *Edut LeYisra'el*, and in it he circulated his ideas about Jesus of Nazareth (publishing sixteen journals).

Pollak Lucky had a strong grasp of the Hebrew language, and in spite of his views, he propagated the study of Hebrew. From time to time he would arrive in Tysmenytsya and spread his ideas about Jesus of Nazareth. In Knihinin (a village near Stanislau) a small sect of devoted adherents was founded, who were called *Luckianim*. World War I found him in Holland; from there he spread his ideas among the Jews of Western Europe. He showed a propensity toward Zionism, planning a visit to the land of Israel in order to spread his missionary views even there. While he was returning from Holland to Stanislau he fell ill, and his fellow adherents brought him to Berlin and they hospitalized him in the Ebenezer Hospital where he died. In accordance with his wishes, they buried him in a Jewish cemetery in the small provincial town of Mecklenburg-Plau.

CHRISTIAN
THEOPHILUS LUCKY

CHAIM YEDIDIAH POLLAK (1854–1916)
INTRODUCTION—RAYMOND LILLEVIK

I am a Hebrew and I fear the God of heaven. I am a Jew and behold, I observe the Torah, the written Torah and the oral Torah, and my soul is inextricably bound to Yeshua the Messiah. He is my life-breath, for he is my Savior King. He is the one HaShem sent to be the resurrection of the soul for anyone who is called "mortal" and to give us eternal life. I am a son of the Mosaic and Israelite faith, and behold, I am also a man of Messiah. I am a disciple of Moses and of the men of the Great Assembly and I am a disciple of Yeshua the Messiah and his apostles.[4]

Chaim Yedidiah Pollak, later known as Christian Theophilus Lucky (1854–1916), from modern-day Ukraine, was a gifted scholar of Jewish tradition who made a significant contribution to missions involved in Jewish evangelism. He was baptized and ordained in a Protestant denomination in the United States. He published mission periodicals for Jews both in Hebrew and English (*Edut LeYisra'el* and *The Peculiar People*), yet he fiercely criticized traditional mission work to the Jews. Lucky maintained that Jewish believers in Jesus should stay within the Jewish people and within traditional Jewish practice.

---

4   "Guarding the Testimony: Introduction."

As editor, activist, and preacher, he was a friend of missionaries but hostile to the theology and methodology of Christian mission societies toward Jews. He claimed that faith in Jesus was mandatory for every Jew, and embracing Jesus as Messiah became to him a core concept for Jewish and Torah-observant identity. Lucky was not the only Jewish believer in Jesus to advocate Jewish believers retaining Jewish identity, but, among Jewish-Christian theologians of his time (the last decades before World War I), he was probably the most controversial and radical voice to champion continuity between Judaism and Christianity, i.e., early Messianic Judaism.

Despite this radical position and its associated notoriety, the details of his own life, particularly how he became a believer in Jesus, remain in the shadows. Lucky's biography is obscured by markedly different versions of the story of how he became a disciple of Jesus. It is difficult to determine which of the conversion narratives is authentic. The primary source for the confusion is probably Lucky himself. Several of those who knew Lucky personally mention that he was reluctant to divulge private information.[5] Moses Löwen tells how, in 1890, Lucky persuaded him not to reveal how he had become a believer: *"Aber nicht war, du sagst es den Leuten jetzt nicht? Sie brauchen nicht alles zu wissen!"*[6] According to August Wiegand, in matters related to his personal life Lucky was practicing the Jewish proverb *"Megalleh tefach u-mekasseh tifchayim."*[7] He probably wanted to avoid being regarded as an apostate from Judaism and the Jewish people, but in any case, he was willing to adapt, use, or obscure his personal story for his own purposes.

---

5   The Norwegian missionary Gisle Johnson described him as a "strange man that it was extremely difficult to get a clear picture of, even for those who knew him." Johnson, "Fra vor missions fortid," 225.

6   "But please don't tell people about it, right? They don't need to know everything!" (Löwen, *Christian Theophilus Lucky*, 6).

7   "Show one palm, when hiding two palms" (Wiegand, *Chajim Jedidjah Lucky*, 46).

CHILDHOOD

Chaim (Wolf/Zeev) Yedidiah Pollak was born on September 11, 1854, in the small town of Tysmienica (Polish)/Tysmenitsa (Yiddish), close to Stanislau in Austrian Galicia, today part of western Ukraine.[8]

The majority of Galician Jews lived in close-knit communities and maintained a traditional economic and religious way of life until World War I.[9] They were mainly Yiddish-speaking, unassimilated, and relatively uninvolved politically.[10] Economically, the Jews were middle-class in a traditional agrarian community. Jews were over-represented in professions such as law, medicine, the arts, and journalism, but the majority lived in crushing poverty that forced many into prostitution or emigration.[11]

According to Löwen, the source that provides essential information about Lucky's closest family and his childhood, Lucky's parents were the shopkeepers Aaron and Esther Pollak.[12] Aaron was an old widower when he married the young Esther, and Chaim—later Theophilus Lucky—was their only son. Lucky never knew his father as Aaron died when he was very young. Thanks to income from the little shop, his mother was able to take care of the boy and afford some education for him. His competence in Hebrew indicates that he probably studied with *maskilim*[13] and later at a yeshiva in his hometown or nearby. He also received some education in German and Polish.

Esther died when Lucky was a teenager. To support himself, he worked as a tutor while he continued his own education in the evenings. He was restless and changed residence and studies frequently

---

8   Wiegand, *Chajim Jedidjah Lucky*, 41. It is today named Ivano Frankovsk.

9   Ibid., 5.

10   Andrei S. Markovits and Frank E. Sysyn, *Nation Building and the Politics of Nationalism: Essays on Austrian Galicia* (Cambridge, MA: Harvard University Press for the Harvard Ukrainian Research Institute, 1989), 154.

11   Ibid., 3.

12   Löwen, *Christian Theophilus Lucky*, 3. According to the SDB *Yearbook* of 1917, Lucky was left an orphan, and was thereafter in care of a relative; cf. "Christian Theophilus Lucky," *Seventh Day Baptist Yearbook* (1917), 22.

13   [Jewish scholars belonging to the Jewish Enlightenment (*Haskalah*) who sought to modernize Judaism and integrate into Eastern Europe society and culture.]

until he came to Berlin at the beginning of the 1870s. He was not only interested in Judaism, but everything religious. In this regard some of the sources include several anecdotes about the little boy's curiosity. For instance, he tried to observe how representatives from the different local religions behaved and practiced their rituals.[14]

As Lucky became familiar with the peculiarities of different religions, he was also confronted with the different factions and movements in the Galician Jewish community. A young Jewish intellectual in the last part of the century in Galicia had a lot to sort through in politics, religion, and conflicting worldviews. The local rabbis in his hometown favored traditional Judaism, but the young Lucky was fascinated by different Chasidic dynasties. He was particularly fond of the rebbe in Ukrainian Wyschnyzja.[15] Although there appears to have been opposition to this movement (e.g., from the local rabbis in Tysmenitsa), by 1830 Chasidut had become the most common form of Jewish life in Galicia.[16] In any case, Chasidic doctrine was only one of several influences on Lucky. During his studies he changed his religious and political profile several times, and he associated himself with Socialism, Pantheism, Anarchism, Reform Judaism, and finally with Jewish nationalism and Zionism (not to mention Christianity and nascent Messianic Judaism). Lucky went from being a German Liberal to a Pole of Jewish confession. Later he was fascinated by Karl Marx, and particularly anarchism as described by Max Stirner, author of *Eine und Sein Eigentum* (1844).[17] His interest in such a broad diversity of secular ideologies was symptomatic of the

---

14 Widauer, *Erindringer*, 168.

15 Wiegand, *Chajim Jedidjah Lucky*, 42. The "Wunderrabbi" mentioned by Wiegand is probably Rabbi Menachem Mendel (d. 1885), author of *Zemach Tzadik* and founder of the Haggar dynasty in Wiznitz. The dynasty is today present in the State of Israel. Cf. Dr. N. M. Gelber, "The Wiznitzer Tzaddikim Dynasty" (trans. Jerome Silverbush) in *History of the Jews in the Bukowina* (2 vols.; ed. Hugo Gold; Tel Aviv, Israel: 1958–1962), 1:89. Cited 16 October 2009. Online: http://www.jewishgen.org/yizkor/Bukovinabook/buk1_089.html.

16 Markovits and Sysyn, *Nationbuilding*, 229; "Horowitz, Arye Leib Ben Eleazar Ha-Levi," *Encyclopedia Judaica Jerusalem* (16 vols.; Jerusalem, Israel: MacMillian. Keter Publishing House, 1971), 8:986.

17 Löwen, *Christian Theophilus Lucky*, 4.

broader *Haskalah* (Enlightenment) movement. In the 1850s, Lucky's hometown was a center for the *Haskalah* movement in eastern Galicia.[18]

STUDIES IN BRESLAU AND BERLIN

During the 1870s, Pollak studied at the three different rabbinic seminaries in Germany, as well as the university in Berlin. The neo-Orthodox *Der Jüdisch-Theologische Seminar* in Breslau (today Polish Wroclaw) was founded in 1854, and was the oldest.[19] In 1872, the Reform-inspired *Die Hochschule für die Wissenschaft des Judentums* was established in Berlin, and in 1873 the competing *Rabbiner Seminar für das Orthodoxe Judentum*, which wanted to combine Torah observance and modern science.[20] Both the Breslau seminary and the institutions in Berlin provided not only traditional scholarship but also modern education for rabbis and teachers.[21]

Pollak began at the school in Breslau about 1871 or 1872. As he apparently had no money, the school sponsored him, only to discover that the restless student was more interested in other subjects than in the Latin and Greek courses he needed to finish high school (the *gymnasium*). In Breslau, Lucky met a man who would become one of his strongest opponents after his conversion: Johann F.A. de Le Roi, the later historian of Jewish missions who had been working in Breslau

18 "Stanislav," *Encyclopedia Judaica Jerusalem* (16 vols.; Jerusalem, Israel: MacMillian. Keter Publishing House, 1971), 15:338.

19 Run by Zacharias Frankel (1791–1875), who tried to balance the religious and historical aspects of Judaism. He also claimed some liturgic reforms, but maintained use of Hebrew. See Nils Roemer, *Jewish Scholarship and Culture in Nineteenth-Century Germany. Between History and Faith* (Madison, WI: University of Wisconsin, 2005), 50–52; and Karl-Johan Illmann and Tapani Harviainen, *Judisk historia* (Åbo: Åbo akademi, 1997), 150.

20 Reinhard Rürup, *Jüdische Geschichte in Berlin. Essays und Studien* (Berlin, Germany: Edition Hentrich, 1995), 201.

21 The studies included Bible exegesis, including the targums, Hebrew and Aramaic, Palestinian geography, historical and methodological introduction to the Mishnah and the Talmud, Babylonian and Palestinian Talmud, classical languages and realia, the history of Judaism in relation to the history of Jewish literature, Midrash, religious philosophy and ethics, ritual practice, and Mosaic criminal and civil law, particularly talmudic family law. In addition pedagogy, catechesis and homiletics were taught. Cf. Schwarzfuchs, *A Concise History*, 101.

as a missionary to the Jews since 1866. Le Roi's condescending way of speaking about "the Jews" and a couple of disingenuous Jewish baptisms convinced Lucky that such missionary efforts were just another expression of anti-Semitism. After some months he left and went to Berlin.[22]

From autumn 1872 to January 1877, i.e., from age seventeen to twenty-two, Lucky lived and studied in Berlin at different religious and secular institutions. If the information from the sources is combined, we see that Lucky became a student at both of the Jewish institutions in the German capital in addition to attending the university. He was admitted as a student at the *Hochschule* under its headmaster Abraham Geiger (1810–1874) during the first year the institution existed. The aim of the *Hochschule* was to study Judaism in the light of modern methods and a modern worldview, and from the very beginning the school was associated with the Jewish Reform movement.[23] Lucky may have been influenced by Reform ideas at the time, or at least he was curious about them. The *Hochshule* also wanted Lucky to finish studying high school subjects, which he then did.

Having finished his work at the *gymnasium*, it seems that Lucky also attended the *Rabbiner Seminar* in 1873. This seminary was founded by the Orthodox rabbi Israel Hildesheimer (1820–1899) in 1873, as a reaction to the establishment of the liberal *Hochschule* the previous year. The seminary was neo-Orthodox in outlook, but Hildesheimer insisted that the students be familiar with the scientific method. The *Rabbiner Seminar* in Berlin became the center for German Jewish orthodoxy, and it tried to combine loyalty to the Torah with scientific methods.[24] Hildesheimer regarded the *Hochschule* as a destructive institution for

---

22 Wiegand, *Chajim Jedidjah Lucky*, 42.

23 Other teachers were David Zvi Hoffmann, Abraham Berliner, and Jacob Barth. Cf. Roemer, *Jewish Scholarship and Culture*, 52.

24 Hildesheimer ran the seminary for the next twenty-six years, so in other words he was Lucky's headmaster. Until it was closed down by the Nazis in 1938 and the library moved to Tel Aviv, the seminary educated a great number of rabbis and lay leaders for Jewish communities in Central and Western Europe. More than one hundred students received rabbinic certification there between 1873 and 1938. Cf. Carolin Hilker-Siebenhaar, *Wegweiser durch das jüdische Berlin* (Berlin, Germany: Nicolaische Verlagsbuchhandlung Beuermann GmbH, 1987), 154.

Judaism and the Jewish community. Lucky's transfer to the new school indicates that he may have sympathized with that view.

Between November 1874 and January 1877, Lucky attended the university for classes in philosophy. At both the *Hochschule* and at the *Rabbiner Seminar,* students commonly attended university lectures in addition to their regular studies. Lucky did not obtain any degree, and, according to university archives, he seems to have been expelled for failure to diligently complete his course work. Lucky's friend August Wiegand describes Lucky as not very successful when it came to classical logic and the art of rhetoric, as he felt more at home in talmudic discourse and with ancient languages than he did with modern academic subjects.[25]

The information about Lucky's stay and studies in Berlin is scanty, although it gives certain background for his reputation as a gifted Jewish scholar. His choice of schools also describes him as an intellectual who sought to be loyal to the Jewish tradition, although not in the mainstream of the Eastern European Jewish communities. His friends describe Lucky as characteristically ambivalent, and seemed to struggle with the tension between traditional Judaism and the liberal Reform movement. The issue of divine revelation in particular seems to have been important to him. This question about the authority of Scripture and its divine origin subsequently became a critical factor in his reassessment of the New Testament's claims.[26]

COMING TO FAITH IN YESHUA

During his time in Berlin or shortly thereafter Lucky embraced the Christian faith, but the sources do not agree on the sequence of events or the details that led him to make this transition. The information is both fragmented and somewhat contradictory particularly when it comes to the question of his baptism.[27]

---

25 Wiegand, *Chajim Jedidjah Lucky*, 43.

26 Wiegand, *Chajim Jedidjah Lucky*, 44.

27 Cf. Löwen, *Christian Theophilus Lucky*, 6 and Wiegand, *Chajim Jedidjah Lucky*, 46.

Some stories report that, at some point, Lucky and a friend began to study the New Testament in Franz Delitzsch's Hebrew translation to prove the superiority of Judaism. In particular, they wanted to compare the life and teachings of Hillel to those of Jesus. In this contact with the New Testament he was especially attracted to the mysticism in the Gospel of John and the Jewish character of Matthew.[28] During these studies Lucky was convinced that Jesus had to be the Messiah. He underwent a private baptism conducted by a friend without becoming a member of any official church or denomination.

The version of the story told by Pastor Max Weidauer recalls that Lucky stated several times that he came to faith in Jeschua (Yeshua) during the night, and that he felt a deeper understanding of the grace of God. Lucky described his new attitude to the message of Christ as feeling the joy of someone who had previously believed there was a precious pearl in a box, but now he had seen it for himself.[29]

Pastor August Wiegand tells how, in Berlin, Lucky came across a Greek New Testament that he read to practice the language. Although the Jewish character of the book struck him, particularly in the writings of Paul, at first he was not very concerned about the person of Jesus. This, however, changed as a result of his struggle over the conflict between traditional Judaism's view of divine revelation and Reform Judaism's view. Lucky had come to the conclusion that if the Torah was genuine divine revelation, the New Testament had to be the same. He came to this conclusion the night before his exam sermon in a Prussian synagogue, apparently as a part of his studies at the *Hochschule*. The following morning he told his teacher Israel Lewy about his decision:

"This night I have become a Christian."

"What's that supposed to mean? Have you fallen into the hands of the missionaries?"

"No, you are the first one I have spoken with. My faith comes solely from the New Testament, which I consider equal with the Old."

"And now you are going to turn your back on our people and its holy religion?"

---

28   Velthuysen, "Christian Theophilus Lucky," 196–98.

29   Weidauer, *Erindringer*, 174.

"Oh no, since Jesus is the promised Messiah, faith in him is not apostasy from the religion of Israel."

"But everyone from our people who goes to this Jesus becomes a *Meshummad* (renegade)."

"I will never become a *Meshummad*."

"And the Torah of Moses—you are going to keep that?"

"Yes, as the New Testament says that the first congregation in Jerusalem was faithful to the law, I will also do that."

"That is not possible. As a Christian you cannot continue to be a Jew!"

"Yes, I will!"

"Then you will become an unlucky man your whole life: You will not be counted among the Christians because you are a Jew, and likewise among the Jews, because you are a Christian."

"That is something I have to bear!"[30]

After the discussion with Lewy, Lucky began traveling extensively. Wiegand says that he was eventually baptized in Belgrade by unregistered Baptists, as he wanted the *tevilah*, i.e., full immersion in water.[31] Both Wiegand and Löwen report that, after Berlin, Lucky moved to Galicia for a short period of time. However, due to suspicion from the Jewish community, Lucky was forced to emigrate to the USA.

Löwen's version of Lucky's conversion is more substantial as well as complex. According to this version, Lucky's first encounter with the New Testament was during his studies in Berlin, where he found a Greek-German version in the belongings of a friend. Somehow the brief excerpts he read fascinated him, and the discovery led him to visit a Sunday service at *Sophienkirche*.[32] After Berlin, Lucky (not yet converted to faith in Jesus) went back to Galicia and Bukowina to work as a tutor. In his spare time he gathered other students around him and introduced them to Max Stirner, anarchism, and esoteric subjects.[33]

---

30   Wiegand, *Chajim Jedidjah Lucky*, 44–45. According to Wiegand, Lewy was a teacher in Breslau from 1883. It is not clear how this information fits with the fact that Lucky then was in New York; see the chapter below.

31   Wiegand, *Chajim Jedidjah Lucky*, 46.

32   Löwen, *Christian Theophilus Lucky*, 6.

33   Ibid., 5.

In Chernowitc some of his sympathizers vandalized and profaned one of the local synagogues and its Torah scrolls, causing great turmoil in the Jewish community. Although he was not involved, Lucky was put under supervision by the Austrian police, who arrested those who had committed the crime. While one of Lucky's friends was able to escape to America and later was baptized, Lucky found shelter in a small village before getting a new passport. At the same time he stopped using his birth name and changed his name from time to time, using a number of aliases, almost like toys: Elik, Elk, Lucki (read "luzki"), and Lucky. During this period Chaim Wolf Yedidiah Pollak changed his name to Lucky, but not yet "Christian Theophilus."[34] The difficulties in Galicia and Bukowina led Lucky to further introspection, and he returned to faith in God.

Wiegand's version claims that, after his conversion and discussion with Lewy, Lucky went back to Galicia and Bukowina, working as a tutor for some Jewish families. In contrast to Löwen, who says that Lucky still had not had a Christian breakthrough at this point, Wiegand says that Lucky used his spare time to share his Christian beliefs and inspire friends and colleagues to study Judaism and stay with their people. In particular he used the Jewish festivals to explain how the New Testament completes and fulfills the Hebrew Bible. According to Wiegand, the story "Eine Pesach-ereignisse" was created during this period.[35] In this story the tutor, Eliakim (who he claims is identical with Lucky),

---

34 According to Unbegaun, the Slavonic surname Lúckij, which derives from a local name, is in Ukrainian pronounced "Lúc'kyj." Cf. Unbegaun, *Russian Surnames*, 282.

35 Wiegand, *Chajim Jedidjah Lucky*, 50. See also "Passah-Ereignisse. Von Eliakim," *Nathanael* 4, no. 6 (1888): 165–86; and K.I.M., "The Story of Passover," *Edut LeYisra'el* 1, no. 7 (1888): 126–140.

not only convinces his Jewish host family that Jesus is the Messiah, but also strengthens their Jewish identity.[36]

In this version of the story, Lucky now wanted to migrate to America. He went to Berlin again for the first time since his studies. He visited the *Sophienkirche* in Berlin at least twice. Although the Christian liturgy felt alien to him, he found some comfort in the sermons about Jesus. Löwen does not cite any particular defining moment in Lucky's conversion process, but from now on he appears to have felt spiritually connected to some Christian leaders, particularly the Old Testament scholar Franz Delitzsch in Leipzig. Delitzsch was already one of the most prominent leaders of the German Jewish missions. Lucky would have a strong affection for Delitzsch and his Hebrew New Testament his whole life. Delitzsch very soon put Lucky in touch with Yechiel Tzvi Lichtenstein, the Messianic Jewish pioneer who was later to become a teacher at Delitzsch's *Institutum Judaicum* for Lutheran ministers.[37]

---

36   The narrative describes "Mr. E," a tutor for a secular Jewish family, who possibly resembles Lucky himself. Through his lessons he is able to make the household more conscious of being Jewish and of Jewish traditions, and at the Passover meal he reveals himself and his faith in Jesus. Ten years later he meets the family in Vienna, and discovers that the wife and her Jewish husband have become Christians. The narrative stresses that Israel is the olive tree into which the Gentiles have been grafted. Without saying it explicitly, the narrative thus is also an attack on traditional Christian supersessionism. Daland claims that the story is true, and that most of the characters were still alive; cf. "A Translated Extract from the Hebrew Monthly 'Eduth l'Israel' (Witness unto Israel)," *The Peculiar People* 1 (1888–1889): 30–53.

37   Jechiel (or Yechiel) Tzvi Lichtenstein (1829–1912), born in Herschensohn in Bessarabia. He was a rabbi in Jassy, where, in 1855, he baptized himself and some of the members of the Jewish congregation in a local river. He thereafter tried to establish a Jewish-Christian congregation in Skolian in Bessarabia. He married the sister of Joseph Rabinowitz, who became a believer in Jesus several years later. After his conversion, Herschensohn-Lichtenstein became interested in Chasidic theology and spirituality, and for a period he went to the Chasidic yeshiva in Liadi (Lithuania) in the 1860s. Consequently he developed a theology combining Jewish mysticism with Protestant Christianity. In 1868 he settled in Leipzig, where he soon became friends with Delitzsch and was employed by different mission societies. In 1886 he was employed as teacher at *Institutum Judaicum* in Leipzig. Here he wrote a commentary in Hebrew on several of the books of the New Testament. Cf. "Jechiel Zevi Lichtenstein," *Missions-Blad for Israel* 86 (1912): 122–27; and Kai Kjær-Hansen, *Joseph Rabinowitz*, 35, 46.

Lucky was particularly inspired by Lichtenstein's views on Jewish Christianity, i.e., Messianic Judaism.

Although none of the sources provide a definite date or place for Lucky's baptism, it probably cannot have taken place until after he left the university. An official baptism would have put him into a difficult situation with the Jewish community in Berlin despite the fact that Jewish conversion to nominal Christianity was a common phenomenon in Berlin of the 1870s.[38] Lucky's later partners in ministry—orthodox Lutherans (such as Delitzsch and later Landsmann and Pohlmann in New York) and Seventh Day Baptists—would argue fiercely against each other on many topics, but neither would have given Lucky a position without some sort of proof of a theologically valid baptism. In this context it is interesting that Lucky became friends with Yechiel Tzvi Lichtenstein in Leipzig, who had baptized himself in his youth. When he first came to faith in Christ in the 1850s, he and some friends had baptized themselves in a river in Romania. Later, Delitzsch persuaded him that this baptism was not sufficient and he agreed to be publicly and formally baptized in a church.[39]

Lucky must certainly have heard about this and been challenged on the topic himself if he was not yet baptized. Further, he must have been baptized before Delitzsch would send him with his recommendation to Britain and the United States. Due to this obscurity it is also not completely clear when Pollak took his new names, and although he continued to use his Jewish name as an editor, among non-Jewish friends and contacts he became known as Christian Theophilus Lucky. However, Theophilus ("beloved of HaShem") is in Hebrew *Yedidiah*, so in this respect he probably wanted to deliberately stress the continuity between his Jewish background and his new Christian faith.

Delitzsch helped Lucky get to London and contact the Jewish missions there. The methods of the British missions appalled Lucky, and he attacked the mission societies for both their methods and their attitude toward traditional Judaism. That provocation followed him

---

38   Todd Endelmann, "The Social and Political Context of Conversion in Germany and England, 1870-1914," in *Jewish Apostasy in the Modern World* (ed. Todd Endelman; New York, NY: Holmes & Meier, 1987), 83-107.

39   Skarsaune, *Israels venner*, 176-77.

the rest of his life. Löwen claims that he was particularly involved in heated discussion with Jewish Christians such as Moses Margoliouth (1818–1881), whom he accused of alienating himself from the Jewish nation.

LUCKY IN NEW YORK

In the 1880s, Lucky spent most of his time in the United States, where he not only received his education in Christian theology but also established an important personal network. Before he began at Union Theological Seminary (UTS) in 1882, Lucky made his living working in a cigarette factory and as a day laborer.[40]

Soon after his arrival in New York, Lucky met people who would become important friends and contacts for him later. Following Delitzsch's advice, he moved in with the Jewish-Christian missionary Daniel Landsmann (d. May 13, 1896), who was working for the Lutheran Church—Missouri Synod.[41] Landsmann was born in Belarus, and he and his German wife were happy to meet Lucky, but the relationship between Landsmann and Lucky was never easy. In fact, their arguments about the national identity of Jewish Christians and arguments about Luther could become so heated that Landsmann's wife had to get between Lucky and her husband several times. Still, they continued to be friends, and Lucky would later recommend Landsmann's books in *Edut LeYisra'el*.[42] After some time in New York, Lucky also became friends with Pastor H. Pohlmann of the Lutheran Independent Church,

---

40   Wiegand, *Chajim Jedidjah Lucky*, 50.

41   Randolph, *Christian Theophilus Lucky*, 206–208.

42   Löwen, *Christian Theophilus Lucky*, 12; *Edut LeYisra'el* 1, no. 2 (1888): 19, and no. 3 (1888): 18–19; Joh. F. A. de Le Roi, "Daniel Landsmann," *Der Messiasbote: Ein Nachrichtenblatt der Berliner Judenmission* (1909): 52–56.

who in 1882 began having services for German emigrants and Jews, and Pohlmann let him preach in his church.[43]

In the fall of 1882, Lucky began a three-year course in Christian theology at UTS, which at the time was one of the two most important Presbyterian institutions in the country, together with Princeton. The relaxed practice of accepting students had one limit: Until 1906, every student had to be a member of a Christian church.[44] For Lucky this was probably Pohlmann's congregation. According to *Sabbath Recorder*, UTS was initially reluctant to admit Lucky to the seminary due to recent thefts by some Jewish students. He was ultimately accepted only on a probationary status.[45] The curriculum for the three years at UTS was largely a prescribed one, and it included studies in Greek and Hebrew. Once a week voluntary classes were held in different oriental languages such as Arabic, Assyrian, Biblical Aramaic, Chaldean, and Syriac. Lucky's friends described him as exceptionally skilled in several of these languages.[46]

LUCKY—A MISSIONARY AND A SEVENTH DAY BAPTIST?

On May 1, 1885, Lucky had his final exam and obtained a graduate diploma in the form of the standard qualification from UTS. A couple of months later, on August 16, he was ordained by Pohlmann in the Independent Evangelical Lutheran Church in New York City. He was thirty years old.[47] However, Lucky did not take work as a pastor. He

---

43 Pohlmann's congregation did not belong to any of the Lutheran synods, and was located in the church building at 87 Attorney Street, which belonged to the Methodists under the name Wesley Chapel. As Pohlmann was allowed to use it for Lutheran services when possible, it was also called "Evangelische-Lutherische Bethanien Kirche." He lived as a widower next door to the church, without any regular salary. Cf. Löwen, *Christian Theophilus Lucky*, 12. Cf. also Andersen, *Israelsmissionen i New York*, 70–75.

44 Robert T. Handy, *A History of Union Theological Seminary in New York* (New York, NY: Columbia University, 1987), 112.

45 Randolph, *Christian Theophilus Lucky*, 208.

46 Philips, *Ch. Theophilus Lucky*, 690; Velthuysen, *Christian Theophilus Lucky*, 196–197, 208.

47 Randolph, *Christian Theophilus Lucky*, 206–208; and Le Roi, *Geschichte* 2:388.

wanted the title only to get American citizenship.[48] Lucky worked as a missionary to the Jews in Strychance, Austria, from 1885 to 1886, after being ordained by Pohlmann. At the seminary, Lucky became acquainted with some Seventh Day Baptist students who would later become significant leaders of their church, such as professor and church president William C. Daland, a man who became Lucky's editorial partner for years to come. On October 1, 1886, after returning from Europe, Lucky began his work in New York as a missionary to the Jews under the Seventh Day Baptist Missionary Society, a ministry that lasted until 1889.[49]

According to the sources, Lucky became a member of the Seventh Day Baptist Church shortly before he accepted ordination in the Lutheran Church, February 14, 1885. None of the sources seem to be bothered by the contradiction. Naturally, both the Seventh Day Baptist sources and the Lutheran sources emphasize their own respective connections with Lucky, but they typically refer to his connection to the other community as well. In the Seventh Day Baptist sources, Lucky's connection to Delitzsch seems to have been highly valued. In fact, Lucky's respect in some Lutheran and German Jewish mission circles (Delitzsch, Landsmann, and Pohlmann) helped him find acceptance within the Seventh Day Baptist Church.[50] Lucky read and spoke several Slavic languages, as well as French, German, English, and later Dutch (in addition to Latin and the biblical and oriental languages studied at UTS), and his competence recommended him to Jewish mission efforts.[51]

Nevertheless, prejudice and suspicion against Jewish converts were widespread among both Christians and Jews. Some Jewish missionaries were involved in scandals related to fraud and financial manipulation. Several papers, such as *The Peculiar People*, attacked the work of one

---

48   Löwen, *Christian Theophilus Lucky*, 15; Wiegand, *Chajim Jedidjah Lucky*, 53.

49   "Christian Theophilus Lucky," *Seventh Day Baptist Yearbook* (1917): 22–23. Editor not given.

50   Ibid., 11; and Randolph, *Christian Theophilus Lucky*, 206–207.

51   According to Lillie Zöckler, Lucky spoke thirteen languages (Zöckler, *Gott Hört Gebet*, 13). Cf. also Kjær-Hansen, "Petra Volf's Reminiscences about Lucky," 37, n. 36.

of them, Hermann Warsawiak.[52] Lucky appears to have experienced the same distrust against baptized Jews in many circles. There are certain hints that various groups in the Seventh Day Baptist Church had problems trusting Lucky in the beginning, reportedly due to bad experiences with former Jewish converts.[53] According to Lucky's obituary in the *Sabbath Recorder* (August 1917), the Seventh Day Baptist leadership suspected Lucky of trying to make "business" when arguing for free agency as a missionary while still receiving financial support.[54]

EDUT LEYISRA'EL AND THE PECULIAR PEOPLE

Already before he finished his studies at UTS, Lucky and Daland established a society for a future journal in Hebrew, the Hebrew Publishing Society.[55] In 1887, Lucky had convinced the leadership of the Tract Society of the Seventh Day Baptist Church to establish two new periodicals: one in English aimed at Christian readers who needed to become aware of the mistakes of Christian mission work

---

52 "Editorial Notes," 112, and "At Least be Courteous," *The Peculiar People* 6 (1893): 94–96 (incomplete pagination in my copy).

53 Randolph, *Christian Theophilus Lucky*, 208.

54 The obituary quotes an observation by one Dr. Main: "Almost, if not quite, the saddest chapter relates to the fact that our people could not understand him. Most of our leaders and people misunderstood him in two particular ways: 1. Jews are full of prejudice against a Christian Jew who receives a salary from Gentiles. Naturally our board wished to pay him a definite salary and receive from him the regular, formal, detailed reports. *He* wished us to give him a modest honorarium, quarterly or annually, and allow him to make, not 'official,' but informal and general reports concerning his fields and labors. *Of course* that was not 'business'! In my judgment his efficiency and joy would have been quadrupled could the board have had some of his idealism. 2. He greatly desired to follow the method of St. Paul, not the methods of a modern board working among the Jews. The modern method is to take converts into the church whose missionaries have been the means of the conversion, Baptist, Episcopalian, Methodist, Presbyterian, etc. Paul's method was simply to urge Jews to accept Jesus as the Savior and Lord, and then allow them to observe honored customs, if they so desired, and would not observe them as essential for salvation, or press them upon others. Here, too, our board and people failed to rise to his level, which was both scriptural and rational." Cf. Randolph, *Christian Theophilus Lucky*, 207–208.

55 Cf. Andersen, *Israelsmissionen*, 71.

among the Jewish people, and one in Hebrew aimed at Jewish readers to establish a stronghold for Jewish Christianity. Both papers were established in the little town of Alfred Centre, New York, and the first issues of *Edut LeYisra'el* were published starting in September 1888. The English paper started in April 1888 under the name *The Peculiar People*. While Lucky was the editor of *Edut LeYisra'el*, *The Peculiar People* was edited by the Jewish Christian Zevi Hermann Friedlander in cooperation with Joseph Landow.[56] However, it is clear from the beginning that *The Peculiar People* strongly identified itself with *Edut LeYisra'el* and its editor.

From the beginning of 1888 to November, Friedlander edited *The Peculiar People* weekly.[57] Christian readers accused *The Peculiar People* of not supporting the Christian mission and not even having its own mission work. Friedlander replied to these criticisms saying that he did not want to talk about their own mission work as they did not meet those "model foes who succumb to the power of our persuasion. Our stories have all no symmetrical endings—they break off at the wrong point." *The Peculiar People* instead wanted the Christian press to report on

---

56   H. Friedlander (1830–1888) was born to a Jewish family in Schneidemuehl, and was baptized in 1852. In 1863, he became a missionary for the London Jews Society. He worked for several years in Jerusalem, and founded the Artuf Colony between Jerusalem and Jaffa. On July 6, 1886, he was compelled to resign from the London Jews Society, and thereafter he had problems supporting himself and his family. Friedlander had commenced keeping the Sabbath and was looking forward to baptism (cf. Le Roi, *Geschichte* 2:190–93; "A Great Need," *The Peculiar People* 2 [1889]: 67–69; and *Seventh Day Baptists in Europe and America*, 386, 1338). Joseph Landow was born in 1859 in Galicia, a descendant of Rabbi Ezekiel Landow in Prague, and grew up within strictly Orthodox Chasidism. In 1886, he met a Jewish Christian in Czernowitz, Bukovina, who preached the gospel to him. He went to the United States to assist with *Edut LeYisra'el*, and was ordained to ministry in SDB in April 1888. Landow was *Edut*'s typesetter in Alfred, where he appears to have suffered from some kind of illness. He was still weak after being ill when he went to Galicia, cf. *Edut LeYisra'el* 1, no. 7 (1888): 120. About Landow's work in Europe, it is mentioned that he gave twenty addresses, no baptisms, but had several adherents (cf. "A Brief Notice of a Brief Life," *The Peculiar People* [1889]: 61–63; and *Seventh Day Baptists in Europe and America*, 384).

57   From July 13 to November 16, sixteen issues were published. See "A Great Need," *The Peculiar People* 2 (1889): 67–69; 67.

the mission's failures as well as its victories.[58] How exactly *The Peculiar People* was financed is not very clear. From its own columns, it is clear that due to the lack of subscribers the periodical suffered from a lack of money.[59] This was apparently the case for *Edut LeYisra'el* as well.[60]

Edut LeYisra'el represented a foreign system of thought even in mission circles, and it did not garner much financial support. The language and attitude of the journal were much more concerned with living a Jewish life in the midst of the Jewish people than traditional missionary tracts in Hebrew. However, it was clear from the beginning that the journal would not be greeted with enthusiasm by the Jewish public. Due to the resentment, *Edut* compares the journal's situation with being lovesick.[61] *Edut LeYisra'el* was supposed to strengthen Jewish values in light of Jesus and to work for peace among Jews, i.e., peace between Jesus-believing Jews and the rest of the Jewish people. Despite its focus on the New Testament and Jesus, when Lucky stated his editorial purposes in the first issue of the journal, he makes reference to spiritual and nationalistic goals, but makes no mention of Christianity, the New Testament, or Christology at all. Still, it was characteristic for *Edut* and

---

58 "Editorial Notes," *The Peculiar People* 1 (1888-1889): 110-112. The "success language" *The Peculiar People* referred to, is also commented on by Kovács in his study of the Scottish Mission. Ábrahám Kovács, *The History of the Free Church of Scotland's Mission to the Jews in Budapest and Its Impact on the Reformed Church of Hungary 1841-1914* (Frankfurt am Main, Germany: Peter Lang, 2006), 365.

59 "Editorial Notes," *The Peculiar People* 1 (1888-1889): 71.

60 Ibid. In the mid-eighties, Lucky and the Tract Society had been promised an inheritance from the Seventh Day Baptists Mr. Delos C. Burdick and Mrs. Hanna Burdick. This, however, never happened, as it was prevented by a court decision; cf. Randolph, *Christian Theophilus Lucky*, 207. As late as 1911, Lucky still thought it would be possible to get this money. He then was trying to establish another periodical in cooperation with Philip Cohen in Johannesburg: *The Messianic Jew.* See "The Work of Brother Ch. Th. Lucky" (by the editor), *Sabbath Recorder* 70, no. 9 (February 27, 1911): 267. In 1888, *Edut LeYisra'el* published a brief obituary about Burdick, see "Memorial Stone in the Book," *Edut LeYisra'el* 1, no. 4-5 (1888): 85.

61 "To the dear readers in the camp of the Hebrews, the *Edut* says," *Edut LeYisra'el* 1, no. 4-5 (1888): 65-67; and "Word to the Reader," *Edut LeYisra'el* 1, no. 1 (1888): 1-8. In the Hebrew text the pagination is 1-6, cf. Hilary Le Cornu, email from September 7, 2012.

Lucky to combine Jewish and Christian writings.[62] Lucky always insisted on rewriting all New Testament names and words in Hebrew using what he assumed were the original terms and names. He referred to Paul as "Shaul HaKadosh" (Holy Saul), and likewise Peter was called "Shimon Keifa."[63] Culturally, the journal had a conservative profile, not focusing much on socio-economic issues.[64] When commenting on the major challenges for contemporary Jews in the United States or Galicia, the journal mainly focused its critiques on national, spiritual, and cultural disintegration, not poverty or socio-economic factors. Lack of assistance to impoverished Jewish newcomers is primarily regarded as a national problem and a national betrayal. In particular, the journal criticizes Marxism, which Lucky depicted as a destructive force for the collective consciousness of the Jewish people.[65]

At the beginning of 1889, the journals met serious problems. Both Friedlander and Landow had died. That tragic loss led to an abrupt halt in the publication of both journals. On June 29, 1889, Lucky returned to Eastern Europe and Galicia.[66] After Lucky's return to Europe, he managed to re-establish *Edut LeYisra'el* in Lemberg/Lvov. In New York, the Tract Society assumed the publication of *The Peculiar People* as a monthly journal from April 1889, with Daland as editor. He served in that position until 1898 when lack of funds caused the journal's closure.

---

62   "This is the task set before 'The Witness,'" in *Edut leIsrael* 1, no. 1 (1888): 6 (the pagination follows the Hebrew text, cf. Hilary Le Cornu, email from Sept. 7, 2012); and "Thoughts from HaEdut," *Edut LeYisra'el* 2 (the volume is not given but from the year I assume it is the second), no. 1 (1890): 5.

63   Wiegand, *Chajim Jedidjah Lucky*, 54.

64   Lucky wanted the journal to be associated with other contemporary Hebrew journals such as *Hamaggid, Hamelitz, Hazephira* and *Chabatzeleth*, see *The Peculiar People* 9 (1897): 237–240. The title of the article is missing and pagination is incomplete in my copy.

65   "Meditations of the Testimony" in *Edut LeYisra'el* 1, no. 2 (1888): 25–29.

66   William C. Daland, "Brother Lucky's Travels," *Sabbath Recorder* 45 (October 10, 1889): 652.

THE RETURN TO EUROPE AND GALICIA

Why did Lucky leave everything that had been built in Alfred, only to transplant the work and replicate it in Europe? As with his arrival in America, the reasons for Lucky's return to Europe are complex. According to *The Peculiar People*, Lucky stopped his work due to bad health, while *Sabbath Recorder* claims Lucky was eager to discuss mission strategy with certain mission societies, which he apparently was able to do in Leipzig.[67] However, Wiegand claims the work and writings of Joseph Rabinowitz and Isaac Lichtenstein enthused Lucky and inspired him to return to Europe. Moreover, an invitation from Wilhelm Faber in Leipzig encouraged him to make the transition.[68] Lucky's return may also have been an attempt to save *Edut* after the death of Landow, whose function was apparently not to do traditional missionary work, but first of all to make *Edut LeYisra'el* known in the Jewish communities in Eastern Europe.

Another possible explanation for Lucky's return to Europe can be found in the narrative by Löwen, who says that at the time *Edut LeYisra'el* was established, a small group of young Jesus-believing Jewish men settled in Alfred Centre. Löwen does not say what they were supposed to do, but probably they were sympathizers who wanted to stay with Lucky. Lucky was registered as a missionary at the time, and gathering a group like this could be counted as part of his work.[69] The plans for them apparently changed after a while, as the whole group left Alfred, and three of them, named Reuter, Karmen, and Japhe, returned

---

67 "Book Review," *The Peculiar People*, 3 (1891): 156–160 (the pagination of the whole article in my copy is incomplete), and excerpts from letters from Franz Delitzsch, William [= Wilhelm] Faber, and Johannes Müller in "Brother Lucky's Work" (by the editor), *Sabbath Recorder* 46, no. 26 (1890): 409. Nevertheless, according to Skarsaune, it appears that the mission leaders in Leipzig had begun their reorientation already in 1888 (Skarsaune, *Israels venner*, 184–86).

68 Wiegand, *Chajim Jedidjah Lucky*, 53.

69 Most Jewish converts were male immigrants; according to Ariel this was due to the different social positions of men and women. There was a widespread feeling of freedom among the male Jewish immigrants, while Jewish women generally held on to Jewish practices (Ariel, *Evangelizing*, 45, 298–299).

to Galicia.[70] According to Löwen, Lucky actually sent them back so "*Sie sollen nichts ganz vergojischen*"—in other words, to avoid their being assimilated into their non-Jewish surroundings.[71] Reuter, who was from Lucky's hometown Tysmienica, later met Löwen in Berlin. Reuter complained that Lucky forced him and the others to stay in the synagogue and the Jewish community, which, according to Löwen, Reuter feared would lead him away from the Christian faith.[72] Lucky seems to have feared the cultural effect of the assimilation process on Jewish Christians in America, a fear that he probably shared with Joseph Rabinowitz, who after his visit to the United States around the same time strongly warned Jews against immigration to America.[73] Philip Roth's comment on the American experience of assimilation expresses what some feared and others hailed: "Immigrants flowed into America, and America flowed into them."[74] Perhaps Lucky believed that if *Edut LeYisra'el* was to reach Jews in Eastern Europe, he and the journal would need a traditional Jewish context to achieve its purpose, and therefore sought to place it in Eastern Europe.

Due to many complications, e.g., Friedlander's and Landow's deaths, Lucky's return to Europe, and the tense fellowship with Löwen that developed later, the publications became irregular. In Stanislau, Moses Löwen, who worked for the *Berliner Missiongeschellscaft*, became

---

70 Löwen only mentions these three names, without identifying them in any more detail.

71 Löwen, *Christian Theophilus Lucky*, 16: "They were not to be totally gentilized." This fear was probably related to intermarriage. According to Ariel, many of the Jewish male immigrants married non-Jewish women and settled in non-Jewish areas. See Ariel, *Evangelizing*, 45.

72 "*Reuter weinte in Berlin vor mir wie ein Kind*" ("In Berlin, Reuter was crying like a child in front of me"). Löwen, *Christian Theophilus Lucky*, 16.

73 Kai Kjær-Hansen, *Joseph Rabinowitz*, 176.

74 Ron Eyerman, "Formation of African American Identity," *Cultural Trauma and Collective Identity* (ed. Jeffrey C. Alexander et al.; Berkeley, CA: University of California, 2004), 110.

Lucky's co-editor. From 1892, *Edut LeYisra'el* was published in Berlin until it was halted at the end of the year.[75]

On July 22, 1889, Lucky arrived in Leipzig and met Delitzsch and his coworkers Wilhelm Faber and Johannes Muller, the secretary of the *Zentralverein*. The friendly relationship between the leaders of the *Zentralverein* and Lucky would prove to be significant for both parties in the following years. Among the leaders as well as the students at the *Institutum Judaicum*, Lucky made friends who would become some of his closest sympathizers as well as coworkers in Galicia.[76]

The next summer the general conference of the *Zentralverein* decided on its new strategy: Its workers should stay away from working as traveling evangelists and establishing homes for proselytes. Instead, they should seek to create Jewish-Christian fellowships that were part of the Jewish environment around them, and they should not let new Jewish believers in Christ become alienated from the Jewish nation. The missionaries should therefore concentrate on building attractive Christian evangelical congregations for the Germans living in the Eastern European heartland of Orthodox Christianity and Greek Catholicism. Then Jewish individuals would come by themselves to observe these fellowships, and eventually establish their own congregations for fellow Jews with help from the evangelical pastors.

There are some indications that the Lucky-Leipzig relationship was not flawless, however. Wiegand, who was a student at the Leipzig institute by then, tells the story of Lucky's visit. He says that Faber was totally unprepared for Lucky's appearance in the summer of 1889, and did not quite know what to do with him in the beginning. Wiegand gives the impression that the journey with Müller and the candidates to Rabinowitz in Kishinev was more like an act of improvisation. In addition, while Lucky established a cordial friendship with several of the German ministers, the friendship he had established with Yechiel Tzvi Lichtenstein before he went to America cooled. Löwen describes

---

75 Zöckler, *Judentum und Christentum*, (1892): 205. Lucky did not accept this situation, and tried several times later to restart the journal. The restart in 1897 was the fourth attempt. Cf. "Zwei neue jüdische Zeitschriften," *Saat auf Hofnung* (1897): 163–168.

76 Löwen, *Christian Theophilus Lucky*, 17.

how Lucky used every opportunity to try to convince the institute lecturer that he should not neglect observance of strict Jewish tradition. Lichtenstein had sympathies in that direction, but when he could no longer tolerate Lucky's pestering, he lost his temper, scolded him, and told him to leave him alone. Lucky apparently never forgot this event. In a letter to Löwen much later, he complained about Lichtenstein's lack of loyalty to Jewish tradition. Lichtenstein's outburst in Leipzig was compounded by two additional sins: His third marriage was to a Gentile woman, and he had shaved his beard.[77]

During his stay in Leipzig in the summer of 1889, Lucky was planning a long journey in Eastern Europe with some of the representatives from the Leipzig institute and *Zentralverein*. But before this journey took place, Lucky first visited the Jewish Christian Moses Löwen in Berlin. He asked him to help with *Edut* and to approach the Berlin Society for financial support. Löwen was from Sambour in Galicia, had been baptized only two years before Lucky turned up, and had been serving the London Society for Promoting Christianity amongst the Jews since 1888. Löwen was perplexed and not very optimistic about asking a mission society to support a journal with *Edut*'s profile, but to his surprise, the Berlin Society accepted the project the same autumn.[78]

The following fall Lucky was traveling with Muller and the candidates Wiegand and Meissner in Austria, Hungary, Serbia, and Bulgaria. In August he was in Constantinople, heading for Palestine, but did not get the *tezkhra* of the Turkish government.[79] Early in 1890, he appears to have settled in Stanislau, although he retained his American citizenship. At the end of August and beginning of September 1889 Lucky stayed with Joseph Rabinowitz, who had led the "Sons of Israel of the New Covenant" congregation since 1884.[80] This visit seems to be the only time Lucky met Rabinowitz. As neither Lucky nor *The Peculiar*

---

77 In light of the enthusiasm toward Herschensohn-Lichtenstein in several issues of *Edut*, where he is called Even-Tzohar, this conflict is surprising.

78 Löwen, *Christian Theophilus Lucky*, 18.

79 The Ottomanian license to enter Palestine.

80 "Brother Lucky's Work" (by the editor), *Sabbath Recorder* 46, no. 26 (1890): 409. According to Lillie Zöckler, this was where Lucky first met August Wiegand and Max Meissner (Zöckler, *Gott hört Gebet*, 14).

People later comments much on Rabinowitz's work, it seems probable that some disagreement took place. As Rabinowitz did not care about observing Sabbath regulations, it is very likely that Lucky was critical of what he saw in Kishinev, particularly in light of his encounter with Yechiel Lichtenstein the same summer.[81]

EDUT LEYISRA'EL AND THE BERLIN SOCIETY

The same autumn, the mission society in Berlin decided to support *Edut LeYisra'el* financially. According to the deal between Lucky and the Berlin Society, Lucky was supposed to produce material for the journal, and was free to live in Stanislau, while Löwen was stationed by the Berlin Society in Lemberg, about three hours away via rail.[82] Lucky did not get any salary; the support from the Berlin Society financed the publication and distribution of *Edut,* as well as the employment of Löwen.

The purpose of the agreement was two-fold: the Berlin Society did not have any responsibility for the Seventh Day Baptist and Jewish nationalist Lucky, and Lucky on his side was not formally connected to the mission. In May 1890, Löwen settled in the Galician capital of Lemberg (today Lviv, Ukraine), and the first edition of the reborn *Edut LeYisra'el* was published the following month.[83] Until 1892, Lucky edited *Edut LeYisra'el* together with Löwen and the Berlin Society, but later, when the society abandoned the journal, he published some issues alone.

Löwen reports that despite the small number of actual subscriptions many Jews were interested in the journal, and he and Lucky received numerous visitors and letters.[84] However, lack of subscribers was not the journal's biggest difficulty. Löwen openly talks about the different problems they met, but according to him, the main challenge was related to Lucky's working habits and personality. In particular, Lucky felt the anguish of being supported by the Berlin Society and still

---

81   Cf. Kai Kjær-Hansen, *Joseph Rabinowitz*, 149; and Kai Kjær-Hansen, "Controversy about Lucky," *Mishkan* 60 (2009): 46–64; 46, note 2.

82   Blom, "Reiseerindringer," *Missions-Blad for Israel* (1892): 123.

83   "A Great Need," *The Peculiar People* 2, no. 1 (1889): 67–69.

84   Löwen, *Christian Theophilus Lucky*, 20.

claiming independence from the mission; he wanted to cut any bond to a mission society, and he wanted Löwen to follow him. Not least, he insisted on observing traditional halachic law, not only for himself, but also for Löwen, who was not willing to do this on principle. Some of the German ministers supported Lucky in these disputes, and one of them, Johannes Müller, claimed that Löwen's non-Jewish wife should agree to conversion.[85] Still, the problems were not always about Löwen and Lucky; the "ordinary" difficulties missionaries expected to meet often made things worse. At the end of 1891, Löwen had fallen into depression, and in January 1892 the Berlin Society had had enough. Löwen went back to Berlin and published a final double edition (issue 8–9) without Lucky's assistance. After the closure of *Edut LeYisra'el*, Lucky waited until 1897 before he was able to establish a new Hebrew journal, called *Ha-Edut*, which at least lasted until the next year.[86] Löwen claims that Lucky also published the journal in 1907. The content and ideology were the same. Except for some sporadic support from the SDB, it is not clear who assisted Lucky in this or from where he received financial support. According to Löwen, Lucky continued to have the same ambivalent attitude toward financial support from mission societies, and he assumes that this was the reason for the new journal's few publications.[87]

In 1898 the American journal closed down as well. In 1910 Lucky established another journal in English, *The Messianic Jew*, together with the Jewish-Christian missionary Philip Cohen from Johannesburg. However, this journal did not survive for long. Possibly only one issue was published, as the partnership between Lucky and Cohen soon came to an end. According to Wiegand, Lucky quit the cooperation with Cohen because of disagreements on some details, and the fact that Lucky did not find it easy to cooperate with partners who held on

---

85 Ibid., 21.

86 Ibid., 22–23.

87 Ibid.

to their independence.[88] The publication of *The Messianic Jew* induced David Baron to write an article against Lucky and his sympathizers in *The Scattered Nation* in 1911.[89] From April 1911, Lucky also wrote some articles in *De Boodschapper* under the name Jedidjah, but from then on, his health began to decline.[90]

LUCKY'S FRIENDS AMONG THE MISSIONARIES

Soon after settling down in Stanislau, Lucky became a voice that missionaries to the Jewish people could not completely ignore. Otto von Harling was somewhat representative of the ambivalent attitude toward Lucky among several missionaries. Once, he witnessed how Lucky criticized the Jewish Christians at a meeting for their lack of Torah observance, while other Jews were present. After a private outburst from von Harling during a break, Lucky began to emphatically explain during the meeting how the Hebrew Bible points to Christ.[91]

For some of the Danish missionaries to the Jews in Galicia, Lucky even became something like a supervisor.[92] Johannes Volf and his wife Petra were the first Danish missionaries the Danish Israel Mission sent to Przmysel (in today's Poland) in Galicia, in 1905. Lucky was his advisor for contact with the Jews. The Volf family and Lucky got along very well,

---

88   Wiegand, *Chajim Jedidjah Lucky*, 61; *The Messianic Jew: Organ of the Jewish Messianic Movement* 1 no. 1 (December 1910). Cited May 14, 2011. Online: http://vineofdavid.org/remnant-repository/_files/The_Messianic_Jew_Volume_1_Lucky.pdf .

89   David Baron, *Messianic Judaism; or Judaizing Christianity* (London, England: Morgan and Scott, year not given). Reprint of David Baron, "Messianic Judaism; or Judaizing Christianity," *The Scattered Nation* 68 (1911): 423–432.

90   Velthuysen, *Christian Theophilus Lucky*, 198; Löwen, *Christian Theophilus Lucky*, 24.

91   Otto von Harling, *Pionerarbeide i Galati* (Oslo, Norway: Den Norske Israelsmisjon, 1948), 14, 25; P. Anacker, "Meine Reise nach Galizien," *Saat auf Hofnung* (1899): 86.

92   Petra Volf, "Mindeblade om Pastor Johannes Volf (27.02.1873–21.10.1911," *Hjemliv og trosliv: Mindeblade fra Indre Missions Vaartid* 13 (1945): 92–118.

and Lucky became the godfather of two of their sons. Several times he also preached in the evangelical church in Przmysel.[93]

In addition to the friendship with the Volf family, Lucky's more lasting friendships from 1889 onward seem to have been with the pastors of small German Lutheran Diaspora congregations in Stanislau: August Wiegand, Theodor Zöckler, and Max Weidauer. Wiegand, as well as his successors Zöckler and Weidauer, were primarily congregational ministers, but nevertheless combined their traditional ministry with mission work among the Jews in the area. Wiegand and Zöckler were trained by the *Institutum Delitzschianum* in Leipzig and influenced by Leipzig's strategic thinking. Wiegand's successor, Theodor Zöckler (1867–1949), became another companion of Lucky's, although he was not as outspoken as Wiegand. He would become the most famous Lutheran pastor in Stanislau and eastern Galicia. He was stationed in Stanislau immediately after Wiegand's departure in 1891, and stayed there until the Germans fled the Red Army in 1944. Like Wiegand he was, in the beginning, dependent on financial support from the Danish Israel Mission, but after some years, in 1893, he was employed by the German Evangelical Church to minister in Stanislau. Until he married in January 1893, Zöckler also lived in Lucky's home, as Wiegand had done, and he even used his home every week for lessons in Christianity for the German children.[94]

Between 1895 and 1898, Zöckler established several institutions in the area, which after WWI numbered about six hundred residents, including an orphanage, a German school that also hosted many Jewish children, a home for the elderly, and a home for disabled and psychiatric patients from all ethnic groups in the area.[95] The institutions were based on a revival in the local congregation in the summer of 1895. Some of the Jewish children were baptized, but to the frustration of

---

93 Another missionary who praised Lucky's friendship was Gisle Johnson from the Norwegian Israel Mission. Johnson met Lucky a few times in 1903 and 1904, during Johnson's first years as a missionary in Galicia, and during the next ten years, they corresponded. Johnson, however, never supported Lucky's agenda in the same way as Volf. See Johnson, *Fra vor Missions Fortid*, 248.

94 Zöckler, *Gott hört Gebet*, 18.

95 Volf, *Mindeblade*, 105.

some Danish mission leaders, Zöckler was very strict about accepting Jewish applicants for baptism.[96]

Zöckler also took care of Lucky's well-being in general, and in the last years before WWI more or less employed him as a teacher of Hebrew, Old Testament, and Judaism for the candidates at the *Paulinum*, a home for theological candidates in Stanislau founded by Zöckler in 1908. The institution was founded to train theologians for ministry in the Diaspora congregations as well as to inspire them for the mission to the Jews.[97] However, considering Lucky's age and economic situation it was just as important that Lucky had a place to live.

Many of the sources comment on Lucky's poverty in Stanislau. According to Weidauer, Lucky lived in several places during his years in Stanislau; one of these was under the Bistritz bridge in a wood shack filled up by his bed, the Talmud, and numerous books.[98] He got clothes from friends, and for Weidauer it was a mystery how Lucky managed to make a living, not to mention how he was able to travel so much. First of all he seems to have traveled a lot in Galicia, visiting neighboring towns and talking with Jews.[99] However, he was also reported to have been in Russia, Romania, Serbia, Germany, England, Holland, South Africa, and the United States.[100] According to SDB sources, he must have been in the United States at least twice after his return to Europe in 1889, in 1893, and 1909.[101] He came to dinner at Zöckler's home twice a week, and later he went to a family by the name of Opdenhoffs, before settling at the *Paulinum*.[102] Although Weidauer assumes that Lucky ate with Jewish friends as well, he believes he was often hungry, but he never begged or borrowed money from anyone. Nevertheless, eating with

---

96 Torm, *50 Aars Arbejde for Israel*, 83.

97 T. Zöckler, "Aus Galizien," *Saat auf Hofnung* (1914): 138. Cf. also Torm, *50 Aars arbejde for Israel*, 83. In Torm's opinion Zöckler sometimes waited too long with the baptism of Jews because he wanted to know their motives. Sometimes Jewish children at the orphanage also were baptized.

98 Weidauer, *Erindringer*, 167.

99 I. Ch. Reinen, "Missions: Correspondence," *Sabbath Recorder* 48, no. 33 (August 18, 1892): 518.

100 Velthuysen, *Christian Theophilus Lucky*, 196–198.

101 Philips, *Ch. Theophilus Lucky*, 690–691.

102 "Missionen i Stanislau," *Missions-Blad for Israel* 82 (1908): 159.

his non-Jewish friends was not without problems, as Lucky expected his meals to be kosher, much to the distress of non-Jewish wives. The Norwegian missionary Gisle Johnson unabashedly described Lucky as "a nightmare for any housewife."

The sources include a detail that perhaps explains why Lucky, in spite of being a rather difficult friend or guest, was not only tolerated, but even warmly welcomed in some places. His ability to remember most people he had met combined with a deep loyalty to those he regarded as friends. When Lucky became friends with several of the candidates from Leipzig and other missionaries, he remembered even the birthdays of their children with visits or postcards. Thereby, Wiegand says, the difficult guest won the hearts of the parents.[103] When possible, Lucky shared social and spiritual fellowship with the German ministers, and he participated more or less regularly in Zöckler's and Weidauer's little staff in Stanislau.[104] Still, Weidauer says that Lucky could become intensely affected during discussions, which made it difficult to talk with him. One of the things Weidauer and Lucky disagreed on was anti-Semitism, an ideology for which Weidauer seems to have had some sympathy.[105]

LUCKY'S JEWISH-CHRISTIAN FELLOWSHIP

Lucky never managed to establish a Jewish-Christian congregation, but that does not mean that he never tried. In Galicia and Bukowina he had a circle of Jewish individuals who viewed him as their leader. Weidauer thought that the circle of Jews who sometimes assembled around Lucky related to him as a person and teacher, rather than being a religious community.[106] Some of these followers of Lucky were probably members of a group in Braila led by a Jewish Christian named L. W. Horowitz, who under supervision by von Harling worked for the Norwegian Israel Mission. However, after some years Horowitz's enthusiasm for the mission as well as Protestant Christianity seemed

---

103 Wiegand, *Chajim Jedidjah Lucky*, 56.

104 Weidauer, *Erindringer*, 171.

105 Ibid., 177.

106 Ibid., 178.

to have left him. According to von Harling this was partly Lucky's fault, as he believes Horowitz gave up his Christian ministry due to broken hopes about a Jewish-Christian colony in Palestine that Lucky had encouraged him to work for.[107]

From the end of the 1890s to 1904, Lucky cooperated with Professor Ernst F. Ströter in an unsuccessful attempt to establish a Jewish-Christian colony in Haifa.[108] This Christian Zionist society believed that Israel's political restoration would precede a national spiritual awakening, inspired by Romans 11 and Ezekiel 37. Their plan was to employ workers and thereby establish some sort of Jewish-Christian colony, unpolluted by influence from the missions. Baptism was not a precondition to being employed, and the group in Braila was now supposed to be the core of this colony.

According to Johnson, the group was excited about these plans for a long time, although it seemed that for group members the main thing was not the Christian aspect but the prospect of making a living in Palestine. Only a couple of them were baptized and took part in Communion. However, after several months in Palestine, in the summer of 1904, group members returned to Europe with broken dreams, as the project seemed impossible to implement. In the fall of 1904 the Norwegian mission society fired Horowitz after he openly expressed his regret at receiving Christian baptism. Despite his antipathy toward the traditional Jewish mission, Lucky was not happy when Horowitz left the Norwegian mission, as the group in Braila seems to have dissolved.[109]

THE STRUGGLE FOR A NEW MISSION STRATEGY

In the decades before WWI, the idea of contextualization of the Christian message and the formation of national churches gained influence among Protestant churches and mission societies in general, and it is only to be expected that similar discussions took place in the Jewish

---

107 Ibid., 3, 19. See also Skarsaune, *Israels venner*, 200–201.

108 Professor Ernst Ferdinand Ströter (1846–1922) founded "The Hope of Israel Mission" in 1892, together with Rev. A. C. Gaebelein in New York. See Strack, *Yearbook* (1906), 115; and Löwen, *Christian Theophilus Lucky*, 20.

109 Johnson, *Fra vor Missions Fortid*, 248, 250.

missions. When they did, it seems that it often was Rabinowitz's work or Lucky's ideas and criticism that came into focus; these also set the agenda for discussions at several international conferences on Jewish mission between 1890 and 1911.

Participants in these discussions were generally inclined to tolerate, or at least listen to, criticism against missionary methods, but they were less willing to entertain the idea of forming Jewish-Christian congregations.[110] Lucky's ideas about Torah observance for Jewish Christians caused the most tension. Lucky's opponents feared that this was a new version of the old Ebionite "heresy," and they considered it to be a form of religious syncretism. Löwen claims that Lucky softened his views in the last years of his life, at least when it came to working for the missions. During their last meeting in 1913, Lucky acknowledged Löwen's position, while regretting his own stubbornness.[111]

THE WAR YEARS IN HOLLAND 1914–1916

During Lucky's last years he became increasingly depressed. This was apparently due to lack of results in his work, as well as the devastation of the war in Galicia. At the outbreak of the war, Lucky was on a journey to the United States, and found himself stuck in Holland. For the next two years, Lucky worked as a preacher in SDB's congregations in Rotterdam and in other places in Holland.

In 1916 he spent some months in England, but as Lucky's sympathy in the war lay with Germany and Austria, the British antipathy toward German Christians was very disappointing for him. According to Lucky, Russia was to blame for the war, and he considered Russia to be the worst enemy of the Jews.[112] Lucky hoped that a German victory would open the doors for a massive Jewish immigration to Palestine.[113] His

---

110 Samuel Wilkinson, "The Moral Defensibility of some of the methods employed in Jewish Missions," in Strack, *Yearbook* (1906), 60.

111 Löwen, *Christian Theophilus Lucky*, 2. Löwen considered this event so significant that it is described already in the prologue of the obituary. Still, the narrative may also serve as a defense for Löwen vs. Wiegand and others of Lucky's sympathizers in Germany.

112 Randolph, *Christian Theophilus Lucky*, 208.

113 Wiegand, *Chajim Jedidjah Lucky*, 61.

opinion about Russia must have been strengthened by reports of the war's enormous destructive impact on society in Galicia, not least for the Jewish population. Between 1914 and 1915, Galicia was occupied by the Russian army, which started an intense Russification campaign with persecution and deportation of Jews from the war zone (Kurland, the kingdom of Poland and Galicia), as the Jews were regarded as hostile by the Russian army.[114] In 1915, the Russians were forced to flee Galicia, but in June 1916, the Russians again occupied Stanislau. Pogroms followed immediately, and the next summer 90,000 houses were burned down and Galicia's economy was destroyed.[115]

Lucky was very worried about his Galician friends. Due to bad health and a general decline due to his age, he had to end his work for the SDB in the summer of 1916. He attempted to return to Galicia via Germany.[116] He was hospitalized around October 1 at *Paulsenstrasser Krankenhaus Ebenezer* in Stegliz, Berlin, where he stayed his remaining two months. On Saturday, November 25, 1916, Lucky died after the conclusion of the Sabbath, on Rosh Chodesh Kislev. He was buried Wednesday, November 29 at 9:30 AM at the Jewish cemetery in Plau, Mecklenburg, seventy-five miles northwest of Berlin.[117] The funeral was arranged and conducted by his friend Wiegand, who had been pastor of the local Lutheran church since he left Stanislau twenty-five years earlier.

Lucky's faith was clearly announced in the German newspapers shortly after the funeral:

> Peace over Israel! Our dear pastor and friend, the Hebrew writer, Rabbi Chajim Jedidjah (Christian Theophilus) Pollak, surnamed Lucky, died Nov. 25th, 1916, just at the close of the earthly Sabbath. His name was filled with care. He was

---

114 Alexander Victor Prusin, *Nationalizing a Borderland: War, Ethnicity, and Anti-Jewish Violence in East Galicia, 1914–1920* (Tuscaloosa, AL: University of Alabama, 2005), iv, 34, 53.

115 Ibid., 51–59.

116 Gerhard Velthuysen (name of article not given), in *Sabbath Recorder* 82, no. 2 (January 8, 1917): 44; and "Deaths" (by the editor), *Sabbath Recorder* 82, no. 5 (January 29, 1917): 159.

117 Velthuysen, *Christian Theophilus Lucky*, 196–198.

a member of the original, apostolic church of Jerusalem, zealous for the law of the fathers and witness of Jeschua in Israel. "There remaineth therefore a rest to the people of God." On behalf of the believing Jews who are faithful to the Law. B. Fliegelman, Lemberg, Galicia, Kleparu 267. On behalf of friends from the Christian Nations. A. Wiegand, Pastor, Plau in Mecklenburg, Germany.[118]

---

118 Translation from Velthuysen's obituary in *De Boodschopper* (December 1916) in Gerhard Velthuysen, "Christian Theophilus Lucky," 82, no. 7 (February 12, 1917): 196.

THEOPHILUS LUCKY'S INTRODUCTION

MEDITATIONS OF THE TESTIMONY

Volume I Issue 2, Cheshvan 5648 (1888) pgs. 18–19

There is one beast under the expanse. It is an incredibly wicked beast. Conceived in darkness and in the shadow of death. Born in hell. This wicked beast devours, kills, and demolishes. There is no good attribute that can overpower it. The souls that it has desecrated are as innumerable as the grains of sand at the seashore. It consumes and destroys man. It brings many epidemics into the world and kills every living thing. What is it? What is its name among the nations and within Israel?

The nations call it Prejudice. It decrees harsh judgments on people without reason. Convicting a man before investigating him thoroughly, believing everything that is said about him without scruple. Even in ancient times this evil beast was known among the Hebrews, but they called it by another name, by its true name: Baseless Hatred.

How dreadful is this name! From the time that the first man sinned until now this evil beast has caused great destruction in Israel. Why did Cain murder Abel? Because of Baseless Hatred. He hated him for no reason other than that Abel did not have to carry a yoke or a plow. And in the days of Noah the wickedness of man was great. God saw that the world was corrupt, and so he brought a great flood upon the earth.

With what did all flesh become corrupt? The sages of the Midrash answered and said that *Androlomosia*[119] came into the world and killed those who were evil and those who were good. It has been so throughout all the generations of Israel. Even King David, the most chosen of all the kings, drank from the cup of Baseless Hatred. The words of his laments came from his viscera, saying:

> Let not my lying enemies rejoice over me, those who hate me for no reason,[120] without cause they laid a net to trap me, without cause they dug a pit for me.[121] Many are those who hate me for no reason; must I return that which I have not stolen?[122] They answer my love with accusation,[123] etc.

At first, those who hated for no reason greatly rejoiced when they saw their fellow fall. Afterward, they set a trap to ensnare the man they hated, and they devised plots against him, seeking from him that which he had not stolen. And why is it thus? They answered his love with accusation. They answered his love with hostility and hate. They did not know how to promote justice, and they did not open their eyes in order to see it. They had a spirit of blindness, and in that blindness they pounced upon their neighbor without cause. Even in our days there has continued to be those in Israel who hate baselessly. They have greatly multiplied among us, and their numbers have become many. They are like gaping wounds on the flesh of our people.

Why do our Jewish brothers hate us, we who follow after Yeshua our Messiah? What evil have we done to our people? Our hearts are filled with love, but their hearts are filled with bitterness and hatred. What sins and crimes have I committed in publishing a Hebrew journal out of concern for the wellbeing of my people? They answer my love with accusations. I am all peace, but when I speak they are for war.[124] Until when, O HaShem God?

---

119 This is a Greek word meaning "hatred of man."

120 Psalm 35:19.

121 Ibid., 35:7.

122 Ibid., 69:5.

123 Ibid., 109:4.

124 Ibid., 120:7.

I am, however, comforted in this: There is still a day coming when the children of Israel will return to HaShem, our God, and they will see their Redeemer. Love of truth will come into their hearts and Baseless Hatred will be wiped off the face of the earth. HaShem will cause this to happen, and on that day law and justice will not be far off. Amen.

הַיְּהוּדִי-לְעוֹלְמֵי-עַד

THE JEW—FOREVERMORE

קֹדֶשׁ יִשְׂרָאֵל לַה׳ רֵאשִׁית תְּבוּאָתוֹ
כָּל-אֹכְלָיו יֶאְשָׁמוּ רָעָה תָּבֹא אֲלֵיהֶם
נְאֻם-ה׳ (ירמיה ב׳ ג׳)

Israel is holy to HaShem, the first fruits of his harvest.
All who eat of it are made guilty; disaster shall befall
them—declares HaShem. (Jeremiah 2:3)

א

I

נָע וָנָד תִּהְיֶה בָאָרֶץ
יִשָּׂא הַיְּהוּדִי חָקוּק עַל מֵצַח:
וּבְכֵן יָנוּד יָנוּעַ מִפֶּרֶץ אֶל פֶּרֶץ
עַל כָּל מִדְרַךְ כַּף רַגְלוֹ יְבוֹאֵהוּ רֶצַח
וְכֹה יָסוֹב הָאֻמְלָל עָיֵף וּרְפֵה-כֹּחַ
מִגּוֹי אֶל גּוֹי—וְלֹא יִמְצָא מָנוֹחַ.

"You shall be a vagrant and a wanderer on the earth"
Carries the Jew, engraved on his brow, unable to hide.
From breach to breach he wanders, bearing his hurt,
As murder stalks him at every pass, at every stride.
Thus turns the miserable, faint, and feeble wretch
From nation to nation—yet he never finds his rest.

ב

II

מֵאֶרֶץ מְכוּרָתוֹ, אֶרֶץ חֶמְדָּה וּרְחָבָה
שֻׁלַּךְ אֲהָהּ! הוּטַל טִלְטֵלָה גָּבֶר—
פֹּה עֲלֵי אֶרֶץ זָרָה, כְּעַרְעָר בָּעֲרָבָה
מִי לוֹ פֹּה וּמַה? כִּי אִם לַחֲצָב לוֹ קָבֶר.
וְכֹה נָגוּעַ וּמְעוּנֶּה זֶה שְׁנוֹת אֲלָפִים
יָתְעֶה כְּשֶׂה פְּזוּרָה תַּחַת הַשָּׁמַיִם.

Expelled from his home, a pleasant and spacious land,
He roams foreign soil, cast from the estate HaShem gave—
Like a juniper planted in the desert, in arid sand.
Who will come to him here, except to provide him his
grave?
And such has been his torment these last two thousand
years,
Like scattered sheep he strays, praying that Heaven
interferes.

ג

III

אֲבָל הִשָּׁמְרוּ לָכֶם עַמִּים! אוֹתוֹ לִנְגּוֹעַ
אַל תָּרִימוּ אֶגְרוֹף רֶשַׁע לְהַכּוֹתוֹ נָפֶשׁ
מַה זֶּה תַּרְחִיבוּ פִיכֶם, עִם בָּזוֹז לִבְלוֹעַ
תַּאֲרִיכוּ לָשׁוֹן, תַּשְׁלִיכוּ עָלָיו רֶפֶשׁ?
הֵן אוֹת שֵׁנִי שָׂם לוֹ אֵל שָׁמַיִם:
כָּל הַנּוֹגֵעַ בַּיְּהוּדִי יוּקַם שִׁבְעָתַיִם.

But beware, O Nations, not to touch his soul!
Raise not your wicked fists to strike him down.
Why do you open your mouths wide to swallow him
whole,
Whilst your tongues spew slime and filth all around?
The God of heaven has placed another sign upon his brow:
"All who touch a Jew shall reap sevenfold; this is my vow!"

ד

IV

עַל שֶׁבֶר בַּת עַמִּי, עַם עָנִי וְכוֹאֵב
אַל תִּשְׂמַח, צַר-נִבְזֶה, מוּסַר פּוֹרֵעַ!
עוֹד יָבֹא יוֹם, וּבוֹשׁוּ פְּנֵי-כָל-אוֹיֵב
מִכְּבוֹד יַעֲקֹב, עַתָּה עַל-יְרֵכוֹ צוֹלֵעַ.
וְאָז אַתָּה, זֶה יָהִיר! אֵלָיו תִּשְׁתּוֹחַח
וְלָנֶצַח יִסָּכֵר כָּל פִּי כֶלֶב נוֹבֵחַ.

Do not rejoice over my broken people, over my daughter,
Who is troubled and despised, whom anguish still afflicts!
A day is yet to come when all those who fought her,
Will be shamed by the glory of Jacob, who still limps.
Then you arrogant will be brought down before him,
looking up,
And like howling dogs your mouths will be forcibly shut.

ה

עוד אראה תקוה טובה לבת עמי
השדודה
נשקפת מן החרבכים, שם בשמי מע...
לא לנצח תראה עזובה, גלמורה
עוד שמיה יאירו, שמשה עוד יעל
שוא לכם חרשים להכין ליהודי
כלי רצח!
„היהודי—לעולמי־עד‟ וזה זכרו לנצ...

V

Yet shall I see hope for the daughter of my plundered
    nation
Peering through the cracks in heaven above.
You shall not see her forever abandoned in condemnation;
Again shall her skies shine bright, and her sun shall rise
    thereof.
In vain, O deaf ones, you fashion murder weapons against
    the Jew!
"The Jew is forevermore" for time immemorial shall
    stand true.

SECTION I

GUARDING THE TESTIMONY: INTRODUCTION

Volume IV Issue 2, pgs. 1–3

I f one of my Jewish brothers approached me and said, "What is the philosophy behind this journal? Teach me the Torah of the Testimony[125] while I am standing on one foot, as well as the spirit of the Testimony—the living spirit that has neither flesh, tendons, nor bones," I would answer him with measured words. I would say, "If your soul desires to obtain life, *guard the faith of Moses and Yeshua*. This is the entire teaching of the Testimony. The rest is commentary and interpretation of this teaching. Go and search them out and you will find the Way, the Truth, and the Life."

Or perhaps I would explain myself a bit more, saying: "If your soul desires to obtain life in this world and possess life in the World to Come, observe the decrees of HaShem. Observe all the commandments of the Torah that were given by HaShem through Moses our teacher—peace be upon him—and interpreted and commented upon by the men of the Great Assembly and their disciples. Observe the testimony of Yeshua, HaShem's faithful Messiah, and take note of the things he did for us. Carefully guard these in your heart. Observe the words that he spoke to us:

---

125 [Lucky refers to the title of his journal, *Edut LeYisra'el* (Testimony to Israel). The title of the journal signifies the testimony of the Messiah and the Torah of Moses to the people of Israel.]

I am the bread of life.[126] I am the living bread that comes down from heaven;[127] everyone who eats of me will have eternal life.[128] I am the entrance. If anyone enters by me he will be saved.[129] My flock hears my voice, and I will give them eternal life.[130] I am the way and the truth and the life.[131]

Guard this Testimony and you will inherit eternal life. This is the teaching of the Testimony and these are the words that were spoken in order to clarify and elucidate the Torah; go and search them and find rest for your soul.

I would say this if the man who came to question me was a wise and learned man with an upright spirit, whose path was straight, who loved knowledge, and sought truth; a man who had prepared his heart to see the heart of Torah before he expounded upon it. I would assure him that if he investigated the words of the Testimony and looked deeply into them, he would find all that he has desired to know.

A STONE OF STUMBLING

I have not been overly verbose trying to clarify and explain the position of the Testimony. It can be compared to a stone in the road over which many will stumble. Yet this is a truly wise generation, filled with knowledge and insight. Nevertheless, no heroes have arisen to sit in the seat of judgment as trustworthy judges, issuing righteous judgments concerning all the new information that comes before them. It is difficult for them to abandon the opinions that they have held since their youth.

Thus, few will be wise enough to understand the position of this Testimony if I do not continue to clarify and interpret this new information. This generation will inherit ignorance from the previous generations.

---

126 John 6:35.
127 Ibid., 6:51.
128 Ibid., 6:54.
129 Ibid., 10:9.
130 Ibid., 10:27–28.
131 Ibid., 14:6.

Consequently, everyone in this generation who holds on to this faulty information will be misled by it—Jews and Gentiles alike—and this new information will prove to be a great obstacle.

People of this generation—Jews and Gentiles—say that there are two religions in the countries in which we live. The first is the religion of Moses (Judaism), which most of the Jews practice, and the second is the religion of the Messiah (Christianity), which most of the Gentiles in these countries practice. Everyone who belongs to the faith of Moses is called a "Jew," and everyone who belongs to the faith of the Messiah Yeshua is called a "Christian."[132] The Jew is not considered a member of Christianity and a Christian is not considered a member of Judaism.

If an Israelite becomes a part of the congregation of Messiah, he ceases to be a Jew, even though he descended from the Jewish people and Israelite blood runs through his veins, for now he is called a "Christian" in the wider community. So too, if a Christian connects himself to the Mosaic assembly through formal conversion, he ceases to be a Christian and is called a "Jew," even though he descended from a foreign people and the blood of that people runs through his veins. This idea is deeply ingrained in the hearts of the people, and even the educated and wise hold on to it.

Therefore, when they see the knowledge of the Testimony they are astonished and ask: "What is this? If the people of the Testimony are Jewish, then they cannot be a part of Christianity. If they are Christians, how can they say that they are Jews? If they become Christians, then they cease to be Jewish. But if they are Jewish, which is what they tell everyone, how can they say, 'We belong to the Messiah'?"

---

132 [Lucky actually uses the Hebrew word *meshichi*, or "messianic," throughout this entire article, but he is referring to a Christian and to Christianity. However, it would appear that he does not use the common Hebrew term *notzri* for "Christian" or *natzrut* for "Christianity," as he does elsewhere, because he is typically speaking about a Jew who believes in Yeshua. When speaking exclusively of Gentile Christians in other articles, Lucky differentiates and uses the term *notzri*. It is important to note, however, that in Lucky's days the words "Messianic" and "Christian" were not as nuanced or distinguishing as they are today. In essence, during this time the term "messianic" may have served mainly to distinguish a Jewish Christian from a Gentile Christian.]

These are the things I hear from the esteemed of this generation. Jews and Gentiles alike disown the people of the Testimony, saying, "You are not a part of us," and, "We do not know you." And so I must communicate to this generation, speaking and writing about the vision of the Testimony, explaining it well on paper, so that they will thoroughly investigate and judge righteously in order that justice will not be subverted.

Because the burden of guarding the Testimony rests upon me, I will stand my watch, answering anyone who reproaches me for it. I belong to the assembly of the Testimony. I am a Hebrew and I fear the God of heaven. I am a Jew and, behold, I observe the Torah, the Written Torah and the Oral Torah, and my soul is inextricably bound to Yeshua the Messiah. He is my life-breath, for he is my Savior King. He is the one whom HaShem sent to be the resurrection of the soul for anyone who is called "mortal" and to give us eternal life. I am a son of the Mosaic and Israelite faith [i.e., Judaism], and behold, I am also a man of Messiah. I am a disciple of Moses and of the men of the Great Assembly, and I am a disciple of Yeshua the Messiah and his apostles.

This is how we guard the Testimony. Now bear with me and I will explain my opinion with God's help.

GUARDING THE
TESTIMONY: PART I

Volume IV Issue 2, Nisan 5657 (1897) pgs. 1–11

Even though the faith of Moses and Judah
is a light unto my path,
Yeshua the Messiah is the life of my soul
and the light of my salvation …

And so he is. The religion of Moses and Israel is the light to my path, for I am a guardian of the Torah and a keeper of the commandments.[133] From my youth I have kept the commands of HaShem and the laws of the Torah. I observe the Sabbath strictly and the appointed times of HaShem, which are all holy and festive days for me. Even the appointed times that were established for us by our sages of blessed memory[134] are just as holy to me as the appointed times of the Torah.

---

133 [Lucky apparently uses the term "religion of Moses" to refer to the Written Torah and "of Israel" to refer to the Oral Torah. He uses the Hebrew word *notzer* (נוצר) for "guardian," which is an allusion to the word *notzri* (נוצרי), which means "Nazarene" and now "Christian" in Modern Hebrew. It appears that in using this specific word, Lucky is subtly communicating to his readers that the Nazarene, the Messiah, was a keeper of the Torah as well.]

134 Rosh HaShanah, Hanukkah, Purim, etc. Rosh HaShanah was established by our sages of blessed memory, for in the Torah there is only Yom Teru'ah (The Day of the Horn Blast). Moses did not expressly command us to celebrate Rosh HaShanah. However, our sages interpreted it as if he had.

No unclean food[135] shall ever enter my mouth, and for seven days—the days of Passover—no leaven can be found in my house. On the tenth day of the seventh month of every single year I afflict my soul.[136] I even observe all four of the fasts mentioned in Zechariah (8:19):[137] the fasts of the fourth, fifth, seventh, and tenth months.[138]

THE UNFINISHED TALMUD

I will be brief. I will recount and account for all the commandments that I perform and do not perform. I observe the Oral Torah, which is the Torah of Moses as interpreted by the men of the Great Assembly and those who came after them. It must be said that the Oral Torah is not a different Torah, for we were not given two Torahs, rather it is an interpretation, and it came about in order to interpret the Torah of Moses. And the interpretation has still not been completed. It has not yet ended nor will it ever end, for the legal rulings (*halachot*) will change in accordance with the spirit of the times and the lives of the children of Israel. This is also the opinion of the great Rabbi Jacob Emden who said that the Talmud is not, and never will be, completed. For the Talmud is comprised of everything discussed and presented in every age by the sages concerning matters of Torah. The investigation into the correct interpretation of the commandments is a tradition of the sages.

In his book *Mitpachat Sefarim,* the great Rabbi Jacob Emden said that the commandments are relative to time, circumstance, and man. He says their applications and interpretations are not sealed and finished all at once, rather they change in every era. It was not just Rabbi Emden who said these things, but all the sages of Israel (with the exception of a few), and this is the foundation of the Talmud. Therefore, all those who

---

135 Pork, shellfish, etc. All the foods that are forbidden to us Jews.

136 [Yom Kippur.]

137 For these days will not become days of celebration for Israel until the eyes of my people are opened and they recognize that Yeshua is the Messiah. Only then will these days change from being fast days to days of joy and feasting, just as Zechariah prophesied.

138 [The fasts of the month of Tammuz, the Ninth of Av, Gedaliah, and the Tenth of Tevet respectively.]

contend with the Talmud are incorrect to lay upon it all of the blame for the unpleasant traditions that Israel practices. This is not the fault of the Talmud. I will speak more on this, lest anyone become upset with me over a subject that I have not fully explained. Rabbi Emden says that the interpretations of the Torah's commands are relative to "time, circumstance, and man," whereas I say that they are relative to "time, place, and man."

THE ONE DISTINGUISHING FACTOR

Even the customs of Israel are like Torah to me if they come from a trustworthy source. Therefore I am a faithful Jew just like all the other faithful Jews who keep the Torah. In every instance we see eye to eye. There is only one area in which I cannot agree; one thing distinguishes and separates me from most other Jews. This one point of difference has assigned me a different destiny in life.

The majority of my Jewish brothers who live in these lands reject Yeshua the Messiah, and for them his name is a horror. This is not so for me. Rather I honor, esteem, and sanctify the name of Yeshua. I believe with a complete faith that Yeshua bar Yosef from Nazareth is the true Messiah sent from our Heavenly Father to all humanity and who suffered in order to redeem them from the coming destruction, bringing them eternal righteousness. I believe there is no other name given to sons of men under heaven by which one is saved. This stone, which they rejected, is the chief cornerstone to the whole structure of the Torah of truth, which HaShem gave to his people Israel and to everyone who belongs to the human race.

Yeshua the Messiah is the life of my spirit. In him I find rest for my soul. He is the light of my salvation. In this one issue am I forced to separate from my other Jewish brothers, even if more and more my soul maintains the desire to agree with them on every matter.

WHAT COMPELS ME?

And what compels me to do this? Who or what was it, even in spite of what our rabbis and sages—both in this generation and in those previous—have said? What compelled me to believe that Yeshua bar Yosef is the true Messiah, even though the majority of my Jewish brothers detested him, rejected him, and would have rather given up their lives than believe in him? Who or what convinced me to leave the path paved by our people (by saying that he truly is the Messiah), especially since my soul is inextricably bound to the soul of our people forever, and I would rather choose death than to be separated from them?

It was the Holy Writings and the interpretations of our sages of blessed memory that convinced me to believe that Yeshua is the Messiah whom HaShem said that he would send to those who dwell in darkness, the shadow of death, in order to rescue them from the coming destruction.

And so I believe that all the Holy Writings were written and spoken through the Holy Spirit (i.e., divine inspiration). The Holy Writings recount the events that happened to us Israelites in ancient times. Their tablets are inscribed with accounts of what HaShem did for our forefathers and for us in every generation, from the day he chose us to be his nation.

WORDS OF COMFORT

Just as a rock in the middle of the sea will be pocked by waves and gusts of wind hitting against it and yet will not be destroyed, in the same way the tradition that we have received from the mouths of our forefathers stands. All the waves of the water—the enemies of the Torah—spill over it but cannot overcome it. The Holy Writings are the words of the living God. Moses and the prophets had visions of HaShem. They recounted their visions from HaShem and his word was on their tongues, and when they spoke words of comfort to the people of Israel they told from the very beginning that HaShem would raise up King Messiah for Israel and for all those who dwell on earth. Through him Israel would have the strength to overpower their enemies among the nations, to remove idolatry from the earth, and to turn all the wicked toward him.[139]

---

139 [From the synagogue prayer *Aleinu/Al Ken.*]

This is not the first time that HaShem has revealed matters pertaining to the consolation, for the river of prophecy is like a river of water. It begins sorrowfully but ends brightly. At its source its waters are few, but little by little its waters strengthen and surge into loud, crashing waves.

In the beginning, even before Moses, HaShem spoke words of comfort to the children of Eve. For the seed of the woman will crush the primordial serpent,[140] trample Satan—who rules death—and the children of Eve (the mother of the living) will be children of life in the World to Come, and children of God in heaven. HaShem said to Abraham: "Through your seed all the nations of the earth shall bless themselves."[141] And through the mouth of Jacob HaShem said to Judah that in the last days a lion, a ruler, would come forth from his loins, from his tribe, and he would have the obedience of the peoples[142] and establish the kingdom of heaven on earth.

In the days of Moses, the most faithful in HaShem's house, HaShem spoke through the man whose eyes were opened[143] that in the last days

---

140 Genesis 3:15. Everyone agrees that the primordial serpent that incites people to sin is a representation of Satan. And it is very surprising that Rashi, z"l, understood the passage as speaking of just a regular serpent. Even *Targum Onkelos* understood the passage as a figure of speech, and *Targum Yonatan* and *Yerushalmi* all understood that the serpent was not just a regular serpent, but rather the primordial serpent (a.k.a., Satan). Rabbi Berechiah said in the name of Rabbi Shmuel that everything was ruined when the first man sinned and would not be repaired until the coming of the son of Peretz (*Genesis Rabbah* 12:5). This is also the opinion of the Apostle Yochanan (John), that the Messiah was revealed in order to destroy the works of Satan (1 John 3:8).

141 Genesis 12:3, 18:18, 22:18. The commentary by the Apostle Shaul (Paul) is beautiful concerning this, for he asserts that it says "seed" and not "seeds" (see Galatians 3:16), because Shaul was interpreting this in the same manner as the rabbis did, who interpreted this to be an allusion. The Torah was thinking about the Messiah, the seed of Abraham, for the nations cannot bless themselves except through the Messiah who is the son of Abraham according to the flesh.

142 Genesis 49:8-12. Even if we say that "Shiloh" is the name of a place and not the name of the Messiah—as many commentators and aggadic writers have supposed—it does not matter, for Jacob was still thinking of the Messiah in his prophecy. For only through the Messiah will Judah have the obedience of the peoples. Only through the Messiah will Judah rule over all those who dwell on earth. However, this dominion is the dominion of Heaven, the dominion of the spirit, and not an earthly dominion.

143 [i.e., Balaam son of Beor.]

a morning star that illuminates the whole earth would step forth from Jacob.[144] Through the mouth of Moses HaShem said that he would raise up a prophet like Moses whom the children of Israel would obey.[145] In the days of the judges of Israel, before Samuel inaugurated a king for them, HaShem said to Eli through the mouth of a man of God that he would raise up a faithful priest who would do the will of God, walking before the anointed one (*mashiach*, משיח) of HaShem all his days. Is this not a prophecy about what will be in the last days?[146]

A RULER WHO FEARS GOD

The days passed, and the scepter of dominion was given to the tribe of Judah, just as HaShem said through Jacob. David son of Jesse was anointed as king over Israel. HaShem said to him through Nathan the prophet: "When your days are fulfilled ... I will establish your seed after you ... and I will establish his kingdom. He shall build a house in my name, and I will establish the throne of his kingdom forever. I will be a father to him and he will be a son to me, and if he commits an iniquity, I will chasten him with the rod of men and with the

---

144 Numbers 24:17. Rabbi Akiva interpreted this passage about Bar Kochba (which means "son of the star") [and proclaimed him to be the Messiah].

145 Deuteronomy 18:18. The commentators were nervous to expound upon this. Many of them thought that these words of Moses would not be fulfilled in the last days. What is even more difficult to comment on are the words "a prophet like me." Is it not written, "Never did there arise in Israel a prophet like Moses" (Deuteronomy 34:10)? Rashi and many others believe this will be fulfilled by another mere Israelite, and he says, "The words 'from your brothers' and 'from among you' mean that just as I (Moses) am from among you, so will he raise up for you [another prophet] in my place" (Rashi to Deuteronomy 18:18). Keifa [Peter] the apostle interpreted this passage about the Messiah, as did other rabbinic commentators, for the Jews traditionally interpreted it this way. From the days of Ezra and on the expositors saw the light of Messiah in these words.

146 1 Samuel 2:35. Rashi, along with the author of *Metzudat David* and others, thought that this priest spoken of was Zadok the high priest, for Zadok ministered in the holy place after Solomon had banished Abiathar. However, it is difficult to accept this interpretation, for neither Solomon nor Zadok did everything that was in the heart and mind of HaShem all their days. This prophecy is a spiritual one. The people of God in that generation awaited the cry of the kingdom, which would be the kingdom of God: a spiritual kingdom.

stripes of the sons of men."[147] David heard and understood that the words of HaShem through Nathan were about the establishment of the kingdom of heaven.

This word took root in David's heart and caused his expectation to grow exponentially. And when the Spirit clothed him he saw the King sitting at the right hand of HaShem and his people surrounding him, radiating in the splendor of holiness.[148] And when David spoke his last words, the Spirit came upon him and the prophetic psalm was in his mouth, and he said that the Rock of Israel, the Ruler of mankind (i.e., the Messiah), the Righteous One, spoke to him.

He will be like the morning light when the sun shines, like a morning without clouds, like sunshine and rain bringing vegetation to the earth. Is not my house with God, for he has made an everlasting covenant with me, fully drawn up and secured. Will he not bring my every desire and all my endeavors to blossom forth?[149] David's son Solomon observed his father's last words. He desired to be this Branch[150] since he built the house of HaShem and prayed, "God, endow the king with your judgments, the king's son with your righteousness," etc.[151] While

---

147 2 Samuel 7:12–15.

148 David made this vision known in Psalm 110. This hymn was about the Messiah, and in Midrash Tehillim on this psalm it says: "This is also about the Messiah, as it says (Isaiah 16:5), 'And a throne is established in mercy and he sits on it in truth.'" Rabbi Yochanan ben Yosei said this, and he added the word "also" because the psalm initially speaks about Abraham. But why does David call Abraham "Master"? Also what does "HaShem will send out of Zion the rod of your strength" mean? And what is "the splendor of holiness"? This psalm is only about the Messiah. The books by the gospel writers and the apostles are trustworthy witnesses, and even the sages of Israel understood this psalm as about the Messiah. Yeshua asked his listeners in the Temple how was it that David called the Messiah "Master" if he is his son (see Matthew 22:32–36; Mark 12:35–37; Luke 20:41–44), and no one responded saying the psalm was not about the Messiah but about Abraham. Yeshua did not say anything that was not already accepted by oral tradition. The tradition that the Messiah sits at the right hand of the Most High is in the writings of the Torah commentators on this psalm, and the phrase, "therefore he will lift up" resembles the words of Shaul (Philippians 2:9): "Therefore HaShem raised him up, etc."

149 2 Samuel 23:3–5. Everyone knows that these are words of prophecy that are clearly about the Messiah who will arise in latter days.

150 [צמח (tzemach)].

151 Psalm 72: the prayer of Solomon.

he was praying the Spirit came upon him and HaShem showed him the form of the Messiah. For all the kings will bow only to the Messiah who is sent from heaven, and all the nations will call him glad. They will not do this to a mere man whose days are numbered or who commits sins.

Even Solomon committed crimes against HaShem, and through his sin David's kingdom was torn in two. From the time Solomon's kingdom was torn in two—from the days of Rehoboam until the days of Hezekiah—the Prophets Obadiah, Joel, Amos, Hosea, and Isaiah arose, but none of them saw the kingdom of heaven in their spirit.

VISIONS OF THE PROPHETS

Obadiah concluded his prophecy with the words, "And the kingdom belonged to HaShem."[152] Joel saw that the day of HaShem was close, the day in which HaShem would pour out his Spirit on all flesh[153] and would reside in Zion.[154] Amos saw HaShem standing beside the altar saying, "In that day I will raise the fallen tent of David."[155] Hosea saw that, in the last days, the children of Israel would return and seek HaShem their God and David their king.[156] Isaiah, the greatest of all the prophets, saw the precious light; mysteries were revealed to him. In his spirit he saw Immanuel,[157] he saw the son that was given to us whose name is Wonderful, Counselor, Mighty God, Everlasting Father, Prince of Peace.[158] HaShem revealed to him that a shoot would sprout from the stock of Jesse, and a branch would grow forth from

---

152 Obadiah 21.

153 Joel 3:1.

154 Joel 4:21.

155 Amos 9:1, 11.

156 Hosea 3:5.

157 Isaiah 7:14.

158 Isaiah 9:5. In his Hebrew translation the righteous Franz Delitzsch of blessed memory separated "Wonderful" from the name "Counselor," therefore there are five names listed here for the Messiah, which is half of the number of holiness [i.e., Ten, as in the Ten Commandments, and ten is represented by the Hebrew letter *yod* (י), which is the first letter of the Tetragrammaton and the first letter of the Master's name.]

his roots.[159] HaShem showed him his Servant. For he shot up like a root out of dry ground, and he was wounded because of our crimes, crushed because of our iniquities, etc.[160]

Micah was able to see even more revelation than Isaiah did. Micah saw that the ruler would come forth from Bethlehem Ephrathah to rule over the house of Israel,[161] and until the time that she who is to bear has borne,[162] until the time when the young woman (or virgin) would give birth to Immanuel, the children of Israel would be under siege. He saw that the ruler born in Bethlehem would shepherd his people by the might of HaShem and that he would be the Messiah of peace. The Prophets Nahum and Zephaniah also saw the kingdom of heaven, which was to come in the last days.

The Prophet Jeremiah, one of the priests at Anathoth, prophesied: "Behold, days are coming when HaShem will raise up a righteous branch whose name will be 'HaShem our Righteousness,'[163] and on that day the children of Israel will serve HaShem their God and David their king whom HaShem will raise up for them."[164]

The prophet in exile, Ezekiel the priest, said in his anger toward Zedekiah:

> You (Zedekiah), dishonored, wicked prince of Israel, whose day has come, the time is set for your punishment. Thus said HaShem: "Remove the turban and the crown ... until he comes, the one to whom judgment belongs, and I will give it to him.[165] I will raise up over them one shepherd, my servant

---

159 Isaiah 11:1.

160 Isaiah 53:2, 5. Rashi and a few others wanted to interpret this chapter about Israel or the righteous in Israel. However, the correct interpretation is about Messiah, just as it says in *Targum Yonatan* and b.*Sanhedrin* 98a and many other places. Almost all the sages attest that these words were spoken only about Messiah.

161 Micah 5:1.

162 Ibid., 5:2.

163 Jeremiah 23:5–6.

164 Ibid., 30:9.

165 Ezekiel 21:30. The turban is on the head of the priest and the crown on the head of the king, and both of them will be given to him to whom judgment belongs: the Messiah.

David, and he will shepherd them. I, HaShem, will be their God and my servant David will be their prince."[166]

This prophecy is about the kingdom of heaven, which is surely coming, and the prophet of exile continued to see visions of God, the form and shape of the Temple, and the glory of thousands in Israel coming with their voices like raging waters. Not everyone who commented on this prophecy understood what the prophets were hinting at. From the days HaShem awakened Cyrus' spirit to build him a house in Jerusalem, the light of Messiah has been breaking and the dawn rising from the dark fog.

The prophets who returned from exile—Haggai, Zechariah, and Malachi—spoke clearly. Haggai said in the name of HaShem: "In just a little while I will shake the heavens and the earth ... and I will shake all the nations, and the delight of all the nations will come and I will fill this house with glory."[167] Afterward he said: "The glory of this latter House will be greater than the first, says HaShem of Hosts, and in that place I will give *peace.*"

---

166 Ibid., 34:23.

167 Haggai 2:6–7. There is no interpretation that sits well with me. Neither Rashi nor the author of *Metzudat David* found the correct interpretation answering this question: What is the glory with which HaShem will fill the House? Or what is the delight of all the nations? According to the author of *Metzudat David* all the nations come with their delight (i.e., their wealth, silver, and gold) and they would be lost and their delight would remain with Israel, and this will be the glory of this House. It is very difficult to interpret it this way. Is silver and gold the entire glory that HaShem desires to give to his people? And with what will this House be greater than the first? Even Abravanel, in his book *Sefer Mashmia Yeshu'ah*, disliked these interpretations. He says that the *Shechinah* will reside in that House and it alone will be the House's glory. This is the correct interpretation. However, the prophecy says that it would occur after this bitter exile. We have been in this exile for 1800 years. Therefore, there is no other way to interpret this. It is about the Messiah. He is the delight of all the nations and to him they will come. It will be through the Messiah that the second House will be greater than the first. Therefore, the Messiah had to come before the destruction of the Second Temple.

Zechariah saw a man, a servant of HaShem whose name is Branch, and he will build the Temple of HaShem.[168] Malachi saw that the Master and Angel of the Covenant would suddenly come to his Temple and they (Israel) would present offerings in righteousness.[169] Before the coming of the great and terrible day, HaShem will send Elijah who will return the hearts of the fathers to their children and the hearts of the children to their fathers.[170]

THE MESSIAH ACCORDING TO THE SAGES

After the prophets ceased, their prophecies and visions were sealed, and scribes took the place of prophets, clinging to hope in the Messiah with growing expectation. They saw the whole congregation of Israel awaiting the coming of the Shoot (*netzer*, נצר) that would sprout from Jesse, coming to proclaim a year of favor and to comfort all the mourners in Zion.

---

168 Zechariah 6:12. Even here Rashi avoids interpreting this about the Messiah. He says: "Some interpret this as referring to King Messiah, but the entire context deals with the Second Temple." He says this refers to Zerubbabel. However, what do the words "from beneath him" mean? Rashi (z″l) interprets these words as from the royal seed. However, it is difficult to interpret it this way. The author of *Metzudat David* (z″l) also interprets this as referring to Zerubbabel, saying that Zerubbabel was appointed with the name Branch and the name Messiah and from beneath him (which he also interprets as "from his seed") King Messiah will sprout forth and build HaShem's Temple in the future. This is also forced. However, at least the author of *Metzudat David* admits that "my servant Branch" is about the Messiah. Rashi does not admit this. Every wise and just judge will pronounce that this prophecy is about the Messiah.

169 Malachi 3:1–3. This prophecy is incredibly clear. Rashi interpreted the "Master" as the God of justice and "the Angel of the Covenant" as the one who avenges the covenant. But who is the God of justice who suddenly comes? The author of *Metzudat David* interprets the "Master" as King Messiah and "the Angel of the Covenant" as Elijah, saying: "Behold he is coming! For when the Messiah comes, Elijah will already have come." The correct interpretation is that the Master and the Angel of the Covenant are one person, described with two different titles. The Messiah—the Master—must be the Angel of the Covenant in order to renew the Sinai covenant through the sacrifice of his blood and purify the sons of Levi so that they may present offerings in the righteousness of Messiah, for the Messiah must be our covering, holiness, and righteousness, just as Shaul [Paul] the Apostle says (1 Corinthians 1:30).

170 The meaning of this passage is clear. Even Rashi does not try to change it!

The sages of Israel—holy men who feared God, filled with his Spirit—described the Messiah in great detail to the Israelites and gave him names such as Son of David,[171] Righteous Messiah,[172] King Messiah,[173] Messiah of Israel,[174] Messiah son of David, our Messiah, etc.[175] They said that the name of Messiah was created before the creation of the universe,[176] and they said that next to the throne of HaShem stands a second throne, and Messiah son of David sits upon it,[177] and they said that the spirit of Messiah hovered over the waters when God created the heavens and earth.[178]

Many other sages have said similar things. Who can count all their words about the Messiah? No one can, for they cannot be counted. The Messiah was their hope and the topic of their daily conversation. Their writings attest to the fact that they were awaiting his arrival. They plumbed the depths of the ideas of the prophets and the seers and they understood that HaShem himself testified about the raising up of the kingdom of heaven by sending his Messiah, and that the Messiah would not conquer through war with sword and spear, but rather with the Spirit of HaShem that rests upon him.

THEY WROTE ABOUT YESHUA

That which the prophets, scribes, Torah teachers, Chasidim, and men of deeds in Israel believed, I also believe. And now behold, the Messiah is Yeshua ben Yosef of Nazareth, the son of David, the shoot from the roots of Jesse, the son of Peretz. He appeared in our holy land and worked wonders in Israel. He showed himself to sons of men as one who is shunned by men; he had no form or beauty. Yet when he spoke, the soul of the people went out to him, for he taught as if from

---

171 b.*Sanhedrin* 95a, etc.

172 Targum to Jeremiah 20:5, etc.

173 *Targum Yonatan* to Genesis 49:12.

174 Ibid., to Micah 4:5.

175 Ibid., to Hosea 3:5.

176 b.*Pesachim* 54a and b.*Nedarim* 39b.

177 b.*Chagigah* 14a.

178 *Genesis Rabbah* 8.

the mouth of the Power and not like the scribes.[179] His disciples were convinced that he was the source of life and that he was the one whom HaShem had sent to bring salvation to this people and to all who believed in his name, and that there is no salvation in any other. He exposed himself to death and bore the sins of many. With his blood he renewed the covenant that HaShem made with our fathers on Sinai, and he opened the gate to all peoples so that a remnant from all nations would seek HaShem.

Now his name is revered in the eyes of all the peoples, for HaShem made him very great and gave him a name that is greater than any other name. Almost all the kings bow to him, all the nations worship him, bless themselves by him, and gladden him. Yeshua ben Yosef fulfilled every prophecy.

What the prophets told us we see before our very eyes. Even that which was not told to us we have seen, for we were not even told the half of what we have seen in Yeshua. How could I abandon this source of living water? Everything that the prophets saw and our sages of blessed memory imagined in their spirits is before us! How could I say, "It is not him," and sin by rejecting his kindness that he gave to me and to all who dwell on earth by sending his Messiah?

Therefore, I have held on tightly to Yeshua and I will not let go while I still have breath in my body. He is the life of my spirit; he is my light and my salvation. He is my glory and the one who lifts up my head. He was sent from our Heavenly Father to bring light to those who dwell in darkness and the shadow of death, teaching them the path of salvation. He came to straighten our understanding.

JUDGE FOR YOURSELVES

And now, beloved children of my generation, draw near and see. Watch closely and judge for yourselves if there is anything with which you

---

179 See Matthew 7:29. The righteous Delitzsch of blessed memory always translated this as "a man of power," and in the later editions of his Hebrew New Testament he translated it as "a man of authority." This is incorrect. The word "power" (*gevurah*, גבורה) is the correct word here. However, we must translate it as "from the mouth of the Power" and not "as a man of power." Everyone who is educated will be happy about my translation, because now the matter is perfectly clear.

can convict me. Listen to me in fairness and weigh all my words. Am I not right? Even though I am a Jew, I am a man who believes in the Messiah with all my heart and soul. Behold, I cleave to Yeshua, even though I am a disciple of the great talmudists and I have charted my course in life by the teachings of the Torah scholars and the heroes of the Mosaic and Judaic faith. I do not speak vilely of the leaders of the Israelite faith. God forbid I should do such a thing! I revere their words.

I answer and say that I am a son of the Mosaic and Judaic faith, and I consistently declare my belief in Moses and the prophets and the words of our sages of blessed memory, who were scholars and heroes of the Jewish faith. In my opinion, their words are holy. For this reason my soul has cleaved to the Messiah, Yeshua ben Yosef, for the Torah, the prophets, and our sages testified about him. He is the objective of the entire Torah. He is the Torah clothed in flesh. To all who believe in his name he gives power and might to be children of God.

Do not ask me: "If he really is who you say, and if our sages really described the Messiah in their spirit and it was Yeshua whom they described, why did his generation reject him? Why did the following generation, the great Torah scholars, not follow after him? And why did Rabbi Akiva cling to Bar Kochba?[180] Why …?"

What can I do? The generation of the first century sat on the seat of Moses and the prophets, and yet their eyes were closed from seeing the glory of Yeshua. They excommunicated Yeshua from the congregation of Israel and they baselessly closed the doors of the house of Judah to the Messiah. The people followed their instruction, for they were the rulers of the Mosaic and Judaic faith, and from these rulers came a great error: a Jew who believes in Yeshua ceases to be a Jew.

This is not the case with me. Behold, I am a faithful Jew, a son of Judah. The blood of Israel is in my veins. I observe the Torah and the commandments. I also observe every prohibition that the ancient and modern sages have taught: that is, if their teachings were founded in the Torah of Moses. And if they forbid me outright from following after Yeshua, the Messiah of the Living God, I will not obey them, for they

---

180 Rabbi Akiva interpreted the passage "And a star arose from Jacob" about him. He did not realize his mistake, for the star arose many years before Bar Kochba.

are in error, yet they do not see it. Yeshua is the fountain of life to those who cling to him. Therefore, I will repeat this over and over again:

Even though the faith of Moses and Judah
is a light unto my path,
Yeshua the Messiah is the life of my soul
and the light of my salvation

GUARDING THE
TESTIMONY: PART II

Volume IV Issue 4, pgs. 1–10

Even though my soul has cleaved to Yeshua
and I am his disciple,
I will not flee from the faith of Moses and Judah,
and it shall give me rest

Beloved brothers of my generation! See, I have shown you in the previous chapter who and what led me to follow the path of Yeshua ben Yosef of Nazareth. I showed you that the Torah and the prophets were my guides. Because of their words and the words of our sages of blessed memory, I took hold of the Messiah and will never let him go. He is the source of life, the one whom HaShem sent to give eternal life to all who desire life. You are mistaken in saying that a son of the Mosaic and Judaic faith cannot walk in the paths of Yeshua. Quite the contrary.

I am a son of the faith of Moses and Judah [i.e., Judaism], therefore it is incumbent upon me to cleave to the Messiah. Moses, David, and the prophets testified about him, prophesying from the very beginning that HaShem would send his Messiah to establish the kingdom of heaven on earth. Yeshua was the one who established it.

If only the children of Israel had not sinned—if only they had not rejected the Master of Life. Now the nations clap their hands and raise a shout to the God of our strength. The nations gather together to give thanks and praise the name of HaShem, and there is not a continent, country, or island in the world where there are not people who worship the God of heaven.

If only my Jewish brothers would cleave to Yeshua, for now everything that the prophets saw in visions is before us. HaShem chose his people Israel to make his name known in all the world and to be his witnesses to the distant islands that he is great and that he alone does wonders. Yet Israel has rejected the Light of the World. Therefore, they sit in darkness and in the shadow of death, and the kingdom that is in heaven has still not covered the face of the earth.[181] I am convinced of this in my heart because I believe that the Torah of Moses is true and that the prophets of Judah spoke the very words of HaShem.

So now why is it necessary for me to continue to say and prove that I—even though I am a disciple of Yeshua—observe the Torah of Moses and the Jewish religion? Have you not heard me say that I regard the Torah as the words of the Living God and I walk according to its ways? Because of its words I run to Yeshua! If the words of the Torah inspired me to run to him, how could I then neglect to observe the Torah's commandments?

Nevertheless, this error is ingrained in the hearts and minds of the Jewish majority, and they say that a disciple of Yeshua cannot be a son of the Mosaic and Judaic religion. Therefore, I must continue to speak about this and show that the majority opinion is incorrect, for Yeshua and his disciples are not forbidden to us, rather we are forbidden from neglecting the Torah.

MESSIAH ON THE MOUNT

In the beginning the Messiah spoke on the mountain and said:

> You who come here, who thirst and hunger to hear HaShem's righteousness in Israel, behold you are the light of the world. You are faithful Jews, and for the Jews the light is the Torah,

---

181 [Lucky is saying that Israel's rejection of Yeshua and disbelief is the reason that the kingdom of heaven has not yet been fully realized or established on earth. When Israel collectively accepts him, then and only then will the kingdom cover the face of the earth.]

for the commandments are the lamp and the Torah is the light. If both the Torah and the commandments are in your hearts, then all of you are lights and your souls are the lamps of HaShem. No one kindles a lamp just to put it under the bushel measure in a dark corner, but on the menorah in an illuminated corner to light the entire house.[182] In the same way it is incumbent upon you to shine your light before men so that they may see your good deeds and praise your Heavenly Father. Your eyes will be enlightened with the light of Torah before your fellow men and they will find the path of HaShem. Their mouths will be filled with songs to our Heavenly Father, who is the true light before you.

When you see that my path is a new one—one that has not yet been trodden by those who preceded me—perhaps it will occur to you to say: "The Messiah came to break and destroy the entire Torah that is with us now, and everything will be new. The old has worn out and ended and the new shall come in its stead. The Torah will be violated and that which we have received—the writings of the prophets—will pass away. The traditions of the fathers will not be remembered or thought of again."

Do not imagine this is so, for this shall never be. In fact, I tell you that I have not come to violate the Torah, but to fulfill.[183] I did not come to destroy, but to uphold and strengthen the entire Torah.

Look, the house of the Torah stands before us in all its splendor; its rooms are spacious and its attics are comfortable. However, people have still not attempted to enter inside and walk throughout the whole house, rather they just remain idle at the threshold. Even this people's scribes, Torah teachers, and guides have still not come into the inner holy of holies.

---

182 See Matthew 5:15 as well as the prayer of Rabbi Alexandri in the Gemara (b.*Brachot* 17a).

183 Matthew 5:17.

I have come to guide you throughout the whole house and to uphold the words of Torah, which originated from the mind of HaShem, the giver of Torah. For, amen, I say to you, until heaven and earth pass away, not one *yod* or one thorn will pass away from the Torah until all has been established.[184] Yes, many people will arise who will attempt to cause the words of Torah to pass away, canceling and violating them. However, they will not succeed. They will be the ones who pass away and their deeds will be like the wind. Not one stroke will ever be canceled.

Therefore the man who violates one of these small commandments and teaches others to do likewise will be called small in the kingdom of heaven,[185] for his deeds are small. And as one who is small and lacking understanding, he attempts to demolish the edifice that HaShem erected. This is the punishment that he will receive: He will be called small. He will not be driven out of the kingdom of heaven, for he, too, belongs to the flock for which I will give my life. Only he will be called small and he will be thought of as small, and the small are exempt from the commandments.[186] In the kingdom of heaven he will stand in the place reserved for the small.

Not so with the man who believes in me and observes the commands of Torah, teaching sons of men to observe them. He will be called great in the kingdom of heaven, and he will sit at the table in the place reserved for the great: at my right hand and in front of me. For he who understands the mind of HaShem and has submitted to his discipline is wise.

I say to you, if your righteousness is not greater than that of the Pharisees, you will not enter the kingdom of heaven.[187] If you do not enter into the house, you will only stand at the

---

184 Ibid., 5:18.

185 Ibid., 5:19.

186 b.*Chagigah* 2b and elsewhere.

187 Matthew 5:20.

threshold all the days of your life. Do not be surprised if I repeat the same concepts as the scribes and Pharisees, for the time has come to take hold of the kingdom of heaven and to enter the rooms of the house.

Behold, up until now you have stood at the threshold of the kingdom of heaven. Now come into the house. Up until now the kingdom of heaven was on earth. The congregation of Israel is the threshold, and the threshold has been accessible to all men. But now the doors of the house have opened and it is time for you to enter the house, dwell within it, and a new light will shine upon you.

On Mount Sinai you heard the voice of HaShem telling you: "You shall not murder." At the threshold of the kingdom it is said: "A murderer is one who kills or beats a man to death, and whoever murders will be liable to a court of law.[188] There they will be sentenced according to the rulings of men."

Yet I say to you that in the house of the kingdom whoever is enraged against his brother baselessly is liable to a court of law. Whoever says to his brother, "*Reka*," is liable to a Sanhedrin, and whoever calls him a reprobate is made liable to the fire of *Geihinnom*.[189] In the court of law in the kingdom of heaven nothing has been overlooked, for there is always a watchful eye and a listening ear. Everything is revealed there.

On Mount Sinai you heard: "You shall not commit adultery." At the threshold of the kingdom of heaven it is said: "You shall not lie with your neighbor's wife to defile yourself by her."[190] Yet I say to you that in the house of the kingdom, whoever gazes at a woman to covet her has surely committed adultery with her in his heart.[191]

---

188 Ibid., 5:21.
189 Ibid., 5:22.
190 Leviticus 18:20.
191 Matthew 5:28.

Moses spoke from the mouth of HaShem, saying: "If a man sends his wife away, he must give her a certificate of divorce."[192] Since you still stand at the threshold, HaShem gave you permission to divorce due to the hardness of man's heart and due to his evil inclination. Hillel and his disciples built on this foundation and said: "It is permissible to divorce her for trivial reasons, even for burning his meal,"[193] because of man's evil inclination. Yet I say to you, you must conquer your inclination and your hard hearts. He who divorces his wife other than for a matter of promiscuity exposes her to adultery.[194] He who divorces his wife sins against his wife's soul. She remains his wife even after he has divorced her. For that which HaShem has bound together let no man separate. Thus, when she is later the wife of another she is an adulteress, and anyone who marries her is an adulterer,[195] for he has taken the wife of another man.

If remaining with your wife is an obstacle to you, if you cannot conquer your hard hearts and you detest the wife of your bosom, then you must act in accordance with the Torah by sending her away and giving her a certificate of divorce. You will be doing a righteous thing, since you will be doing what the Torah says. However, HaShem cries because you will not spare your covenanted wife and because you will not have compassion upon your neighbor. That which HaShem has bound together you are separating.

Does it not seem good to you to conquer your evil inclination and stop hating your wife to whom you have cleaved, to have mercy and compassion upon her, to forgive her of her sins if she committed any, and to remain with her until death separates you? You will be doing an even greater righteousness, even greater than that of the scribes and Pharisees,

---

192 Deuteronomy 24:1.

193 b.*Gittin* 90a.

194 Matthew 5:32.

195 Ibid.

for you will be doing that which is in the heart of HaShem. You are children of HaShem, children of the kingdom, and as children of the kingdom you must be warriors who rule and overpower your inclination.

FASTING IN SECRET

Our Master Yeshua spoke about these things on the mount. Do you find anything forbidden in them? Has he forbidden us from observing the words of Torah that HaShem gave to us on the mount through Moses? Watch and pay attention to how our Master Yeshua penetrates the innermost thoughts of the Torah, looking through it and revealing its true countenance as yet unseen until his day. Yeshua our Savior also did not violate the prescribed fasts, rather he taught us: "When you fast, do not be gloomy like the hypocrites."[196] He did not tell us, "Do not fast," rather, he said that *when* we fast, we should not be like the hypocrites.

Therefore, it is our duty to fast and deny ourselves, but it is also our duty to search out the opinion of HaShem. If we deny ourselves and everyone who sees us recognizes that we are fasting, then we have already received our reward. For man's joy—the joy of the flesh and not of the Spirit of God within him—is when men praise him and surround him saying: "You are a pious man because you fast and worship HaShem." The fast that HaShem desires is this: that man denies himself *in secret*, before God alone, not in front of anyone, that it be a day when man pardons his neighbor of his sins, and that it be a day when he is focused on HaShem.

Yeshua was not speaking of a communal fast,[197] for on a fast day that includes the entire assembly of Israel, it is forbidden for everyone to bathe and put oil upon their heads. Everyone in the assembly looks gloomy, weeps, and rends their hearts, and everyone who does not do these things betrays his people, for he has withdrawn from the community. If he is truly afflicting himself with the entire assembly, then

---

196 Ibid., 6:16.

197 [Fasts that are prescribed to the Jewish people in the Torah and by rabbinic decree.]

there is no hypocrisy in that. It is only if he is fasting privately—even if he is truly afflicting himself—that there is hypocrisy if he distorts his face so that everyone knows he is fasting.

THE VOICE OF THE POWER

This is what our Master Yeshua said and taught. He did not teach violating the words of Torah, rather, he taught us to strengthen them, observe them, and to raise them up, entering into the inner chambers of HaShem's heart to do as he desires. Not judging according to the letter of the law but according to the spirit of the Torah. Thus, it is no surprise that when Yeshua ended his teaching on the mount the crowd was astonished,[198] because he taught them as if from the mouth of the Power and like a man who stands before the king in his house, not like the scribes who stand in the courtyard. A prophet like Moses arose before them, and when he speaks, it is HaShem answering us audibly. The voice from the mouth of the Power was the voice of Yeshua speaking to them.

When Yeshua descended the mountain, a leper approached and Yeshua healed him. He commanded the man to show himself to the priest and to bring the offering Moses commanded the leper to bring.[199] And when our Master Yeshua came to the other side of the sea, to the land of the Gadarenes, men who were gripped by demons met him. Yeshua drove the demons out and gave them permission to enter the herd of pigs that was grazing by a slope. The herd rushed down the slope into the sea, and all the pigs drowned in the water.[200]

Why did Yeshua allow the demons to kill the pigs? Because the Gadarenes transgressed the law, violated the Torah, and raised pigs, which HaShem said not to eat. The Torah is holy and whoever defies it will surely be punished. Therefore, Yeshua did not have mercy on the property or finances of the Gadarenes, even if in every instance he would do good to sinners and reward them with loving-kindness.

---

198 Matthew 7:28.

199 Ibid., 8:1–5.

200 Ibid., 8:28–32.

LOVING-KINDNESS TO SINNERS

And when Yeshua dined in the house of Mattai [Matthew] the tax collector,[201] and many tax collectors and sinners also came to dine with him, the Pharisees complained that our Master Yeshua was eating with them, and Yeshua, with a heart of compassion and loving-kindness, said:

> The strong do not need a healer, but those who are sick. I came to the earth to heal the sicknesses that come from sin—bodily sicknesses—which Satan has introduced to mankind, and to call those who have been wounded through transgression and sin to repentance so that they will know and pursue the knowledge of HaShem.
>
> Behold, I am like rain pouring down on them and on the land, just as Hosea prophesied concerning me.[202] For the world shall be built upon loving-kindness. And you scribes and Pharisees, you who judge the tax collectors harshly and regard them as Gentiles and heathens, what you are doing is not good, for HaShem has not desired this. Go and learn what Hosea the prophet said by the mouth of HaShem: "I have desired kindness and not sacrifice." HaShem is saying that the kindness you show to each other is dearer to him than every sacrifice that Solomon offered.
>
> Yes, you Pharisees refrain from sin, and you do very well in this, but be very careful and guard yourselves against pride. Those who are humble are great in HaShem's eyes; it is as if they had offered up every single sacrifice.[203] You must show kindness to these unhappy people who fell into the web of sin, and you must accept the sacrifices from the criminals in Israel so that they may return to HaShem.[204] If I do not dine

---

201 Ibid., 9:10 and on.

202 Hosea 6. Every interpretation on the words of this prophet point to the Messiah Yeshua.

203 b.*Sotah* 8b.

204 See b.*Eruvin* 49b.

with these tax collectors, if I do not allow them to serve me, I would be withholding kindness from them and preventing them from fearing Heaven. HaShem sent me to do good and to show loving-kindness."[205]

This is what our Master Yeshua said to the Pharisees who truly desired to venerate and glorify the Torah.

THE PRESENCE OF THE BRIDEGROOM

And when the disciples of Yochanan [John] asked him why his disciples did not fast, he answered them that his disciples are members of the wedding party. As such they are not able to mourn while the bridegroom is still with them.[206] Behold, days are coming when the bridegroom will be taken from them, and then they will fast; then they will mourn. What need is there for mourning while the bridegroom is still with them?

Since Yochanan's disciples asked him this and understood his answer, and since they were truly pious men who feared Heaven, Yeshua answered them with a parable saying that no one puts a new patch on a worn out garment, for the patch tears away and the tear is made worse. Also, no one puts new wine into old wineskins, for the wineskins will split open and the wine will spill out, rather they put the new wine into new wineskins, thus both are preserved.

Our Master, Teacher, and Rabbi Yeshua spoke to them in parables and riddles, for this was his manner of speaking to his disciples. The disciples of Yochanan were students of the Torah of truth and they did not harden their hearts. They understood Yeshua's words.

This is what Yeshua said:

> What is a personal fast? Behold, you and the Pharisees fast often. Why? You fast and deny yourselves because of your sins. Is this not like a new patch on a worn out garment and new wine in an old wineskin? It is good to return to HaShem

---

205 See b.*Ketuvot* 96a.

206 Matthew 9:14–15.

in true repentance and to renew your spirits. Look, I am right in front of you. Look, it is my wedding day and my heart is overjoyed. Look, I am here to renew you, to give you new life. All your sins will be cast into the deepest depths of the sea if you rend your hearts instead of your garments. From then on you will be like new wine skins that contain new wine. After I am taken from you, then you can fast and afflict yourselves. But now, while I am still with you, you are unable to fast and mourn. If you mourn, you are testifying against yourselves that you are still old wine skins.

HARSH JUDGMENT

On the second Sabbath of the Counting of the Omer, when Yeshua was passing through the fields, his disciples were hungry and plucking heads of wheat,[207] rolling them in their hands, and eating. The Pharisees complained very much, for there was a great rivalry between them and all the other factions and sects, such as the Sadducees, the Boethusians, and so on. Thus they scrutinized every new sect that arose in Israel. Every little thing that diverged even slightly from the order they had instituted frightened them, for they were always afraid that their order would be destroyed.

They could have judged Yeshua's disciples favorably, with kindness and righteousness, saying: "They have committed no sin or crime in picking the wheat, for they were forced to do so because they were hungry." Instead they judged harshly and said within their hearts that Yeshua's disciples did what is not to be done on the Sabbath. They said this to Yeshua: "Look, your disciples are doing what is not to be done on the Sabbath!"

In reality, Yeshua's disciples did nothing wrong. What could they do? Could they not go and hear teaching and knowledge from the lips of the Anointed Priest?[208] Every word that came from his mouth was

---

207 Ibid., 12:1–9.

208 [*HaKohen HaMashiach* (הכהן המשיח), which can also be translated literally as "The Priest, The Messiah," which is what Lucky wanted his Hebrew readers to notice.]

more valuable to them than gold or any fine thing. Had they not seen wheat in the field they would have forgotten their hunger altogether. However, they saw the wheat and their hunger compelled them, for they too were merely flesh and blood. They said in their hearts: "What evil would we be doing if we just picked the heads of wheat? Our scribes forbade us from picking heads of wheat on the Sabbath, and we do not want to go against their decrees, but we are extremely hungry now and we have nothing with us to eat, and to disregard the words of Torah is like disregarding life itself. Who will save us from this pressure? What if we allow ourselves this time? Picking and eating is not truly work nor commerce."

This is what they said within their hearts, so they picked and ate. If only the Pharisees had not judged them so harshly, they would have perceived that the disciples did not want to go against the sayings of the scribes.

Thus, when the Pharisees scolded Yeshua regarding his disciples he responded to them, saying:

> Your judgment is not correct, for you have judged harshly. When David was in trouble, what did he do? He took the bread of the Presence and ate, and he also gave it to his men and they ate, even though the bread of the Presence is only for the priests. And what do the priests do on the Sabbath? They desecrate the Sabbath and yet they have not transgressed, for they do the work of holiness and serve in the Temple. But something greater than the Temple is here. Before you is the Torah clothed in a fleshly body. These disciples have come to hear the Torah and to serve in holiness. You Pharisees, is this the loving-kindness that you show your neighbors?

> If only you had shown kindness, for you have certainly not convicted the innocent ones of a crime. In your zeal to make a show of your righteousness and to propagate your teachings you have forgotten that HaShem said, "I have desired kindness and not sacrifice." Why did the scribes prohibit the picking of wheat on the Sabbath? Because the Sabbath was given to sons of men for their body and soul as rest

from every labor. Are we given over into the hands of the Sabbath? No! The Sabbath is given over to us,[209] for it is said that the Sabbath is to be a delight to us. Is there any greater delight than to hear the words of Torah, which is the bread that comes down from heaven? Would my disciples abandon hearing the words of Torah for the sake of the decree that the scribes made to be a fence to the words of Torah? Your sentence is not just.

SAVING LIFE ON THE SABBATH

It was our Master's custom to heal the sick on the Sabbath, even if it was not a matter of *pikuach nefesh* ("saving a life," פיקוח נפש). But who can truly measure or weigh what is truly a matter of *pikuach nefesh* and what is not? If a man has an affliction, pain, or ailment and yet there is no danger to his life, should we not heal him even on the Sabbath? Even the scribes and Pharisees discouraged doing so for fear lest others might want to demolish the structure that they built. If only their structure was not a structure made out of pieces of paper!

See, they were cruel and attacked everyone who so much as touched that structure. As a result of the wars that the scribes and Pharisees fought with the Sadducees and Boethusians, they were like savages in the wilderness who knew no compassion. They guarded their teachings and decrees like the pupils of their eyes. Lest a man grind spices on the Sabbath[210] in the desire to heal his sick neighbor, they decreed that he should not heal his neighbor—who was also created in the image of HaShem—if it is not a matter of *pikuach nefesh*. Our Master asked them: "Is there a person among you with a sheep, that if it were to fall into a cistern, you would not take hold of it and lift it out? How much more precious is a man than a sheep?"[211]

---

209 "The Sabbath is given over into our hands; we are not given over to it" (b.*Yoma* 85a). In the *Mechilta* on Parashat Ki Tisa it says: "The Sabbath is given over to you, and you are not given over to it."

210 One of the thirty-nine forms of prohibited actions on the Sabbath.

211 Matthew 12:10–13.

WASHING HANDS

There was also another time that the Pharisees argued with Yeshua. Our sages commanded us to perform a small deed, which is that every man who is going to dine must first wash his hands, for his hands touch everything and for this reason are not clean. The sages of blessed memory named this commandment *netilat yadayim* (ritual hand washing), and they guarded this command like watchmen on a wall, never sleeping, assuring that no man transgressed this command.

It happened that when the disciples of Yeshua were under pressure, being hungry and having no water with which to wash their hands before the meal, that they ate without ritually washing their hands. So the scribes and Pharisees came to Yeshua and said: "Why do your disciples transgress the tradition of the elders? They do not ritually wash their hands before the meal?"

Yeshua was not able to refrain himself, and he spoke with them sternly, saying:

> The disciples who follow me transgress *your* commands and *your* tradition, but you transgress the commandments of *God* for the sake of your tradition. You observe the tradition that you received. What you are doing is good. But be careful not to be filled with too much zeal and not enough understanding. If you do not have understanding, you will be capable of transgressing the commands of God. God is holy and it is incumbent upon us to be holy as he is, and everything that we do must be in accordance with his will.
>
> I will give you an example: HaShem gave the command "You shall honor your father and mother" in thunder and lightning. His words were interpreted by Moses: "He who curses his father and mother shall surely be put to death." If a man makes a vow, he must keep it. Whatever comes out of his mouth he shall consider holy. If he takes an oath, he must fulfill it. Now, if the two things occur at the same time, that is, if a man says to his father and mother, "*Korban* is anything you would receive as my beneficiary," what are you to do? Keep the vow, desecrating the Word of HaShem and

not honoring your father and mother, or honor your father and mother and desecrate the words of your vow?

In your great zeal for the tradition of the elders you carefully watch, making sure no one breaks the vow he made, and he must go to a sage to ask if he can break it.[212] You have violated the Word of HaShem for the sake of your tradition. If only you had truly grasped HaShem's words! You have said that whoever withholds his assets from his father and mother speaks in vain. He does not need to inquire the opinion of a sage, for his words have violated the Torah before they were even spoken. This is what Isaiah proclaimed from the mouth of HaShem: "This people approaches me with their mouth, and with their lips they honor me, but their heart is distant from me. Their fear of me is empty; it is taught as a commandment of men."[213]

If only you would open your eyes and see that in the house of the kingdom it is the heart that matters! We honor the things that are in our hearts. What are you, O religious people? What is your desire? Why do you scold me about my disciples? Did they *disregard* the ritual washing of hands? Certainly not! They do not disregard nor question the tradition of this commandment. However, those who are forced into such a situation are exempt from a commandment. What can they do? And what is the evil of eating without ritually washed hands? Are you so afraid of ritual impurity?

It is not what enters the mouth that contaminates the person. If the thing that enters our mouth is permissible—that is, if it is kosher—it will not contaminate us. But what comes out of the mouth—evil, murderous thoughts, lying testimonies, abusive words—contaminates the person, and that person rebels against the words of HaShem and distresses his Spirit.[214]

---

212 See b.*Nedarim* 64a.

213 Isaiah 29:13.

214 Matthew 15:1–20.

OBSERVING THE DECREES OF THE SAGES

This is what our Master Yeshua said to the Pharisees in order to teach them to delve into the thoughts of HaShem through the words of the Torah. However, Yeshua observed everything that the sages, scribes, and Pharisees enjoined upon us. When the collectors of the half-shekel asked Shimon Keifa [Peter] if Yeshua and his disciples paid the half-shekel, Yeshua commanded Shimon Keifa to throw a fishhook into the sea and to pull a fish out and to pay with what was in its mouth, even though the children of the kingdom are exempt from this.[215] The scribes and Pharisees sit in the seat of Moses, and it is our duty to do everything they tell us to do.[216]

This is what our Master Yeshua said. However, he rebuked the scribes and Pharisees for widening their *tefillin* and lengthening their *tzitziyot*.[217] It is our duty to lay *tefillin* and wear *tzitzit*, but it is our duty to be careful not to become prideful by them before sons of men, for in our boasting we will have received our reward.

Indeed, to love HaShem with all our heart, all our soul, all our strength, and all our knowledge is the first and greatest commandment, and the second greatest is to love our neighbor as ourselves. It resembles the first, and it is greater than all sacrifices and burnt offerings.[218] Yet, the entire Torah, the prophets, and the traditions are all dependent upon these two commandments. It is our duty to guard justice, kindness, and faith, but also to lay *tefillin*, affix *mezuzot*, wear *tzitzit*, to give the tithe, and everything that our sages of blessed memory enjoined upon us.

OBSERVING THE DECREES OF THE MESSIAH

This is what Yeshua our Master, the Messiah of the Living God, taught us. This is what he commanded us to do. His disciples and emissaries never deviated from the path that Yeshua paved for them. The disciples of his day and those who came later—the disciples of the disciples—all

---

215 Matthew 17:24–27.

216 Ibid., 23:2–3.

217 Ibid., 23:5. [Fringes.]

218 Mark 12:29–31.

observed the Torah and the commandments just as they were taught, in accordance with the tradition they received: the tradition of the elders, sages, and Pharisees who sit in the seat of Moses.

Therefore I, one of the disciples of Yeshua, observe the Torah and the commands in accordance with the tradition of the elders, scribes, and Pharisees. I do so because of what King Messiah said, and I observe all the ordinances of the Mosaic and Judaic faith. What else should I do? And you, O people of my generation, an error has clung to your hearts. You think that every disciple of Yeshua turns away from the faith of Moses and Judah by following the ordinances of Yeshua. Therefore, I will continue to repeat this over and over again, time and time again:

> *Even though my soul has cleaved to Yeshua*
> *and I am his disciple,*
> *I will not flee from the faith of Moses and Judah,*
> *and it shall give me rest.*

GUARDING THE
TESTIMONY: PART III

Volume V Issue 2, 5658 (1898) pgs. 25–35

Thus far I have shown that the Torah and the gospel are complimentary sisters. The Torah teaches the path that leads to the gospel and the gospel supports the legs of the Torah. The writings of Moses and the prophets proclaim good news, namely that there will be redemption for this people and the words of the gospel writers and the emissaries make this known in that Yeshua is the Savior who redeems all who believe in him through his blood.

The writings of Moses and all the other prophets say that when the Messiah comes the Torah will be made great and truth will shine through at evening time. The gospel writers and the apostles proclaim good news, saying that the light that shines through the darkness has come,[219] the light of the world has dawned on all who dwell on the earth and on all who seek life. The Torah has dressed itself in flesh and has been revealed before every creature, so that all that is called "mortal man" will walk in the paths of Torah. I have also attempted to show that Yeshua the Messiah taught all his disciples to obey everything written in the Torah that HaShem commanded us through the mouth of Moses.

Now please bear with me, my brothers and beloved peers, while I continue to clarify my words. There are many who say to me: "What you

---

219 John 1:5.

say is true. Yeshua indeed did not violate the Torah and he was careful to perform the commandments according to the customs of his generation. But he laid his hands upon his disciples, his first emissaries, and said, 'All that you forbid on the earth will be forbidden in heaven and all that you permit on the earth will be permitted in heaven.'[220] These apostles changed word, law, and statute, and interpreted the Torah in contradiction to the customs of the elders, and everything that the Sadducees and Pharisees forbade they permitted. They even violated the commands of Moses!"

This is what many people say to me. Therefore I must act as a watchman at his post, proving that what they say is not true. So I ask you, my brothers and peers, to take up my cause and walk with me into the rooms of the annals of the first century so that you will see they are mistaken. If only you would! Now please, ascend with me to Jerusalem along with the elders of Yeshua's assembly, and let us listen to what they decreed.

COMPASSION ON THE NATIONS

In the beginning, HaShem chose Israel to be his treasure, and he gave them the Torah and the commandments, laws, and statutes in order to purify and sanctify them as a people while all the other nations wandered aimlessly off the path. The nations did not know God nor did they honor him, rather they strayed after the vanities that they were counseled to follow. Because of this, God gave them over to impurity, handing them over to futile knowledge, and they did every vile thing. Afterward, HaShem's compassion was stirred for the nations, and he proclaimed to them good news through the mouths of the prophets, saying:

> Days are coming when all the peoples and nations will obey
> the voice of the Torah, for the Righteous Messiah is coming—
> the Root of Jesse—who stands as a banner to the peoples.

---

220 Matthew 18:18. First Yeshua says this only to Shimon Keifa, and then afterward to all his disciples, for Yeshua laid his hands upon them and gave them authority to teach, to permit, and to forbid.

The nations will seek after him,[221] and he will teach justice to them.[222] I will make him a light to the nations to be my salvation to the ends of the earth,[223] and the nations will walk by his light.[224] The nations will see his righteousness,[225] and he will say, "Here I am, here I am!" to a nation that does not call on my name.[226] Nations from the ends of the earth will come to him,[227] and he will say to Lo-Ammi (Not My People), "You are my people."[228] In him my name is glorified, from the rising of the sun to where it sets.[229]

This is what HaShem said through the mouths of the Israelite prophets and seers. The pious of Israel awaited the coming of these days, when HaShem would have compassion on all the nations of the earth.

IMMANUEL IS BORN

Then came days of joy and gladness; days of kindness and salvation arrived. Unto us a child was born, unto us a son was given! He is called a prophet of the Most High, for he walked before HaShem to clear the way, to teach the path of salvation to his people, and to bring light to all who dwell in darkness and the shadow of death.[230] He was the salvation that HaShem established before creating all the peoples;

---

221 Isaiah 11:10.

222 Ibid., 42:1.

223 Ibid., 49:6.

224 Ibid., 60:3.

225 Ibid., 62:2.

226 Ibid., 65:1.

227 Jeremiah 16:19.

228 Hosea 2:25. [Here Lucky ascribes the prophecy in Hosea concerning the Jewish people to the Gentiles as well. He is showing that through the Messiah the Gentiles also enter in to HaShem's favor and, instead of being cast off for previous wicked acts, he will take them in with compassion, just as he does to the nation of Israel. Cf. Romans 9:25–26; 1 Peter 2:10.]

229 Malachi 1:11.

230 Luke 1:76–77 in the song of Zechariah.

he is the light to illuminate the eyes of the nations and the majesty of his people Israel.[231]

Yeshua is his name. Immanuel is his name. He is the Messiah that HaShem sent from heaven to save *all* who dwell on the earth, and through him *God is with us*. And with his holy mouth he said: "Many will come from east and west to recline with Abraham, Isaac, and Jacob in the kingdom of heaven,[232] for I have other flocks that are not from this sheepfold, and I must lead them as well."[233] Oh how great is the hope that all the nations will be assembled and gathered at the feet of Messiah!

The Messiah was killed. He was put to death on a tree of execution. They stripped the Prince of Life, crucified him,[234] hung him on the tree, and drove nails into his hands and feet.[235] Even his disciples experienced great persecution, so much so that they had to flee the city of Jerusalem.[236] They killed Stephen, stoning him to death,[237] and a man named Shaul of Tarsus, who was a disciple of Rabban Gamliel, was filled with rage and murder. He demolished the assembly, going into their houses and carrying off to prison men and women who believed in Yeshua.[238] Thus the disciples were scattered all around, yet they passed through the land and proclaimed the good news of the redemption.[239]

---

231 Ibid., 2:30–32. Shimon the Elder, a righteous and pious man who used to await the comfort of Israel, said this in the Temple. He is a credible witness, representing the expectations of all pious Jews. The pious in the house of Israel hoped for the day when HaShem would pour out his Spirit even on the Gentiles.

232 Matthew 8:11.

233 John 10:16.

234 Matthew 27:35; Mark 15:24; Luke 23:33; John 19:18.

235 John 20:25.

236 Acts 8:1.

237 Ibid., 7:59.

238 Ibid., 8:3.

239 Ibid., 8:4.

CORNELIUS THE RIGHTEOUS GOD-FEARER

Shimon Keifa [Peter], disciple of Yeshua, also left Jerusalem and went to Jaffa, staying there for many days.[240] A Gentile man named Cornelius was in Caesarea. He was a centurion with the Italian Regiment and he was a pious God-fearer, as was his entire household. He was charitable and kind to the people. He always prayed to God and he had a good name among the entire Jewish people.[241] An angel of God appeared to him in a vision in the ninth hour of the day and said, "Your prayers and your charity have risen as a memorial before God. Now send men to Jaffa and call Shimon, surnamed Keifa, to come to you." Cornelius did so sending two men who were servants in his house and one soldier to go with them to Jaffa.

Shimon Keifa was a Pharisee and thus very concerned about ritual purity. He would not eat anything that was served by someone who was not ritually clean, as was the custom with all the Pharisees of his generation. In his day it was forbidden for a Jew to associate with a foreigner, and had not HaShem commanded him through his angels to go to the foreigner's house, he would not have gone to Cornelius, nor would he have even sent any emissaries in his stead.

Therefore, HaShem showed Keifa a vision. In the sixth hour he went up to the roof to pray; he was hungry and wanted bread, and while it was being prepared for him he fell into a trance. He saw heaven opened and an object descending toward him that appeared like a large sheet bound at the four corners. Within it was every type of earthly creature, beast, creeping thing, and bird of the air. There was a voice that said to him: "Arise Keifa, slaughter and eat." Keifa said: "Heaven forbid, my Master! For I have never eaten anything profane or impure." The voice replied, saying: "That which God has purified you must not treat as an abomination."

The voice came to him in this manner three times, and afterward the object returned up to heaven. While Shimon wondered about the meaning of this vision, the three messengers of Cornelius came toward him, standing at the entrance and asking, "Is there a Shimon, surnamed

---

240 Ibid., 9:43.
241 See Acts 10.

Keifa, here?" He was still pondering the vision, and then the Spirit of HaShem said to him: "Here are three men who are seeking you; get up, go down, and leave with them. Do not ask them their reasons for coming or burden them with many questions, for this is why you saw the vision. I sent these men."

Shimon obeyed the voice of HaShem and went with Cornelius' messengers to Caesarea, and a few other brothers who lived in the city of Jaffa went with him. He came to Cornelius and found many gathered there to hear the Word of HaShem from Keifa. Keifa said: "You all know that up until now it has been forbidden for a Jew to associate with or draw near to a foreigner. However, HaShem God in his grace taught me through a vision to never again say that a man is profane or impure. HaShem desires to purify every single person and to bring them close to him. Therefore, I did not avoid coming to you. Now tell me why you called for me." Then Cornelius recounted his vision of an angel commanding him to send for Shimon Keifa. He said: "I have done everything that HaShem commanded me and you have done well, for you came to us and we are all here before HaShem to hear everything he has commanded you."

EVEN TO THE GENTILES

Keifa opened his mouth and said:

> Now I truly know that HaShem shows no favoritism, for in every single nation one who fears him and does what is righteous is worthy before him. He sent his Word to the children of Israel and he gives peace through Yeshua the Messiah. HaShem anointed him with the Holy Spirit and with might to heal all those oppressed under the hand of Satan. The people of Judah killed the Messiah, hanging him on the tree, but HaShem raised him on the third day and he appeared to us. He chose us to be his witnesses, and he commanded us to make this known and bear witness that HaShem gave him the authority to judge the living and the dead. In his name HaShem will forgive all our sins, just as the prophets prophesied from the very beginning.

While Shimon was still speaking the Holy Spirit fell on all those who heard him. The brothers who came with him from Jaffa were very astonished, because they saw that the gift of the Holy Spirit was poured out even on uncircumcised Gentiles. Even the brothers in Jerusalem were exceedingly astonished when they heard of this, and they gave glory to God, saying: "HaShem has opened the path of repentance that leads to life even to the Gentiles!"[242]

Other disciples who had fled from Jerusalem came to Phoenicia, Cyprus, and Antioch, and relayed the good news to our brothers, the children of Israel. Yet many of the Greeks in Cyprus and Cyrene also became believers in HaShem and his Messiah when they heard the word of the good news, and a great many people were gathered to our Master in Antioch.

This is how HaShem demonstrated the signs of his loving-kindness. Not one word that HaShem spoke ever fell void. He spoke and it was so; he commanded and it endured. He said that even to the Gentiles the gate would be opened, the one through which the righteous enter, and it was opened. Then HaShem demonstrated yet another sign.

THE BENJAMINITE

Shaul of Tarsus, a Benjaminite, who persecuted the disciples, locking them in prison, went to the city of Damascus in order to destroy the devout disciples of Yeshua who were there. But HaShem had other plans.

HaShem had decreed that Shaul, this Benjaminite, would be his chosen vessel to lift up the name of Yeshua the Messiah before the Gentiles and their kings, and before the children of Israel. So when he was walking and came near to Damascus, suddenly a light from heaven shone upon him all around and he fell to the ground. He heard a voice saying to him: "Shaul, Shaul, why do you persecute me?" And Shaul said, "Who are you sir?" Yeshua answered: "I am Yeshua, whom you persecute." Shaul was afraid and said, "What shall I do?" Yeshua

---

242 Acts 11:18.

answered and said, "Get up and go to the city. There you will be told what you must do."

He came to the city and heard that he was called to lift up the name of Yeshua before the Gentiles and their kings, to suffer and be tortured for the sake of this name. Shaul became a disciple of Yeshua and soon thereafter he proclaimed in all the synagogues that Yeshua was the Messiah, the son of the Living God. Upon his return to Jerusalem from Damascus he proclaimed the name of Yeshua with great courage. Bar-Nabba [Barnabas] accompanied him and he became a faithful, beloved friend.

When Bar-Nabba came to Antioch by the order of the elders of the Assembly and saw that the work there was prosperous, he went and sought after Shaul the Benjaminite to stand with him at his right hand.[243] He brought him to Antioch where they lived together for a full year within the assembly, and they taught many.

THE ASSEMBLY PRAYING FOR THE GENTILES

The leaders of the assembly in Antioch saw HaShem's grace upon the Gentiles in that he pulled them out of the darkness of worshiping mute idols to serve him in holiness. Their hearts cried out for all the nations and peoples, and they wept before HaShem. While they were worshiping him and fasting, the Holy Spirit said to them, "Separate for me Bar-Nabba and Shaul from among you for the work to which I have called them." They fasted, prayed, and laid their hands upon the heads of Shaul and Bar-Nabba and then sent them off.

The two of them went to Seleucia, Cyprus, Pamphylia, Pisidia, and other regions and they proclaimed the good news of redemption in every place. They raised up many disciples, established congregations, chose elders and teachers for those congregations, and placed them in the hands of the Master. Then they returned to Antioch and gathered the assembly and told them about all the wondrous things that HaShem

---

243 [A play on words by Lucky, for Benjaminite in Hebrew is literally *ish-yemini* ("man of my right hand," איש־ימיני). Lucky is looking for a prophetic significance to the tribe of Israel from which Shaul comes, and finds it in his devotion and fortitude when proclaiming the Messiah, standing firmly alongside Bar-Nabba.]

had done among the Gentiles, and how HaShem had opened up the entrance of faith to them.

OPPOSITION TO THE UNCIRCUMCISED PROSELYTES

Hearing this brought great joy to every person in the Messiah's assembly at Antioch. In every place that this news reached, the joy of the believers was great. But there were a small few in Judea who became exceedingly disturbed when they heard that the uncircumcised were coming to believe in the Master Yeshua the Messiah, and yet not one of them was circumcised. They thought to themselves: "Will these uncircumcised obey the Torah of Moses and the tradition passed down by the elders and scribes? Will they do all the deeds of the Torah, which those who are circumcised must do? And how will they be saved if they do not do all that Israel does?"

These zealous disciples thought that the uncircumcised would, for the rest of their lives, retain the foreskins of their hearts if they did not remove the foreskins of their flesh, and that if they did not obey the Torah of Moses then they would not be able to serve HaShem and his Messiah. These zealous Pharisees, disciples of Yeshua in Judea, judged that if the uncircumcised in Antioch did not become like the Jews[244]—following all the Jewish laws—then they could not be disciples of Yeshua.

In their minds the Torah of Moses was the only gate through which believers in Yeshua could enter, and everyone whose flesh was not circumcised was impure. Thus, it would be forbidden for a Jew to associate or break bread with him. They believed that the decrees and edicts that issued from the schools of Hillel and Shammai would never be canceled,[245] and they did not accept proselytes until they were circumcised and immersed. After all, just like our fathers who could not enter into the covenant until they were circumcised, so too, proselytes

---

244 [i.e., convert to Judaism.]

245 b.*Pesachim* 92a. Hillel and Shammai debate whether or not a proselyte who converted and immersed himself on the Eve of Passover could eat of the Passover offering. Shammai ruled yes, while Hillel ruled no.

could not enter in unless they did the same. Even Abraham was not called perfect until he was circumcised.[246]

These zealous disciples knew that in generations past, the decree of the Greek Empire would put Israelites to death over this command of circumcision.[247] They wondered how it was that this command can now be canceled and no one raises a voice of protest? They thought that non-circumcision was as defiling as a grave was,[248] and that the *Shechinah* could not rest upon the uncircumcised. They hoped that if the Gentiles sought the Root of Jesse that they would cleave to Israel and attach themselves to the house of Jacob, becoming children of Israel themselves, and that they would become circumcised and observe the Torah of Moses. Thus, they were exceedingly disturbed when they heard that Bar-Nabba and Shaul accepted proselytes who were not circumcised.

They came from Judea and went to Antioch, teaching the uncircumcised proselyte brothers: "If you do not become circumcised according to the faith of Moses you will not be saved. If you are not circumcised then you are impure, even if you are immersed. You are impure and you are sinners just like all the other Gentiles who have not yet been immersed, and it is forbidden for us to associate or dine with you. If you are not circumcised you are not able to gain access to HaShem."

The hearts of the uncircumcised believers became faint and afraid. They did not know what to do. If the words of the zealous Pharisees were correct, why did Shaul of Tarsus—disciple of Rabban Gamliel—and Bar-Nabba not teach this as well? Why did they not command them to become circumcised prior to immersion? The uncircumcised proselytes desired to serve HaShem with all their hearts, and if it was incumbent upon them to circumcise their flesh, then that is what they would do, even though this would be an exceedingly difficult act. They did not know whose halachah to follow: that of Shaul the Benjaminite and Bar-Nabba or that of the zealots from Judea?

---

246 b.*Nedarim* 31b.

247 See b.*Shabbat* 130a.

248 As discussed previously in b.*Nedarim* 92a.

THE JERUSALEM COUNCIL

Shaul and Bar-Nabba were greatly agitated concerning this matter with the uncircumcised proselytes, for they did not want to burden them with the yoke of Torah. The yoke of Torah was placed upon the necks of the children of Israel, not upon the necks of any other people group. Shaul and Bar-Nabba argued and disputed with the zealous believers from Judea about placing the yoke of Torah on the uncircumcised Gentiles who were turning to HaShem.

They argued with each other. But this was not an argument of hatred or jealousy; this was an argument between brothers. They had an argument over Torah and a battle over the study of the words of HaShem. And the brothers issued counsel saying, "Shaul, Bar-Nabba, and the other brothers with them shall come to Jerusalem and they shall present this argument to the apostles and elders, and whatever they decide, so shall it be."

Shaul and Bar-Nabba came to Jerusalem and recounted to them all the great things that HaShem had done with them; then the believing disciples who belonged to the Pharisaic sect arose and said, "Make a decree to all the uncircumcised who are turning to HaShem to circumcise their foreskins and observe the Torah of Moses in accordance with the tradition of the elders."

THE COUNCIL'S VERDICT

The apostles and the elders gathered together to look into this matter further. After all the arguments, they decided that Shaul and Bar-Nabba were correct, and that their opinion did not deviate from the path of Torah in what they were doing. Even the brothers who argued against them saw the validity of their words. Shimon Keifa arose and said:

> Men, brothers, you know that from the beginning HaShem chose me from all of us to make the good news known to the Gentiles, and they heard it and believed it. And God, who knows the heart, testified about them when he gave the Holy Spirit—the Spirit of Torah—to them as well, just as he gave it to us. In terms of the Holy Spirit, he has not differentiated

between them and us. The *Shechinah* has also rested upon them, because he has purified their hearts through faith.

Are we now to test God by placing a yoke upon the necks of the Gentile disciples, a yoke that even our fathers and us have not been able to carry? Indeed the yoke of Torah is a heavy one; it is heavy even for us. However, since HaShem placed this yoke upon us, we must carry it with love, and we must never remove it. Nevertheless, in giving them the Holy Spirit prior to circumcision and prior to receiving the yoke of Torah, HaShem has testified that the Gentile disciples will be saved even if they are not circumcised. All of us believe that through the kindness of Yeshua the Messiah we are saved—them just as much as us—so why would we place a yoke upon them that HaShem has not already placed?

The whole assembly fell quiet and listened to Bar-Nabba and Shaul the Benjaminite. Shaul relayed all the signs and wonders that HaShem continually did through them among the Gentiles. The elders of the assembly were convinced by the words of Shimon ben Yonah—surnamed Keifa—and so it was. For the *Shechinah* rested upon people who were not circumcised and who did not observe the Torah of Moses.

YAAKOV DELIVERS THE RULING

When they finished speaking, Yaakov[249]—the head of the Assembly—confirmed the judgment, saying:

Men, brothers, listen to me. You have heard what our brother Shimon has said to us. From the beginning God saw fit to take for himself a people for his name from among the nations, and he gave them the Holy Spirit even though they did not accept the faith of Moses and Israel upon themselves.[250] Behold, they are HaShem's people! The name of HaShem is upon them because they expelled all foreign gods from their

---

249 [i.e., Jacob, or James, the brother of the Master.]
250 [That is, full conversion to Judaism, which included circumcision.]

midst and now they bow down to the God of heaven, even though they did not become a part of the house of Jacob.

The prophets of HaShem made this fact known to us even in ancient times, as it is written: "On that day, in the last days, when there will be Gentiles in the land who bear my name, and after I scatter the house of Israel among the nations, on that day, when I sit in judgment over Israel and the nations, I will raise the fallen tent of David and repair the breaches of Israel. I will raise up the ruins of Jerusalem and rebuild her. I will raise up David's tent so that the rest of humanity and *all the nations that bear my name* may dwell within it. And the rest of the peoples who have still not obeyed the good news will later obey it, and all the nations that bear my name—for they heard the good news before that great and terrible day—will also have their hearts renewed. Their spirits will seek HaShem in faith and truth, for their eyes were opened and they saw that they strayed from the path.

This is what HaShem said, and this is what he decided. He knows his creatures and loves all the works of his hands. This is what was written in Amos.[251] Therefore, after having weighed these words with the Torah, I decree that we should not make it difficult for the Gentiles who turn to God. We cannot burden them with the yoke of Torah. They can worship HaShem even if they are not circumcised. Let everyone walk in the ways of his own people, for they are not of the seed of Abraham so they do not need to observe the covenant of Abraham as we do. They will have the name of HaShem upon them, even if they did not become a part of the house of Israel. They are our brothers even if they belong to a different people.

These are the only commandments that they are bound to: They should refrain from the impurity of things sacrificed to foreign gods, from prostitution and sexual immorality, and

---

251 Amos 9:11–12.

from meat or poultry that is strangled or found in its blood. These three things they shall observe for the sake of their souls, for these three things will defile a person. They shall not transgress any of these. They are not bound to anything outside of these three things.[252] For in every generation there are those who teach the Torah of Moses, and in every city it is read aloud every Sabbath in the synagogues. When the Gentiles go into the synagogues they will hear the Torah of Moses and the laws of HaShem. They will hear that which is good to do and that which should not be done, and they will choose what is good and the paths of Torah from the desire of their hearts. The Torah will find favor in their eyes, for the Spirit of HaShem will guide them. Little by little their eyes will be opened and they will see how good our ways are compared with the ways of the nations, since we walk the paths of Torah and they do not know its ways, and they will also choose to walk in our ways. This is my ruling.

A LETTER TO THE GENTILE DISCIPLES

Then they deliberated, and Yaakov's ruling seemed good to the elders, apostles, and the whole assembly. They sealed the decree by sending two men of good reputation: Yehudah Bar-Shabba [Barsabas][253] and Sila [Silas],[254] along with Shaul and Bar-Nabba, were sent to Antioch.

---

252 These three laws are not a part of the seven Noahide laws. But even though the elders did not caution the Gentiles returning to HaShem to follow the Noahide laws, they surely did not forget to caution them about murder and theft. Why then did they choose these three things? Well, it is not true that they only chose these three. They added these three to the Ten Commandments, the words of the Sinai covenant. This is my opinion. The proselytes accepted the Ten Commandments and they summarized the rest of the words of the Torah of Moses with these three additional commands.

253 Bar-Shabba is the same as Bar-Shabtai (i.e., son of Shabtai or son of the Sabbath).

254 This should say Shila (שילא), and this name can be found in the Gemara. Professor Delitzsch, in his Hebrew New Testament translation, wrote his name as Sila (סילא). In my opinion it should be written as "Shila" because the root of this name is actually Hebrew.

They wrote a letter and sent it with them, saying:

> To our Gentile brothers in Antioch, Syria, and so forth:
>
> Greetings,
>
> Since we have heard that men have gone out to you from among us troubling and confusing you, frightening and unsettling your souls with teachings that we did not command them to teach, we all thought it good to send you our brothers Yehudah Bar-Shabba and Sila, who have risked their lives for the sake of the name of our Master, Yeshua the Messiah. They have risked death in order to glorify and sanctify the name of our Messiah. They are trustworthy and unbiased, and they will explain to you the ruling that we agreed upon unanimously, for it was good to the Holy Spirit and to us to not place a burden upon you, except for these three things, which you shall not violate: Refrain from things sacrificed to foreign gods, from prostitution and sexual immorality, and from meat and poultry that is strangled or found in its blood. If you guard yourselves from these things it will be good for you and your hearts will have peace.
>
> Signed by us, the apostles, elders, Yaakov, etc.

The two delegates—Yehudah Bar-Shabba and Sila—delivered this letter to the congregation in Antioch. The people in that congregation were overjoyed. The words of that letter were a comfort to them, for they saw that they were deemed worthy in HaShem's eyes and in the eyes of the pious in Israel, even though they were not circumcised. They blessed HaShem.

UNDERSTANDING THE VISION

And now my brothers and beloved peers! Now that I have shown you what occurred in those days and what the disciples of Yeshua did, judge for yourselves. Tell me, is there anything here that is not in the Torah? That which the elders of the Messiah's assembly permitted was not for us but for the Gentiles. The strap was loosened and the dividing wall between the nations and Israel fell.

HaShem showed Shimon Keifa through a vision that it was permissible for an Israelite to associate and eat with a foreigner, and Keifa acted according to the vision that HaShem showed to him. He went to the house of the uncircumcised and ate with them. Yet he did not eat that which is forbidden to eat.[255] He did not eat anything forbidden in Cornelius' house, for he explains his vision to us, and it had nothing to do with the abrogation of dietary laws.

It is incredibly important to understand this. That which Shimon ben Yonah saw in a vision was supposed to reveal to us the truth concerning ritual purity. The dividing wall between the nations and *the* nation (Israel) fell and was demolished. The uncircumcised man is not impure anymore if he has turned to HaShem. If he has immersed but has not undergone circumcision, he is pure and it is permissible to eat with him. This is also the halachah of our day and age. This is taught in all the study halls. It is permissible for us to sit at a table with the uncircumcised, and it is permissible for us to eat with them—that is, anything that is not forbidden for us to eat.

When the elders of the congregation of Messiah and the apostles heard about this vision, its interpretation, and the great things that HaShem was doing through Shaul and Bar-Nabba among the Gentiles in Antioch, Syria, Cilicia, and so on, they permitted the Gentiles to enter the Assembly of HaShem as righteous converts:[256] converts to the name of Love[257] and the covenant of truth. They accepted them without requiring them to be circumcised.

---

255 [Foods that are *treyf* or not butchered properly, i.e., he did not eat anything that was not kosher.]

256 [The Hebrew term Lucky uses here is *ger tzedek*, which ordinarily refers to a Gentile who fully converts to Judaism and is bound to the entire Torah of Moses. Lucky uses the term to indicate that these Gentile believers were able to experience the spiritual benefits of a convert to Judaism (i.e., access to HaShem, salvation through Messiah, acceptance among the Jewish believers, and membership within the commonwealth of Israel, etc.) but without the full obligation to the Torah.]

257 [Yeshua, who is the personification of HaShem's love.]

A NEW PRECEDENT

It was not like this in the schools of Shammai and Hillel. This was different from the fixed halachah of that time. But did these Gentiles not also see the wonders that HaShem worked? For he raised the nations from the dead and opened the path of repentance that leads to life. He testified about them in giving them the Holy Spirit. They realized that HaShem desires to open the gate to all who turn to him. In giving the Gentiles the Holy Spirit, God testifies that they are righteous converts, for they inherit righteousness through the Messiah who came to bring an end to iniquity, to do away with sin, and to bring eternal righteousness.

The Gentile disciples of Yeshua—who are righteous converts and fellow inheritors of the kingdom of heaven—were born from above, from water and spirit. They are true converts, for they desire to be close to God, and they are our brothers, even if they have not come into the covenant of Abraham, since they are not of the seed of Abraham. They are just as much our brothers as other Jews are, for everyone who forsakes idol worship has similar religious views and practice as a Jew.

However, the elders of the assembly of Messiah did not permit us Jews to stray from the paths of the Torah of Moses. The Torah belongs to us. It is our inheritance and we must walk in its ways, for its ways are ways of peace and its paths are pleasant paths that do not lead to death. They are the paths of the Messiah, the Prince of Peace.

אַהֲבָה תַּחַת אֵיבָה
REPAYING HOSTILITY WITH LOVE

(מתי ה':מ"ד–מ"ו)   (Matthew 5:44–46)

אהוב את אויביך, ברך מקלליך
גם אם ישטנוך בחמת אפים
גמלם אהבה, תן למו ידיך
כי אהבה לבדה תירש שמים.

Love your enemies, and those who curse you bless,
Even if they accuse amidst their burning rage;
With love repay them, extend hands of gentleness,
For none but Love alone inherits Heaven's praise.

היטיב למשנאיך, מנדיך, חירפיך
הקמים עליך לבלעך חיים
השב־נא אהבה אל חיק רודפיך
אהבה נאמנה בת אל שמים.

Do good to your haters, banishers, and disgracers,
Those who rise up against you to swallow you alive;
Now return love deep into the bosom of
          your pursuers,
She, Faithful Love, that daughter of Heaven's Light.

רעה אם יביאו עליך משנאיך
יביאוך במצוק באש ובמים
העתר בעדם, האר למו פניך
באהבה, מלכת ארץ ושמים.

If those who hate you approach with evil design,
If they make you pass through water and through fire;
Petition on their behalf, and make your face to shine
With Love who reigns queen of heaven and earth entire.

אז תקרא בן לאביך, חסד נוצר
ומזריח שמשו לטובים וגם לרעים
אז תשוה לאלהיך, תדמה ליוצר
הממטיר חסדו על צדיקים ורשעים.

Call to your Father, O son, who causes grace to sprout,
On the good and on the bad he makes his sun to shine;
Now resemble your God who fashions the devout,
Who showers his grace on every righteous and
          wicked kind.

SECTION II

THE SPIRIT OF GOD: ITS PURPOSE AND FUNCTIONS

Volume II Issue 7 and 8, Tishrei-Cheshvan 5650 (1890)
pgs. 109–112; 122–126

The words "Spirit of God," "Spirit of HaShem," "Holy Spirit," or "my Spirit" (referencing God), are found in many places in the Torah and the prophets, and they are found especially in those Holy Writings that speak to the fulfillment of Israel's hope. For example, when Isaiah promises that a Redeemer will come to Zion, he adds:

> "As for me, this shall be my covenant with them," said HaShem. "*My Spirit*, which is upon you, and my words, which I have place within your mouth, shall not depart from your mouth." (Isaiah 59:21)

In the same way Ezekiel proclaims the good news of the return of Israel, saying:

> And I will take you from among the nations and I will gather you from all the lands, and I will bring you to your own soil … and I will place my Spirit in your midst. (Ezekiel 36:24, 27)

Similarly, the Prophet Joel, after advising us of the future mercies of God upon Israel, says:

> And after that I will pour out my Spirit upon all flesh. (Joel 3:1)

Thus every member of Israel who yearns to understand the Torah, which is the "inheritance of the assembly of Jacob," who waits in humility and faith, and who longs for the fulfillment of the promise of God, is required to look into what Moses and the prophets wrote, examining the nature of the Holy Spirit, its workings and effects. Indeed we know that it is a difficult thing for flesh and blood to accurately depict or even understand the nature of a human being's spirit; how much more so is it difficult to acquire knowledge of the Spirit of God!

However, in order to arrive at some sort of comprehension, we must first dispel all our imaginations, preconceptions, and mental images. We must let the illumination of the Word of God direct our intellect.

THE SPIRIT AS MERELY AN INFLUENTIAL EFFECT

The first question that arises in examining the words "Spirit of God" is: What do these words mean? Do they refer to one of the attributes of God? Is the Spirit of God merely the effect of the divine will, the influence brought and birthed through the emanation of the Divine Power? Or does it have an actual, intrinsic reality? For example, when God said to Moses, "I will draw upon the spirit that is upon you and I will put it upon them" (Numbers 11:17), was there truly a spirit upon Moses from which God drew and placed upon the seventy elders, or should these words be understood figuratively to mean that God was merely giving the seventy elders wisdom as he had done for Moses?

It would appear that the Rambam (in his book *A Guide to the Perplexed* Part I, chapter 40) thinks that the words "Spirit of God" do not indicate merely influence or divine will alone, but also wind, breath, will, and inspiration, for he says concerning the Spirit that it is "the Divine Inspiration by which the prophets prophesy." He employs this opinion when describing the various degrees of prophecy (Part II, chapter 45), saying that "the Spirit of God" and similar titles refer to a heavenly force that is given to mankind:

> It compels him to do something good and grand, like rescuing noble men from evil men, or to influence many people for good. Concerning the man who takes this task upon himself, it is said that the Spirit of HaShem came upon him or that the

Spirit of HaShem clothed him (or gripped him), and other names are also used. This is the degree that all the judges of Israel reached, as it says: "The Spirit of HaShem was upon Jephthah" (Judges 11:29); and of Samson it is said, "The Spirit of HaShem came upon him" (Judges 14:19), and it is said, "And the Spirit of HaShem came upon Saul" (1 Samuel 11:6).

What the Rambam means here is that the Spirit of God is simply the heavenly force through which great and mighty things are done as was distributed to Jephthah and Samson, or the inspiration that compelled the prophets such as Daniel and Job and through which they wrote their books. The Rambam also says (Ibid.):

> The second degree of prophecy is when a man feels as if a matter has been impressed upon him and as if he received a new power that encourages him to speak, and he speaks with wisdom, praises, words of caution, useful things, political matters, or theological topics... and it is said of such a one that he speaks by the Holy Spirit. In the same way, David composed psalms by the Holy Spirit, Solomon composed Proverbs, Ecclesiastes, and Song of Songs. So too, Daniel, Job, Chronicles, and all the other writings were composed in this manner: by the Holy Spirit... In reference to this Holy Spirit, David says: "The Spirit of HaShem spoke within me" (2 Samuel 23:2).

According to this passage the Holy Spirit is not an actual separate entity, rather it is merely the title for an inspired action that was done or some inspired notion conceived in the mind of Moses or any one of the prophets. According to this interpretation the Spirit remained with the prophets continually throughout the course of their lifetimes, but its effect ceases and amounts to nothing when they died. Thus it resembles a voice that is ever shifting in the wind, and when the wind stops blowing every trace of the voice ceases to exist.

However, this is not what was handed down to us by Moses and the prophets. When they spoke about the Holy Spirit they never used language that would give us the notion that the Spirit was merely an effect or an influence. Rather, in every instance, they employ words that imply essence, being, actuality, and existence. We are able to see this in the example before us, "And I will draw upon the spirit that is upon you and I will put it upon them" (Numbers 7:11). The wording of this passage clearly indicates that some eternal substance or thing rests upon Moses, from which God draws in order to place it upon others.

Likewise, in Numbers 11:25 it says, "And when the spirit rested upon them they began to prophesy, but they did not continue." The word "rested" that was used here was undoubtedly a very bad choice if it is only depicting an effect of the Divine Power that was influencing them. On the contrary, this type of language implies an external presence—outside of their human spirits—which comes and rests upon them. Likewise, the notion that the Holy Spirit is merely a spiritual influence will be repudiated by all other passages that use the word "rested" or that speak to this concept of the Holy Spirit.

THE CAUSE AND EFFECT OF THE SPIRIT

HaShem said that he would fill people with his Spirit, "And you shall speak to the wise of heart whom I have filled with the spirit of wisdom" (Exodus 28:3), and that he would pour out his Spirit, as it is written: "I will pour out my Spirit upon all flesh" (Joel 3:1). And in another place in the Scriptures it says that the Spirit will come upon mankind, and that "the Spirit of HaShem will grip you, and you will prophesy along with them" (1 Samuel 10:6). Concerning its departure is says: "And the Spirit of HaShem departed from Saul" (1 Samuel 16:14). And concerning its enveloping of all those to whom it comes it says: "And the Spirit of HaShem enveloped Gideon" (Judges 6:34).

Not one of these passages teaches that the Spirit merely performs actions, rather, the Spirit is something that God pours out on us, that fills the soul, or envelops a man; it is something that comes and departs. There is certainly much evidence to support this. Nowhere in the Holy Writings does it speak of the Holy Spirit as one and the same as the power to prophesy. Rather, it is depicted as *the reason* that the power to prophesy occurs. It is the resulting action, as we find in Samuel's words to Saul: "The Spirit of HaShem will grip you, and you will prophesy along with them."

Accordingly, if the Holy Spirit is the cause, and the power to prophesy is the effect, then the Holy Spirit and the power of prophecy cannot be one and the same; rather, they must be two separate issues entirely. Therefore, the Holy Spirit cannot be something merely internal, rather, it must be something external, which distinguishes between those upon whom it resides.

Now all that remains for us to do is to investigate whether the Tanach speaks of the Holy Spirit figuratively to mean the inspiring will of the Divine Intellect, or if it speaks of the Holy Spirit as the actual agent who enables and empowers the worker. Let us test this line of reasoning and replace the word "spirit" with "will" and say: "And I will draw upon the *will* that is upon you and I will put it upon them"; or "I will pour out my divine *will* on all flesh"; or "The *will* of HaShem will grip you"; or "The *will* of HaShem departed from Saul." This is strange and fails to convince. The words "Holy Spirit" cannot be synonymous with "the will of God," nor does the Holy Spirit equal the actions that result from its inspiration; rather, the Spirit is an actual force that can come and go, be poured out, and apportioned to others.

SPIRIT AND WIND; INTELLIGENT OR INDISCRIMINATE

The next question is this: is the Holy Spirit lifeless and does it work indiscriminately without sentience, resembling an erratic force such as electricity, or is it living and sentient like a human or an angel? As we attempt to answer this question, we must first look at how this word "spirit" (*ruach*, רוח), which is included in the divine appellation of "Holy Spirit" (*Ruach HaKodesh*, רוח הקודש), sheds light on this question.

Indeed we find that it is used in the Tanach in terms of air and wind that blows: "And HaShem drove back the sea with a strong east wind (*ruach*) all night long" (Exodus 14:21). In many other passages this *ruach* is lifeless and without sentience. However, we also find that the word *ruach* is used to indicate a vibrant, sentient, and immortal force, for instance: "His *ruach* was agitated" (Genesis 41:8), and "The *ruach* returns to God who gave it" (Ecclesiastes 12:7), and many other similar passages.

We have determined that when the Spirit attaches itself to man it becomes an intelligent, divine instructor. This leads us naturally to suppose that the Spirit is also attached to God. It stands to reason that if God had wanted us to understand this word differently, he would have used a different word. He knew that this word had two meanings, thus he knew that it is possible that people would misunderstand this. Nevertheless, it was his will to use this word.

Without any doubt he desired to lead us down the path of truth and not down the path of error, therefore we must conclude that it is to be understood as a natural, actual force. And this is the teaching of its nature: that the Spirit of God remains joined to the Divine Essence, resembling the human spirit that remains joined to man, and it would be incredibly strange and contradictory to nature if we imagined that the spirit of man was living and intelligent and yet the Spirit of God, on the contrary, is lifeless and unintelligible and indiscriminate.

APPORTIONING WISDOM AND KNOWLEDGE

The job of the Holy Spirit is to apportion wisdom and knowledge, as it is said concerning Bezalel: "See, I have called the name of Bezalel son of Uri son of Hur of the tribe of Judah, and I will fill him with the Spirit of God, with wisdom, understanding, and knowledge in every craft" (Exodus 31:2–3). It must also make the will of God known, girding mankind with prophetic ability in order to recount that same will to others. Thus, when the Holy Spirit came upon Saul and his messengers, they were given the ability to prophesy, and when HaShem promised through Joel that he would pour out his Spirit on all flesh, the effect was that "your sons and daughters will prophesy, your old men will dream dreams, and your young men will see visions" (Joel 3:1).

Another charge of the Holy Spirit is to sanctify man so that he will be holy, as it says in Ezekiel (36:27): "And I will put my Spirit within you, and I will cause you to walk in my laws and to observe my statutes and perform them." Therefore, the Spirit of HaShem is called a spirit of wisdom and understanding, a spirit of counsel and valor, a spirit of knowledge and fear of HaShem (Isaiah 11:2).

THE HOLY AND EVIL SPIRITS

So how could we even entertain that this Spirit, which has all these designations and functions, could be merely a lifeless influence, without wisdom, knowledge of God, and holiness? Therefore, it is clear that the Spirit who does all these things must be intrinsically wise, intelligent, and holy.

This concept finds solid substantiation in Scripture, which contrasts the Spirit of HaShem with the evil spirit. It is said (1 Samuel 16:14): "And the Spirit of HaShem departed from Saul and an evil spirit sent from HaShem began to torment him." In another place HaShem promised to pour out a spirit of grace and supplication on Israel, and he also promised to expel the spirit through which the lying prophets prophesied, saying: "And on that day, says HaShem of Hosts, I will wipe out the names of the idols from the land. I will also make the prophets and the impure spirit vanish from the land" (Zechariah 13:2).

Therefore, if the evil spirit, or the impure spirit, is actual and intelligent, then so, too, is the Holy Spirit. Indeed, the evil spirit is an intelligent, sentient being, which is clear from the vision of Micaiah son of Imlah (1 Kings 22:19–22):

> I saw HaShem seated upon his throne … And HaShem said, "Who will entice Ahab to rise up against and fall at Ramoth-Gilead?" Then a certain spirit went out and stood before HaShem and said, "I will entice him!" And HaShem said, "With what?" And he said, "I will go out and be a lying spirit in the mouths of all his prophets."

Here it is completely clear that the lying spirit is not a lifeless, unintelligent force; rather, we find that it possesses sentience and a will of its own. Thus, it stands to reason that the Holy Spirit must as well!

PHYSICAL ATTRIBUTES TO THE SPIRIT

We see that this Spirit is described with physical attributes. The Holy Writings speak of the Holy Spirit as one who judges, speaks, mourns, can be set to rest (Zechariah 6:8), and many other such things. For instance, it says (Genesis 6:3): "My Spirit will not contend[258] in man forever." Jewish expositors debate about the meaning of "my Spirit," but it is imperative that we first look at what these words mean.

Abravanel says: "The spirit of my intellect is my spirit that I put within mankind, and it will not judge within him forever." It appears that Ibn Ezra also agrees with this. He says: "[The spirit] decrees justice, for it judges in the body." Rabbi Joseph Kimchi, whose words are cited in the book *Michlol Yofi*, also speaks in a similar manner: "My ethereal spirit that I breathed into mankind is forever contending with the body, because it does not delight in the lusts of the body, and the body is drawn after base, fleshly desires."

According to these opinions, "my spirit" is not the Spirit of God, but the spirit of man. Yet it is clear that this cannot be. If God intended to indicate the spirit of man, would it not have been just as easy for him to say so? If the meaning were "spirit of man" then this distorts the Scriptures and makes them merely senseless words.

The expositors sensed the difficulty in their interpretation, and so they were forced to come up with a new explanation, using another word. Just as they make "my spirit" to mean "spirit of man," so too, they make "man" to mean "man's body," and the words "my spirit" never contained this meaning at all! We have two points to contest in this interpretation. "Man" never means anything other than all of mankind—men and women—as well as all of man in his entirety: body, spirit, and soul. "My spirit" cannot just refer to the intellect; rather it must mean the Spirit of God that is spoken of by the mouth of God himself.

We cannot find any passage that might support the idea that the words "my spirit" (when spoken by God, about God) can mean anything other than God's Spirit. It cannot mean the human spirit! Hence this explanation by the rabbis is not plausible at all. Rashi interprets

---

258 [*Yadon* (ידון), from the root literally meaning, "to judge." Some loose translations render it as "reside" or "rest."]

the words "my spirit" in their simple, literal sense, saying: "Let my spirit not be contentious or quarrel (as to whether to destroy or have compassion) with me because of man."

SPEAKING WITHIN

All the functions of the Spirit—judging, ruling, tarrying in arrival and departure, even doing evil deeds (in the case of the lying spirit)—must be sentient acts, and arguing that they are not is an exercise in futility. Therefore, even if we only had this passage (Genesis 6:3), it would still provide adequate evidence to prove our claim. Yet we have more passages at our disposal.

David says, "The Spirit of HaShem spoke within me and his words were on my tongue" (2 Samuel 23:2). The Hebrew word *bi* (בִּי) can be interpreted as "through me," or "within me," or "with me," and the reader may choose between any of these three options, for its meaning does not change at all depending on the translation. The important part in this text is the obvious subject, the Spirit of HaShem who is speaking, and there is no difference if it is speaking through, in, or with David.

This is best explained by Radak[259] and Rashi. Radak says: "I recounted the songs that the Holy Spirit spoke within me." Rashi says:

> He lodged his Holy Spirit within me and it spoke within me. Every expression of prophecy is indicated through speaking, just as it says, "Did he only speak within Moses? Did he not also speak within us?" The meaning of this is that the Spirit enters within the prophet and speaks within (or through) him.

Here Radak and Rashi are both in agreement that the Holy Spirit is the one who is speaking, and that it is not just influence alone that causes the prophet to speak. And if it is the Holy Spirit who is speaking, then it most certainly cannot be a mere lifeless influence, but a personification of a sentient being.

---

259 [Rabbi David Kimchi.]

Another passage to consider is the one in Isaiah (63:10): "And they rebelled and grieved his Holy Spirit." We are told that the Holy Spirit can be grieved or incited to anger. Something that is lifeless cannot be incited to anger, and only living, sentient beings can become grieved. Therefore, the Holy Spirit must be alive! However, Radak attempts to dissuade us from this obvious conclusion by saying: "His *Holy Spirit* means the words of his prophets that were spoken from the Holy Spirit." His comment rather changes the content instead of clarifying it.

If God had meant "the words of the prophets," would it not have been just as easy for Isaiah to write it? The passage says "his Holy Spirit," so we must accept it. The one who argues and changes the content of the passage is essentially saying that it is not to his liking and that he opposes it. If we take the words at their literal meaning, then it is very explicit and clear that the Holy Spirit is much more than what Radak says it is.

THE ARGUMENT IS SUBSTANTIATED

We now need no more documentation. These passages tell us that the Spirit judges, speaks, is grieved, and this is enough to prove our point. Concerning the Divine Intelligence we know nothing, thus we must simply gather the evidence given to us in the Holy Writings. We understand "Spirit of HaShem" to mean the "Spirit of the Eternal God," and we see that if he is eternal, then his Spirit must be also.

When we speak about the goodness of God, or about his loving-kindness, or about his might, we mean that all these attributes are everlasting and will never be separated from the Divinity. Is it possible then to imagine that the Spirit of HaShem was created in time and space, and that before it was created HaShem did not have a spirit? Indeed we know that man's spirit is finite, that it had a beginning, yet will we say that HaShem's Spirit belongs in this same category?

The name that Scripture gives to this Spirit strengthens the point and makes it all the more explicit: the Holy Spirit, or the Spirit of Holiness. David says: "Do not take your Holy Spirit from me" (Psalm 51:13), which is as if to say, "The Spirit of your holiness." And Isaiah says: "And they rebelled and grieved his Holy Spirit" (Isaiah 63:10), or even more literally, "the Spirit of his holiness." The holiness of God is infinite, as he is, thus this Spirit of his holiness cannot be finite or created, rather it must be a divine entity.

ANY PRAYER AND ANY SUPPLICATION BY ANY PERSON

2 CHRONICLES 6:29

Volume I Issue 1, Tishrei 5648 (1888) pgs. 8–10

Prayers, supplications, and requests have been precious treasures to our people since biblical times—since the world began. We have always known how to offer prayer to HaShem. While Adam and Eve were walking with God, they asked him for anything that their hearts desired. Even after they sinned, their grandson Enosh still continued to call on the name of HaShem. What is this if not prayer?

Noah walked with God and even built an altar after the flood,[260] Abraham planted a tamarisk tree[261] and, according to the words of the Talmud, he prayed. Israel obtained nothing, whether great or insignificant, apart from prayer. King David prayed day and night, Solomon prayed a great prayer, and so it was among all the generations and chronicles of Israel.

---

260 [Genesis 8:20.]
261 [Genesis 21:33.]

RELINQUISHING TREASURES

However, miraculous wonders began occurring less frequently in Israel. Israel no longer wanted their precious treasures. The peoples ascended in stature, nations were advancing ahead of Israel, and it was only our people—Israel and Judah—that diminished in stature. Our scepter of strength fell limp. Today, Israel follows a path to cancerous sickness.

The peoples whose fathers worshiped idols have opened their eyes and have come to your Heavenly Father at all times with prayers, supplications, and requests. When they gather together they do not say a word until after they pray and until their lips engage in conversation with the Master of the whole earth, God of heaven, Creator and Savior. Their deeds are no longer wily human ploys; rather they only seek to do the will of their Father, their gracious Savior. This is what they do in everything. However, this manner of prayer has ceased in Israel. Israel has given away his portion to the peoples and then walked away.

I still remember the words of Shimon Sofer, a rabbi and religious teacher in Krakow. Once, when he was speaking from the bimah about the new path that many of the children of Israel have chosen, he said, "Isaiah prophesied about this: that the Torah would go out from Zion and the word of HaShem from Jerusalem (Isaiah 2:3). The Torah would go out and leave forever, and the word of HaShem would go off to others, never to return to Jerusalem."

This is how the people of our generation think, and they conduct themselves accordingly. It was not so long ago that the congregations of Israel, which are dispersed throughout all these foreign lands, sent their emissaries, and even their rabbis, to gather together. One of these emissaries felt moved to honor a certain Dr. Hirsch—rabbi and teacher at Adath Israel in Philadelphia—by asking him to pray to God on high who had sent his help to the council gathered there. Why did he do this? Rabbi Dr. Hirsch does not even believe in God, let alone would he take pleasure in the prayers and supplications of Israel.

And so it is just as Shimon Sofer had said. The Torah of Israel has gone out from Zion, the word of HaShem has left Jerusalem, and the voice of HaShem can be heard in the houses of all the foreign peoples.

The land of Israel spread across all the lands, just as the sages of the Talmud prophesied, yet Israel has abandoned his estate. And like a voice calling in the wilderness was the author of the American Jewish newspaper, *The Menorah*, yet he found no answering voice. The author's name was Aryeh Levy, and he sent his words to all the rabbis throughout the Diaspora, asking them thirty questions. One of his questions to them was this: "Nearly the majority of Israelites deny the existence of God; does not a Jew cease to be a Jew in this denial?" But Levy called out in vain, and it was for nothing that the lion[262] roared, for no one answered him.

Nevertheless these rabbis and congregational members presume to bear the name "Jews," but we who have also descended from Judah (just as they have), who come in the name of HaShem, and who pray to him through Yeshua his Messiah, are despised by them. It is as if we had exchanged our faith and the faith of our forefathers. Our Jewish brothers are called "enlightened" and "intellectuals," and yet they are very far from true intelligence.

ISRAEL IS NOT ALARMED

"If a shofar is blasted will not the people be alarmed?" This is what Amos the prophet and shepherd asked (Amos 3:6), for he was a man of God and feared the word of HaShem. He was a prophet of HaShem, pure in heart. And so he was astonished. A lion roared; who cannot be afraid (Amos 3:8)?

Our time is quite different from the time of Amos the prophet and shepherd. In our days a shofar is blasted and the people are not alarmed; the lion roars and no one is afraid. It is now the month of Elul, and what do we see in the camps of Judah in these foreign lands in which we live? The people of our generation have become "wise" and they have discarded the shofar so that they will not be alarmed. Israel has abandoned every goodness. Israel has distanced themselves from God. All of Israel's righteousness has become merely external, like a decorated garment that is embellished in vain; in the same way they

---

262 [Lucky refers to the author's first name "Aryeh," which means "lion." Cf. Amos 3:4, 8.]

enter the houses of prayer in vain. There is no prayer in these houses of prayer. They thrust out God, their Redeemer, so now where is the one who will listen to their prayers?

However, HaShem will have mercy and our Jewish brothers will concede, for the name of HaShem is called upon them. They will turn from their evil ways and they will pray and seek the face of HaShem. Then he will pardon their sins and heal their land. Just as he did previously, so too, will he do even now. Just as it happened in the days of Solomon, so too, will it happen even today. For now we have an intercessor who stands between the Father and us: He is Yeshua the Messiah who sits at the right hand of the Power. May his name be blessed forever and ever. Amen.

GAINING INSIGHT INTO THE WORDS OF TORAH

NEHEMIAH 8:13

Volume I Issue 4–5, Tevet 5648 (1888)

Then on the second day the heads of fathers' households of all the people, the priests, and the Levites, were gathered to Ezra the scribe that they might gain insight into the words of Torah. (Nehemiah 8:13)

I t was their dream to gain insight into Torah in the days of Ezra and Nehemiah, and those who fear HaShem and revere his name do so even today. But it was not merely the heads of the fathers' households or the priests and Levites who gathered to hear Torah—as if only the lips of a priest such as Ezra should guard knowledge—but even the poor and common folk came together to turn their ear to the lesson of Torah. "For Moses has from generations past those who study his Torah in every city, and his words are read in synagogues every Sabbath" (Acts 15:21).

To what may I compare the books of the Torah? I shall compare them to the angels of God in the throne room; I shall compare them to the *seraphim* of God who stand above him. Each calls to the other, saying, "Holy, holy, holy is HaShem of Hosts; the fullness of the entire earth is his glory." The holy books say, "Holy is HaShem of Hosts," and they proclaim to us, "You shall be holy, for HaShem your God is holy." To make this known, HaShem gave us this Torah to meditate upon until the end of life. This will be what we do: *gaining insight into the words of Torah.*

Behold, the Garden of Torah is before you. It is a desirable garden, the Garden of Eden, the Garden of HaShem. In it is every succulent tree. In it is every morsel of heaven above. In it are blossoms, flowers, pleasant rows of branches clothed in splendor, and every kind of beauty. If your soul longs to delight in abundant goodness, please come into this garden and be sated with its honey, its sweetness, and its produce. Its dew is the dew of life. Drink from it and let your soul live.

NEHEMIAH AND EZRA HIS HELPER

The days of Ezra and Nehemiah brought the resurrection of Israel from the ash heaps of the great destruction that began in the time of Nebuchadnezzar and lasted until the days of Artaxerxes I. Overwhelming sufferings befell our people in those days. Our enemies beat us into dust. Then they took all of Israel's glory for themselves. Great turmoil came upon us, and Israel dwelt without Torah and without joy.

However, HaShem had compassion on his people and gladdened them in the days of Ezra and Nehemiah. After days of storm and cloud came days of sunlight and blue skies. The generation of Hachaliah[263] departed, and the generation of Nehemiah arrived.

Nehemiah was a truly precious man. Not every generation produces a man who so loved his people as he did. His faith in HaShem was stronger than boulders, his heart stronger than rocks. Had he known what he had to do from the start, neither mountains nor hills would have been able to stop him from accomplishing his task. He would return glory to Israel through his faith, wisdom, and courage.

HaShem sent Ezra the priest and scribe—who speedily transcribed the Torah of Moses—to be a helper[264] to Nehemiah in his holy work of rebuilding the breached walls of our people. This was a new era

---

263 [Hachaliah was the father of Nehemiah.]

264 [Lucky is employing a play on words, since the word used here is *ezrah* (עזרה), which means "help" in Hebrew, just as the name Ezra (עזרא) does.]

for Israel, an era of strengthening and building the nation, an era of resurrection and revitalization. Ezra and Nehemiah built the wall of the Torah in those days. Dew from heaven came down and the dry bones lived. Israel became a brave and mighty people.

The mighty Torah worked wonders—as it always does—and Ezra proved himself as a glorious priest of HaShem. He strengthened it, enhanced it, and placed a crown of splendor upon it. Thus our sages admired Ezra for his righteousness, and they gave his name honor and praise, because he built the fortresses of the Torah and placed a wall and armed guard around it.

READING THE SCROLL EXPLICITLY

> And they read in the scroll—in the Torah of God—explicitly, giving insight into it, and they understood the reading (Nehemiah 8:8). Rabbi Ika said in the name of Rabbi Chananel in Rav's name: "'And they read,' this refers to the Scriptures; 'explicitly,' this refers to the Targum; 'giving insight into it,' this refers to the division of verses; 'and they understood the reading,' this refers to the accentuations, and others say the *masorot*." (b.*Megillah* 3a; b.*Nedarim* 37b)

Now, I will speak with you about the words of Rav. Rav was the greatest *amora*[265] of his generation. He was called Abba Arika[266] (meaning, "the tall one") by the sages of his generation. He had the eyes of an eagle and he perceived with eyes of wisdom that if the people of Ezra's generation had not looked into the Torah in order to understand it, given insight into it, and had they not transcribed every single letter, the sages would not have been able to build this wall of Torah that has been handed down to us. Therefore, he drew upon the passage

---

265 [Aramaic word for a teacher who taught by speaking the words of the Oral Torah from roughly 200 CE to 500 CE in the land of Israel and Babylonia.]

266 Abba Arika, also called Rav, was the head of the *amoraim* and he taught Torah along with "Rabbi" and Rabbi Chiya in the land of Israel, and later he went to Babylonia. From there he returned to the land of Israel; afterward he went a second time to Babylonia and established an institute of learning.

(of Nehemiah 8:8) in order to show us that this is truly what Ezra and his generation did.

Behold, we also have days of bitter sadness now in the nineteenth century. The time of the end and destruction has come upon us: the destruction of our Torah and our nation together. But even though we are unworthy and our portion is by no means large—for we no longer have men like Nehemiah to rebuild the destroyed wall of our city, nor men like Ezra to rebuild the wall of the scattered Torah—our portion is nevertheless a pleasant one. For we do possess the trustworthy Scriptures. Moreover, the dew from heaven descends upon our fields. This is what the words of Ezra and Nehemiah have been to us.

Therefore, let us do as they did, and HaShem will help us. Let the aforementioned words of Abba Arika be our guide. Let us gain insight into the words of the Torah, let us read the Scriptures and the Targum, let us gain insight into the division of the verses, and through them we will even understand the accentuations that the ancients handed down to us. We will understand their pure understanding, and then we will enjoy great peace. Behold, I descend to the depths of the sea in order to bring up precious stones and sandalwood from the deepest depths of the Torah!

THE TORAH CYCLE

The words of Rav inform us of a great principle. He says that the words "and they read" refer to the Hebrew Scriptures; the word "explicitly" refers to the Targum, etc. But what are the Scriptures? In the days of Ezra and Nehemiah did they know from where the Scriptures came? According to the sages of the Talmud, Ezra fixed a set order to the reading of Scripture. We also have a tradition that Nehemiah, with the authority invested in him by the king, established a library, and Ezra himself recorded and documented all the books in which the genealogies of Israel and the history of the Torah were written. The deuterocanonical books, the books of Josephus, and the Babylonian Talmud all attest that the Torah reading cycle was established by Ezra and his household in the days of Artaxerxes.

However, if you examine closely, you will find that the reading cycle has been a point of contention and argument all throughout the generations up until the Council at Yavneh. But even if we were to say that the Torah cycle was indeed established by Ezra and Nehemiah during the reign of Artaxerxes, then why is it that in the days of Rav they did not know this reading cycle?

> And they read in the scroll—in the Torah of God—explicitly, giving insight into it, and they understood the reading. (Nehemiah 8:8)

Rashi (whom the sages of Israel correctly called "*Parshandatha*," i.e., "Torah Expositor"), says, "The word 'reading' (*mikra*, מקרא) is the Hebrew word for the Pentateuch." This is consistent with the words of Rav. Ezra swayed the spirit of his time and strengthened the hearts of the Israelites by reading the Torah and explaining the Word of HaShem. He made the Scriptures "explicit" through the Targum, and he provided insight into the Scriptures through the division of the verses. I believe the words of Rav are correct. Israel read the Scriptures, making the meaning explicit, and providing insight into their words. In the Scriptures they found hope for a secure future.

A SPIRIT OF CRITIQUE

And now, beloved reader, you are also reading the Scriptures explicitly and gaining insight into them. Come now into this garden and your soul will delight in its goodness. If the words of *Parshandatha* (Rashi) are correct, the Scriptures spoken of here in the books of Ezra and Nehemiah are the five books that our brothers in Greek lands called the Pentateuch. You can also find this word in the Talmud (see b.*Menachot* 39a; y.*Megillah* 1a). However, in the Scriptures we will find many names for the Pentateuch: "the book of the Torah" (Deuteronomy 31:26), "the Torah" (Nehemiah 8:2, 7, 13, 14), "the book of the Torah of HaShem" (2 Chronicles 17:9, 34:14; Nehemiah 8:3), and "the book of the Torah of God" (Nehemiah 8:18, and see Joshua 24:27). These names accurately teach that the words spoken in the Torah of Moses did not come from the heart of a man, for the witnesses who attest to its divine source lived not long after it was written. They saw the signs and wonders of HaShem that he showed to his covenant people. The Torah of Moses is the Torah of the covenant.

Moses took the book of the covenant and read it in front of the people. He took the blood of the sacrifices and threw it on the people, saying, "This is the blood of the covenant," and the people responded, "Everything that HaShem said we will do and we will obey" (see Exodus 24:7–8). Moses came in the name of HaShem, who made a covenant with his people Israel. If a member of our people arises today and speaks deceitfully against the words of this covenant, he is no longer a member of our people.

To the anguish of our souls, men have arisen in our age, striving with all their might to search for defects in the words of HaShem with a critical spirit.[267] Those who are critical—and their numbers increase daily—will say that the Torah of Moses is but mere plaster on a flimsy wall,[268] the hallucinations of dreamers. They say the things written in the Torah never happened, and they say that Israel's scribes fabricated these things in order to bring glory and praise to their own race. Indeed, even today's Torah teachers speak like this from the bimah!

However, these people have already ceased being teachers to the children of Israel. They have already cast off the crown of their nation from their heads. And even if they pretend to bear the name of "Israel," their hearts are not the heart of Israel.

---

267 Criticism is nothing new. The spirit of criticism has always and will always be part of the human mind. Its attributes include: carefully searching and examining, judging by thorough research and investigation, and deciding what is true. The meaning of the root of this word in Hebrew (*bikoret*, ביקורת) is first of all "to cut" or "to break through." From this root comes the word "morning" (*boker*, בוקר), for it is light that breaks through the darkness of night. The second meaning of this root is "to penetrate" the secrets of any given thing, to investigate and extrapolate, analyze, dissect, and to elucidate the matter. The third meaning is "to render a judgment." Ezra was indeed critical and he investigated every single word of the Torah. The talmudists, the sages, and their disciples all had a critical spirit in that they critiqued, investigated, and sought to know every matter. However, this is not the spirit of criticism of which we are speaking. We are speaking of the new critics of our generation, the ones who destroy every holy thing.

268 [Ezekiel 13:10.]

136 TESTIMONY TO ISRAEL

THE HEART OF ISRAEL

I now turn to my brothers whose hearts still remain one with the heart of Israel. For the people of Israel are well versed in miracles. Thus we know that the things written in this scroll were not fabricated by man nor are they hallucinations. These things really happened. And if the Torah contains things that are difficult to solve, God is the one who holds all the solutions. By the testimony of two to three witnesses—from which this Testimony has arisen—shall these difficult matters be decided.

Therefore, gracious and beloved reader, let us gain insight into the words of Torah and understand them through studying both the linguistics and the narrative. In doing so we will procure a heart of wisdom, for this Torah makes even the foolish wise. I trust, beloved reader, that you are neither foolish nor a buffoon, but rather one who loves truth and seeks wisdom:

> For if you acknowledge with your mouth that Yeshua is the Master, and you believe in your heart that God awakened him from the dead, then you will be saved. For man will believe in his heart and it will be righteousness for him, and with his mouth he will confess and it will be salvation for him. (Romans 10:9–10)

THE FUTURE OF OUR PEOPLE: JUDAH AND ISRAEL

Volume I Issue 1–2, Tishrei-Cheshvan 5648 (1888), 11–15; 21–24

> For the children of Israel will live a long time without a king and without a prince, without a sacrifice and without a sacred pillar, without an ephod and without images. Afterward, the children of Israel will return and seek HaShem their God and David their king, and they will fear HaShem and his goodness in the last days. (Hosea 3:4–5)

Israel has always been both a miraculous sign and an enigma. He is the firstborn of all the nations of the earth; his history was written before any other people knew how to find their origins, and he is the only nation who is able to trace his lineage all the way back to Adam and Eve. He is old, advancing in years with gray hair, yet he still possesses his strength. He is like a tree whose roots are many, whose branches are few, and who is firmly planted. All the menacing winds come and blow against him, yet they are unable to displace him.

Countless wars have been waged against him. Many rulers and kings have captured him, persecuted him, and overpowered him. The wars have passed; those who have waged them are no more and their names are no longer remembered, yet Israel still lives and endures. He still stands and laughs at all their weapons of war.

A MIRACULOUS SIGN AND ENIGMA

He has been scattered and dispersed to the four corners of the earth for eighteen centuries. He has endured severe governments. They have taken righteousness and justice from him, and they have devastated him. Yet when they afflicted him he grew numerous, spreading throughout the earth. In the course of his lifetime he has seen many other nations fall into oblivion, and yet he still retains a surviving remnant. He still exists today. Israel stands as a miraculous sign; many nations marvel at him. He is an enigma, for neither Israel nor the nations have an answer for this phenomenon.

However, God *does* have the answers. Who is still unable to see that the hand of HaShem accomplished all this?! HaShem's counsel will eternally endure through each and every generation. He said that Israel would arise and live and that he would be forever faithful to his desired people throughout all the ends of the earth; and he has been! Does he say and not perform or speak and not do? If HaShem has said it shall be so, who can intervene?

HaShem has bestowed his loving-kindness upon Israel, giving him life, giving him an inheritance, and sustaining him so that Israel stands as an enigma before all the peoples. And yet even more goodness and kindness is in store for Israel in the coming days—a greater kindness that is unfathomable. HaShem knows the future of his people Israel and he knows the plans that he revealed through his prophets and through the apostles two thousand years before they would occur. Not one word will be left unfulfilled.

THE EXAMPLE OF HOSEA

This was spoken 2,500 years ago, before the city of Rome was built, and HaShem spoke to Hosea son of Beeri in the days of Uzziah, Jotham, Ahaz, and Hezekiah, kings of Judah, and Jeroboam son of Joash, king of Israel, saying:

> Take for yourself a woman of whoredom and children of whoredom [Hosea 1:2] so that you can be a sign and an example to Israel that the whoring wife represents Israel's

relationship with me. Israel has surely whored, so much so that he has awakened my wrath, and he has become Lo-Ammi (Not My People), and the daughter of Jacob has become Lo-Ruchamah (Not Pitied) [ibid., 6, 9]. Therefore, the fate of Gomer daughter of Diblaim shall be their fate. Just as Gomer was not a lonely and single widow since you were living with her, neither will she be a married woman, because you shall not take her as your wife nor shall you enter into a covenant with her.

Israel shall live thus for a long time, without a king and without a prince, without a sacrifice or offering and without a cult pillar, without an ephod and priest and without images [ibid., 3:4]. This is also how Israel will live in exile among the nations. He shall not be the people of HaShem nor shall he be the people of other gods. He shall not worship HaShem nor shall he sacrifice to other gods. He shall neither possess priest nor ephod, nor shall images and idols be found with him. Prince and judge, king and ruler, will not come from his tribes, and yet he will not walk in the ways and customs of the Gentiles. This is how Israel will live for a long time: neither in heaven nor on earth. The dew of heaven will not fall on him, neither will the delicacies of the earth sweeten his palate.

This is what HaShem said over 2,500 years ago. Not one letter has gone unfulfilled.

A NATIONAL SIN

When did these things occur? Before the time of the Babylonian Exile the children of Jacob had a Judean king. Even if the majority of Israel went into exile, leaving the kingdom of Israel destroyed and no longer extant, the kingdom of Judah nevertheless persevered with its monarchy, and it also possessed the priesthood and ephod. Although images and idols polluted the kingdom of Judah, the priest and ephod remained in place.

Zerubbabel was a great prince in Israel and belonged to the family of David, even though he himself was not a king. Although he was conceived in Babylon,[269] he drew his lineage from David, the Root of Jesse. Nehemiah, also a great prince in Israel, was a comfort[270] to Israel in his time of trouble. He rebuilt the Temple and witnessed power and might in Israel, such as there had never been, and the Spirit of HaShem was with him. The Maccabees domineered over those who hated Israel, and they were great princes and trustworthy judges in Israel and Judah. So when was the time of destruction when Israel would cease to have a prince or judge, priest or ephod, ruler or sovereign?

That time of destruction, horror, and desolation came after the wicked Titus destroyed the Second Temple. Our Holy Temple was destroyed, our Holy City was demolished, and her children went into exile. The people of Israel were dispersed and scattered among all the peoples without altar or sacrifice, without peace offerings or burnt offerings, without priest or ephod, and even without images or cult pillars. They were left without prince or judge, king or ruler. Others from among the Gentiles ruled over Israel, and the days of exile have lasted for a very long time.

Eighteen centuries have passed and Israel has still not returned to his former glory. He is still scattered and hated among the nations. Almost all hope of returning and rebuilding the fallen national walls has been lost. The sin of Israel is a national sin. This national sin was committed approximately forty years prior to the destruction of the Temple when the nation gathered in Jerusalem to celebrate the Passover and sacrifice the Passover lamb.

The nation of Israel committed a horrible sin and slaughtered the Lamb who came to bear the sin of the world. They hung the Messiah on a tree, the Messiah whom HaShem sent in order to bring an end to sin, atone for iniquity, and usher in eternal righteousness. They pierced

---

269 [A play on words in Hebrew to interpret the meaning of Zerubbabel's name. Lucky uses the words "he was conceived in Babylon (*zarua be-bavel*, זרוע בבבל), which, when written, looks and sounds very similar to the name Zerubbabel (*Zerubbavel*, זרובבל).]

270 [The Hebrew word used for comfort here is *nechamah*, directly relating to Nehemiah's name (*Nechemyah*), which means "Comfort of HaShem."]

him between his ribs. They despised and abhorred him, even while they dearly longed for his arrival. Herod judged him and the leading priests and scribes sentenced the Messiah of Life to death and executed him. They derided him and said, "He is not the one." With a loud voice they cried out with great zeal, "May his blood be upon our heads!"

Even now this transgression has not been atoned for. The blood of the Messiah is upon the heads of our people. We are in exile and there is no one to return us, and when the nation rejected him—the very nation that he came to redeem—that nation became rejected and despised amongst the nations even to this day. And now the time that Hosea saw in a vision is upon us. Israel is in an awful state.

WE HAVE NO KING

We have been without a king for so many years. Indeed our number has grown to more than seven million souls, and we have had opportunities to appoint leaders over us, yet we have not done this, nor will we. We are not able. We have no hope of reestablishing our kingdom, neither in Palestine nor in any other country, until the sin of our nation has been covered over.

Thus shall we live amongst the Gentiles. Their kings shall be our rulers and our land shall remain in the hands of strangers. If we were to say, "Let us use wisdom and appoint a king over us," we would be in rebellion against HaShem and his word, and our designs would fail.

HaShem said to David (2 Samuel 7:8–14), "From the pasture I took you to be a ruler over my people Israel, and after you I will raise up *your descendant* from your own issue, and your throne shall endure forever." Who amongst us can say, "I am descended from the house of David"? When the city was demolished and the Temple set aflame the genealogical records were lost and are no longer in existence. HaShem, in his holiness, said once and for all—and he does not change his mind—that the king of Israel would be a descendant of David. HaShem will not recognize anyone else. And if a man should dare to say, "I am a descendant of David," and he is not, HaShem will not bless him and all his labors shall be futile.

From the day that we rejected King Messiah whom HaShem sent to us from on high, despised the greatest gift of all that HaShem gave us in his great mercy and faithfulness, loathed the great King of Kings who was appointed over us by our Heavenly Father, we have not had a king from our tribe, nor will we until HaShem has compassion upon us.

NOR DO WE HAVE PRINCES

Indeed many from our Jewish brothers have become quite wealthy and made their houses opulent as any sovereign would, and yet these rich men from our people have not achieved the status of king or ruler. Nor is there anyone among us to whom a foreign king would give such authority to rule or serve in any sort of governing role. There is also no one among us whom this king would trust as an advisor in matters pertaining to matters of state.

We no longer have a high priest as we did when the Persians, Greeks, and Romans conquered our land. And even though we are a nation, we have lost all the characteristics of a nation. We have rejected the Prince of Life and we have detested the high priest of the order of Melchizedek; therefore we have neither prince nor priest. Just as we do not have a government, we also do not have a Temple or any of the necessary utensils with which to worship HaShem as we did when we were in our own land.

WE HAVE NO SACRIFICE

We have no altar; therefore we have no sacrifice. HaShem commanded us to sacrifice in the land and not outside of it. The Romans burned down the Temple and destroyed our sanctuary. Ever since, all sacrifices and offerings have ceased. We do not have a sin offering or a scapegoat to carry our iniquities to a remote land. Every year our Jewish brothers come only with prayers on Yom Kippur—the tenth of Tishrei—yet there are no goats, no lots are cast, and no offerings. If there are no sacrifices, then of what use are the priests? Therefore, even the priests were taken from us, and we will not build altars.

WE HAVE NO CULT PILLARS

We have ceased offering incense to idols and sacrificing to demons and false gods long ago, for we have received double punishment from HaShem for all our sins[271] and seven-fold for our disobedience. We are like Hosea's wife, for she was not married yet she was no longer a prostitute once Hosea took her for himself.

We have ceased being idolaters. Idols have become defiling and strange to us. Yet we are also not worshipers of HaShem, the Living God, for we have not obeyed his words or performed his commands. HaShem commanded us to bring an offering for our crimes, yet we have no offering. HaShem brought the greatest offering on our behalf in giving his Son, his Messiah, as a sacrifice during the same month he had made a covenant with us.[272] Many of our Jewish brothers are still protesting: "We do not want him!" So thus we remain.

WE HAVE NO EPHOD OR IMAGES

Our Jewish brothers have not recognized the high priest after the order of Melchizedek that HaShem appointed,[273] and they have not obeyed the Word of HaShem. The Urim and Thummim have left us. A priest cannot be found. Thus we cannot inquire of HaShem as we did in ancient times when we were truly a nation. Yet, unlike those nations that walk in darkness, we will not request counsel from the mouths of mute idols nor will we obey them.

This is how Israel has lived for a very long time. Just like Gomer he is not consecrated to HaShem nor is he whoring after other gods. Gomer was neither discarded nor betrothed while living with Hosea. She was not *consecrated* to Hosea as his wife, for he did not marry her, and she was a whoring woman even to him. However, she was no longer a whore and she no longer sat at the gates or covered her face with a veil, rather, she worked in Hosea's house.

---

271 [Isaiah 40:2.]

272 [During the month of Nisan, the month in which Passover occurs.]

273 Psalm 110:4.

This is how it is with Israel, and he will not be able to see past the veil covering his face until HaShem removes it and opens his eyes.

REJECTION AND RETURN

Just as HaShem rejected Israel and gave him the name Lo-Ammi (Not My People), and his sister Judah was named Lo-Ruchamah (Not Pitied), so too, will HaShem take pity on his people, and the children of Israel will return and seek HaShem their God and David their king, and they will fear HaShem and his goodness. After Israel has lived a long time thus, the time of his regeneration will come. The Spirit of HaShem will blow on the dry bones and Israel will arise like a gallant warrior. He will arise from his long, comatose slumber of death.[274]

What a wondrous time that will be for Israel! The resurrection of faith that will occur will be astonishing to all who hear. Israel will repent, receive consolation, and return to his Heavenly Father and be healed. However, HaShem says that this will happen only *afterward*: after Israel has lived a long time in the desert without producing any fruit. Only afterward will the Jewish people return and embrace the husband of their youth. It has not happened yet. It will happen afterward.

AWAKENING FROM EXILE

This will signify the end of the most difficult period; this is the resolution to the unsolvable enigma. Israel will return to his Father who loves him and he will embrace his Beloved with both arms. His compassionate Father will once again gather him under his wings of mercy, and he will betroth Israel to himself forever in righteousness. He will call him *Ammi-Atah* (You Are My People), *Cheftzi-Becha* (I Delight in You), and Israel will also respond and call him *Eli-Atah* (You Are My God) and *Abba Avinu* (Our Dear Father). We see the signs of these good times to come even in this generation. The days of revival are coming. This is just the beginning.

---

274 See Ezekiel 37:1–14.

For a long time Israel has neither progressed nor regressed. He has slept like Choni the Circle Maker, who slept for seventy years.[275] His rabbis, leaders, and guides have made the yoke around his neck heavier every day and tightened the band around his waist. They have legislated harsh laws, which our fathers could not bear. They have bound him by his hands and feet with doubled and tripled fetters that are not easily loosed. He was mute; he followed them like a lamb to the slaughter.

The house of Israel is filled with the corpses of those who were slain. Yet HaShem called out to the Spirit and said, "Look at these dead bodies, and bring the four winds—whether calm or raging—and initiate the revival of the house of Israel. Then Israel will return and seek HaShem his God and David his king."

Once the scales fall from Israel's eyes and he recognizes his transgression and sin, then will he repent. He will see that he has strayed from the path thus far. Then he will be ashamed and distraught, and he will hide his face. The spirit of repentance will come into his heart. His heart will be contrite; he will anguish and confess his sins in detail.

AND HE WILL SEEK HASHEM HIS GOD

He will go and seek HaShem together with all his property and his entire household. He will seek his love. He will search and diligently read through HaShem's scroll. He will not seek HaShem in the teachings of men that come from the mouths of rabbis and teachers who

---

275 [Choni the Circle Maker was a first-century sage known for drawing circles in the ground and praying for rain. Once, while traveling, Choni came upon a man planting a carob tree, and the man advised him that it would take seventy years for the carob tree to bear fruit. Choni fell asleep and awoke seventy years later to find the grandson of the man picking the fruit of the carob tree (b. *Ta'anit* 23a).]

teach according to their own caprice, rather he will seek teaching directly from HaShem.[276]

The Jewish people will search the Scriptures, as they are life to all who search them and they contain in them everlasting life. Those Scriptures attest that Yeshua, the Messiah of the God of Israel, was sent from God. All who hear his words and believe in the one who sent him will pass from death to eternal life.[277] Israel will then seek HaShem like a deer panting for water, and the many waters will not be able to extinguish the flames of Israel's love.

HASHEM HIS GOD AND DAVID HIS KING

He will seek HaShem and the Messiah together. The glory of the latter house shall be greater than that of the first,[278] for the Master that Israel seeks and the Angel of the Covenant that he desires will suddenly come to his Sanctuary.[279] He came to bring crime to an end, to put a stop to sin, to atone for transgression, and to bring eternal righteousness.[280] And he was wounded for our crimes, beaten for our transgressions, and by his bruises we are healed.[281] Yeshua the Messiah grew up like a tender shoot, like a root from arid ground. He came from Nazareth and he corrected and instructed by the power of God. He performed signs and wonders for a few years, then he offered up his own life to be slaughtered to atone for our iniquities.

---

276 [Lucky's dissertation thus far must not be misread as an anti-Judaism or anti-rabbinic polemic. Lucky states emphatically many times throughout his articles that he adheres to Rabbinic Judaism and its interpretations. However, here Lucky is stressing the change that will occur when Israel no longer seeks the judgment of the rabbis that are at times just and at times not, and will actually have direct communication with HaShem. He harshly criticizes the abuse of the religious elect, but his critique is not intended to serve as an all-out invalidation of Judaism.]

277 John 5:24, 39.

278 Haggai 2:9.

279 Malachi 3:1.

280 Daniel 9:24.

281 Isaiah 53:5.

Then the Israelites shall be astonished and ask in amazement, "What caused our forefathers to despise the Messiah of HaShem? Is he not the delight of all the Gentiles and the one to whom every knee must bow? Do not all the nations worship him?"

The stone that our forefathers—the builders of HaShem's Sanctuary—rejected has become the chief cornerstone. This is the Son of David, who appeared in Jerusalem before the Temple was destroyed. He is the Master of David.[282] This Master sits to the right of HaShem the Most High in might, and at the end of days he will return to judge the living and the dead.

The Son of God will then descend from his place of glory and come in the form of Yeshua, the form of flesh, blood, tendons, and bones, in order to rescue the sons of men from sin and crime. And he is the one of whom the sages of the Talmud said over and over again: "The Holy One, blessed be he, will reduce his *Shechinah* and cause it to reside in the temple of the human body."[283]

This is what the Jewish people will realize. The light that is coming upon them will be a light of life, a light that awakens them from the slumber of death, a light of resurrection and revitalization.

THEY WILL FEAR HASHEM …

They will not fear HaShem in the sense of fright and terror, for in those days they will sing: "*Violence is no more and plundering has ended, and marauders have left this land.*"[284] Their fear will be out of love. They will scrupulously observe every word of HaShem, and they will carefully listen continually to every whisper from his mouth.

Just as a bride continually concerns herself with pleasing the beloved of her youth, so will the Assembly of Israel for her Beloved. Her

---

282 Psalm 110:1.

283 [Cf. Philippians 2:6–8; John 1:14; 2 Corinthians 6:16. Perhaps Lucky is also paraphrasing a sentiment based on interpretations of Exodus 25:8: "They shall make a sanctuary for me so that I may dwell in their midst." E.g., Sforno's comments on the passage.]

284 [Isaiah 16:4.]

love will grow stronger each day, and the only desire of the daughter of Judah will be to find favor with her Beloved.

... AND HIS GOODNESS

The Messiah is the goodness and kindness of Israel. The Torah was given through Moses and kindness and truth came through Yeshua the Messiah.[285] The Lamb who takes away the sin of the entire human race embodies the eternal kindness of HaShem. In those days the children of Israel will love God's kindness,[286] and they will praise and bless him. It will be a time of favor and salvation for Israel, and the words of the holy Shaul will be fulfilled: "If their rejection means favor for the world, what will their acceptance be but life from the dead?!"[287]

ONLY A MOMENT LONGER

In the last days all these things will occur. HaShem has not deserted his people whom he has known since the very beginning of time. Israel will be everlasting, for HaShem will not act falsely or break the eternal covenant he made. Who can understand his ways? He desires to grant pardon to every rebellious person. Israel waits with a hard heart, but only for a little while longer until the fullness of the Gentiles enters in, and afterward all Israel will be saved.

The people whom HaShem chose to be his treasure, and through whose descendant all the nations of the earth will bless themselves, will return to being his treasured people once again. They have abandoned HaShem only for a short instant. They will be the least among the nations only for a moment. Then, in great compassion, HaShem will gather them and the last will then become the first.[288]

---

285 John 1:17.
286 Titus 2:11.
287 Romans 11:15.
288 Matthew 19:30.

Behold, that time is now! God is awakening a time of lavish affection. The eyes of Israel will be opened and they will see Yeshua the Redeemer. All anguish and lament will vanish, and the exile will come to an end. Amen; may it be his will.

DEW FROM HEAVEN

Volume I Issue 3, Kislev 5648 (1888) pgs. 6–8

"May God give you dew from heaven and the fat of the earth" (Genesis 27:28). "Dew from heaven," this is the Torah, and "fat of the earth," this is the Prophets. (*Midrash Tanchuma*, Parashat Toldot 15)

How lovely is this saying! The Scriptures and the Word of HaShem are like the dew of Hermon that falls on the mountains of Zion within the hearts of men, for through his word HaShem ordained the blessing of everlasting life.[289] Dew symbolizes blessing to those who inhabit the earth, for it gives life to everything that grows.

DROPLETS OF DEW

Have you ever awoken to a springtime morning without clouds,[290] when the time of pruning has come and the voice of the turtledove is heard in our land,[291] the dawn's awakening and rising seen through the window of your house with its rays shining, peeking through your window slats? Did you leave your room to see and consider the marvels

---

289 Psalm 133:3.
290 2 Samuel 23:4.
291 Song of Songs 2:12.

of him whose understanding is perfect,[292] who guides his world with loving-kindness,[293] in order to perceive his ways through creation? Have you? What did you see?

Everything before you tells you of his attributes: the flower buds that can be seen on the ground, the mandrakes giving off their scent, the blossoms and the flowers wearing a crown of splendor. On all of these are drops of dew, sparkling like crystals, like rays of light at dawn, like pavement made of sapphire, as clear as the sky itself.[294] The grasses absorb their life force from these droplets of dew; they drink, saturate themselves, and are satisfied, thereby becoming a blessing of beauty to mankind. If you beheld all this beauty, then your head would also be moist with dew. Droplets of life would glide gently down into your heart and into your very being; a new spirit would enter you.

THE WATERS OF SCRIPTURE

> For there shall be a seed of peace, the vineyard shall bear its fruit, the land shall yield its produce, and the heavens shall give their dew. (Zechariah 8:12)

If the heavens withhold their dew, the earth will withhold its produce (Haggai 1:10). When Job spoke to his faithful companions about bygone days when he still enjoyed God's protection, he took up his theme, saying, "My roots reached water, and dew rested upon my branches" (Job 29:1–2, 19). With these two images that he described he indicated all the wealth, happiness, and gladness that he possessed before HaShem's affliction took away everything he had.

In the same way, if Israel obeys the voice that calls, "Return, O Israel ... for you have fallen because of your sin,"[295] and if Israel returns to HaShem his God, then HaShem would be like dew upon him and he would blossom like a rose and strike root like a tree of Lebanon. His boughs would spread out, his glory would be like that of an olive tree,

---

292 Job 37:16.

293 From the prayer *Nishmat Kol Chai*.

294 Exodus 24:10.

295 Hosea 14:2.

and his fragrance would be like that of Lebanon.[296] Indeed, the dew is the Word of HaShem. The word does not return void, rather it does what HaShem desires and accomplishes what it was sent to do. Like dew, the Scriptures spread within the hearts of men, and good fruit will sprout and come forth from them: the fruit of love and the fruit of repentance that will rescue them from the coming wrath (Matthew 3:7–8).

Happy is the man whose portion is the Scriptures, who delights in the Torah of HaShem day and night![297] Wherever he may dwell, the words of HaShem are like songs.[298] The Scriptures are the dew of life that flow from the never-failing source of living water. Past generations thirsted, drank, and were satisfied. Until the heavens and the moon no longer exist, the spring will be open to every human being. Let them come, drink, and marvel at the beauty of heaven—the mighty waters— in which the *seraphim* above delight. These waters are the Scriptures.

The Scriptures possess an eternal power. The Word of HaShem stands forever. Even the heavens will pass away with a loud roar, and the elements will be destroyed with an intense heat (2 Peter 3:10), yet the Word of HaShem will remain. The Word of HaShem guards light and expels dark clouds. Every place where the Scriptures have reached, darkness flies away in an instant and the light of life comes to those who dwell there.

THE POWER OF THE HOLY WRITINGS

Now lift up your eyes to the east and west, north and south, and look.[299] Pay attention. What do you see? Light has come upon the peoples who once sat in darkness. Desolate wastelands have become vibrant cities and bustling towns. Savages in the desert turned into civilized men, men of understanding. Suddenly they became scholars and men of stature, walking in the paths of discipline and good character. Who or what accomplished this? It was the power of the Holy Writings!

---

296 Ibid., 14:6–7.
297 Psalm 1:2.
298 Psalm 119:54.
299 Genesis 13:14.

Up until this very day, those who proclaim the good news of redemption go out crossing distant lands, seas, and islands. They take with them the books of the Bible—the Holy Writings—to the inhabitants of those lands. The wilderness of India was glad and the arid desert of Kush rejoiced; the Arab desert blossomed like lilies, and places that had never been trodden were paved with roads. For the dew of heaven descended upon the inhabitants, giving life to the dry bones, giving them sinews and placing flesh upon them,[300] and they became a people.

This did not occur in places where the Scriptures do not reside, and the dew of heaven does not fall upon them. Their inhabitants are as lifeless corpses. They possess no understanding. Wickedness and folly are in their midst; sin and death in their hearts. Disaster and catastrophe come upon them; desolation and devastation are their portion. For the rays of light from the Torah have not shone upon them, and they walk in utter darkness. Therefore they are fading away. What Rabbi Elazar said is beautiful:

> The illiterate will not be resurrected, as it says, "The dead will not live"[301] ... For all who make use of the dew of the Torah will be resurrected by the dew of Torah, and all who do not make use of the dew of Torah will not be resurrected by the dew of Torah. (b.*Ketuvot* 111b)[302]

Nevertheless, may the name of HaShem be blessed, for he has done something new in our age. HaShem has bared his holy arm before all the nations and all the ends of the earth have seen the salvation of our Master. Those who were anticipating this went out and raised their voices, saying, "Ho, all who are thirsty come for water. Come buy food without money, at no cost."[303] Many peoples inclined their ears and

---

300 Ezekiel 37:8.

301 Isaiah 26:14.

302 [This passage from the Talmud resembles the statements of Yeshua when he says: "Amen, amen, I say to you, if you do not eat the flesh of the son of man and drink his blood, you do not have life within you. One who eats my flesh and drinks my blood has eternal life, and I will raise him on the last day" John 6:53–54. Lucky, in line with Yochanan and his gospel, is equating the Torah to the "Word" of HaShem, i.e., the Messiah.]

303 Isaiah 55:1.

many nations gathered around to listen: those from the east and the west; those from the south and the north; those from India to Kush, and those from China. Every single day the number of those who hunger for the bread of life and thirst for the waters of salvation grows, and with joy they draw water from the fountains of Yeshua. For the Holy Writings are a lamp to their feet and a light to their paths.

LOVE INSCRIBED ON TABLETS

The Scriptures were written for every single people group, tongue, and province. The words of Moses, the words of the prophets, the words of Yeshua, and the words of his emissaries have been translated into three hundred languages in this generation. The Scriptures are a tree of life, and the tree bears leaves of medicine for every anguishing soul and for every broken and beaten heart. The love of HaShem erases those ailments. The love of HaShem is inscribed on tablets.[304]

Therefore, the tree is desirous to the eyes and it is a pleasure to study it. Everyone who touches it has his eyes opened and his ears unplugged and he hears the voice of the good news, *for faith comes from hearing.*[305] "Look among the nations, observe well and be utterly astounded, for a work is being done in your days which you would not believe, even if you were told."[306] The blind are seeing, the lame are walking, lepers are being cleansed, the deaf are hearing, the dead are rising, and the poor are receiving the good news of salvation.[307] The end of visions has not yet come; greater things than these will our eyes behold in the coming days. Just as the earth brings forth its growth and a garden makes its seed shoot up, so too, HaShem God will make his righteousness and praise shoot up before all the nations.[308]

The Scriptures are a gem: a stone more precious than the stones of Ophir. The Torah and the words of the prophets are jewels, more

---

304 [In other words, the love of HaShem is exemplified through the Torah given by Moses.]

305 Romans 10:17.

306 Habakkuk 1:5.

307 Matthew 11:5; Luke 7:22.

308 Isaiah 61:11.

valuable than pure gold, the gold of Ophir,[309] onyx, or sapphire. Even all the golden vessels of the Temple cannot compare to their worth. By the grace of God,[310] the peoples from a wild olive tree have been joined to the root of the cultivated olive tree and are nurtured by that root. They cherish these precious jewels because the light,[311] which is the gift of heaven,[312] has dawned upon them. He has given them their portion in the Holy Spirit,[313] and they have tasted the good word of God and the powers of the World to Come[314] (Hebrews 6:4–5).

RECLAIMING OUR ESTATE

How is it that we, who are the natural branches of the cultivated olive tree and who have sprouted forth from the root, have failed to cherish this good gift of Heaven thousands upon thousands of times more than the multitude of peoples cherish it? We receive the law of the firstborn.[315] We hold the status of children; we have the covenants, the giving of the Torah, Temple worship, and sacrifice. To us belong the patriarchs, and the Messiah issued from us (according to the flesh). Pleasant places have fallen to us as an inheritance.[316] Despite all this, how is it that we have failed to profit from our estate?

---

309 Isaiah 13:12.

310 The "grace of God" is the Messiah. See Titus 2:11.

311 The Torah, for the commandments are the lamp and the Torah is the light.

312 This is the gift of God (of which John 4:10 speaks), and the gift of God is faith (Ephesians 1:8), as Rabbi Pinchas son of Yair said: "Torah brings one to vigilance, vigilance to alacrity, alacrity to cleanliness, cleanliness to abstinence, abstinence to purity, purity to piety, piety to humility, humility to fear of sin, fear of sin to holiness, holiness to the Holy Spirit, and the Holy Spirit brings one to the resurrection of the dead" (b.*Avodah Zarah* 20b; *Mesillat Yesharim* 1:9).

313 That is, the gifts of the Holy Spirit (1 Corinthians 12:7–11). "Holiness brings one to the Holy Spirit" (b.*Avodah Zarah* 20b). And everyone (priest) who does not have the Holy Spirit in him will not be inquired of [for prophecy] (b.*Yoma* 73b).

314 The powers of the Holy Spirit are the powers of the World to Come; for it is through them that man gets a taste of the World to Come.

315 [The double portion given to the firstborn son as prescribed in Deuteronomy 21:17.]

316 Psalm 16:6.

I implore you, my Jewish bothers, let us cling to our estate and not slack away from it, for it is our life and the lengthening of our days. In it is every honor we could ever receive in life. Let us take refuge in the shadow of this wall[317] so nothing evil will befall us. The sun will not strike us by day, nor the moon at night,[318] for HaShem is our guardian. He is our shadow, and the dew of heaven will fall during our harvest time, for he will never abandon us all the days of our lives. May the name of HaShem be blessed. Amen.

> Do not let this book of Torah cease from your lips, but recite it day and night, so that you may observe faithfully all that is written in it. Only then will you prosper in your undertakings and only then will you be successful. (Joshua 1:8)

> Search the Scriptures in which you say you have eternal life. They testify about me. (John 5:39)

> And from your youth you have known the Holy Writings, which are able to give you the wisdom that leads to salvation through faith in Yeshua the Messiah. For all of Scripture was written through the Spirit of God and is useful for teaching, for reproach, for correction, and for training in righteousness. (2 Timothy 3:15–16)

---

317 The wall is the Torah (b.*Bava Batra* 8; b.*Pesachim* 87).

318 Psalm 121:6.

וְאַתָּה ה' בְּרָחוֹק תַּעֲמוֹד!
BUT YOU, HASHEM, SO FAR OFF STILL REMAIN!

אִם גַּם חָדְלוּ לוֹחֲצֵינוּ
לְעַנּוֹתֵנוּ בָּאֵשׁ וּשְׁפָטִים רָעִים
עוֹד קוֹדֵר נְהַלֵּךְ וְתָשׁוּחַ נַפְשֵׁנוּ
וְאֵין מִסְפָּר לְרִשְׁמֵי הַפְּצָעִים.
בִּלְעֲגֵי לָשׁוֹן יִשְׁאֲלוּ שׂוֹנְאֵינוּ:
תִּפְאֶרֶת צִיּוֹן הֲתָשׁוּב עוֹד?
מָתַי לְכִסֵּא יֵשֵׁב מַלְכֵּנוּ?
וְאַתָּה ה' בְּרָחוֹק תַּעֲמוֹד!

Even if all our oppressors should cease
To afflict with harsh judgments, torment, and flame,
Still we'd aimlessly wander, our souls still deplete,
For no list can scarce number our wounds and our shame.
With contemptuous tongues those who hate us ask:
"Will Zion's splendor again return one day?"
O when will our King take up his throne at last?
But you, HaShem, so far off still remain!

מֵאֶרֶץ לְאֶרֶץ וּמִפֵּאָה לְפֵאָה
מִבְּלִי מָנוֹחַ יֵתַע עַמֶּךָ
וּמְאוֹד יִכְסוֹף אֶל-הַמַּרְגֵּעָה
אֲשֶׁר נִשְׁבַּעְתָּ לוֹ בִּדְבָרֶיךָ.
וְיִשְׁאַל: מָתַי יִבָּנֶה הַמִּזְבֵּחַ
עֲבוֹדַת הַקּוֹדֶשׁ בּוֹ נַעֲבוֹד
מִשָּׁנָה לְשָׁנָה אֵלֶיהָ נִתְיַפֵּחַ?
וְאַתָּה ה' בְּרָחוֹק תַּעֲמוֹד!

From land to land, corner to corner we roam,
Ever your people wander void of rest;
How greatly we long for the recreation of home,
A promise you made, which your words still attest.
We ask: "When will the altar be built and made great?
Yearly we weep with sobs and we pray.
Please return it to us and the holy rite reinstate!"
But you, HaShem, so far off still remain!

עַד שְׁאוֹל שָׁחָה נַפְשֵׁנוּ
וְקִלְלַת חַטֹּאתֵינוּ עָנְתָה בָּנוּ.
הָרוּחַ תִּמָּלֵא מִקּוֹל יְלָלָתֵנוּ:
מָתַי גְּאוּלָה תִּהְיֶה לָנוּ?
נְשָׂא בִדְמָמָה זְרוֹעֶךָ, אָיוֹם!
וְנִמַּסֶּה פָּנֵינוּ הַנְּקֻמָטִים לִמְאוֹד
בְּדִמְעוֹת-נוֹחַם לַיְלָה וָיוֹם
וְאַתָּה ה' בְּרָחוֹק תַּעֲמוֹד!

Until Sheol's depths our souls finally reach,
And we stand to answer for our sins' curse,
Our spirit with a wailing voice will beseech:
"When will it be that our redemption occurs?"
Most Feared One, from quietude raise up your arm high!
So that we, with tears of comfort shed night and day,
Will see the marks on our face melt away as we cry,
But you, HaShem, so far off still remain!

SECTION III

I AM MY BELOVED'S AND MY BELOVED IS MINE

אני לדודי ודודי לי
(ELUL)[319]

Volume 4 Issue 4, Tishrei 5650 (1890) pgs. 95–97

My beloved extended his hand through the opening, and my feelings were aroused for him. (Song of Songs 5:4)

I have sought you, I have called for you, my Beloved,
> And my feelings were aroused for you.
You will come and you will elevate my glory,
> And now I shall not fail you again.
Even my brothers will seek you again,
> They will lift up their eyes toward heaven,
And they will see you on the throne of your glory,
> And their feelings for you will be aroused.

Behold, the first day of the month of Elul has come. Behold, it has come with noise and a great roar, and it reminds us that the "Day of Judgment" draws near. It is the custom of Israel in the Diaspora to

---

319 [The month of Elul (אלול) is an acronym for "I am my beloved's and my beloved is mine" (אני לדודי ודודי לי).]

blow the shofar every single day, from the beginning of the month to the end. Those who are pious and very devout fast frequently during this month.

PREPARING FOR REPENTANCE

According to the tradition given to us by our sages of blessed memory, on the first day of Elul Moses ascended the mountain a second time, after he had broken the first set of tablets. HaShem told Moses to take a shofar and sound it throughout the entire camp, and the blowing of the shofar announced that Moses was ascending the mountain a second time. It warned them not to go astray again as they did the first time when they made the golden calf. Moses did as HaShem had said. Therefore, we also blow the shofar on every first day of Elul, and once we have begun to sound the shofar, we do not stop blowing it until the end of forty days of repentance, until the end of the tenth of the next month, for Moses descended the mountain on the tenth of the month of Tishrei.

Just as the Israelites fasted and afflicted themselves in those days, so too, even now, many fast and afflict themselves during this month. If the people of our generation were not so weak, we would fast for all forty days. Just as in the days of Nineveh—the days of repentance—so it is now. Jonah proclaimed, "Yet forty days and Nineveh will be overthrown!" They believed in God and proclaimed a fast, putting on sackcloth and ashes, from the greatest to the least, and God saw and relented from the disaster that he was going to inflict upon them.[320] Even our sages appointed forty days for repentance: thirty days to prepare the soul, search the paths of God, and awaken the heart, and ten days to truly repent, from the Day of Judgment until the Day of Atonement.

---

320 Jonah 3:4, 5, and 10.

AWAKEN FROM THE SLUMBER OF SIN

The soul that has been given over to trouble and captivity must weep over her father and mother for a month, and this is the month of Elul.[321] Therefore, man must weep and supplicate before HaShem and blow the shofar morning and night for the entire month, instilling fear in the heart of man and arousing him to do something to escape the coming wrath. The Rambam explained the commandment of blowing the shofar. He said that the sound of the shofar inspires fear in the heart. The sound of the shofar blast calls to the man who hurries along the wide path that leads to Sheol and Avaddon, and the voice of the shofar says, "Stand still for a moment and think upon your deeds, for the Day of Judgment is near and none can withstand it." The sound of the shofar awakens sinners from the slumber of sin.[322]

Man's heart cannot find rest until it rests in HaShem, until he knows that he has crossed over from death to life, and that HaShem has forgiven him all his sins. Long ago, in Israel's past, when we still dwelt in our land and the Temple stood in its proper place, we offered up burnt offerings and sacrifices. Now the Temple has been destroyed and the place of the altar is a desolate hill; the burnt offerings and sacrifices have ceased and it is no longer possible to offer up a pleasing aroma to HaShem. Now fasting and affliction have taken the place of sacrifices, and prayers and supplications have become substitutes for burnt offerings. Therefore, we weep and lament during this month, according to the counsel of our great luminaries.

DAYS OF FORGIVENESS

Anyone who is concerned about the salvation of his soul will not give sleep to his eyes nor slumber to his eyelids until he sees the light of the first of the days of forgiveness. He will soak his couch with tears, and when midnight comes he will arise like a lion and run as fast as

---

321 The *Zohar Chadash* 46:4 says concerning the verse, "And she shall mourn her father and her mother for a full month" (Deuteronomy 21:13) that the month mentioned is Elul, and the Arizal interprets that "her father" is the Holy One, blessed be he, and "her mother" is the children of Israel.

322 From the Rambam's *Hilchot Shofar*.

he can to the house of prayer to request HaShem's pardon. He will pour out his heart like water and he will cry out, "We have no power to appease you, my Master! Act in accordance with the covenant that you made with our forefathers, for we trust in your abundant mercy."

My brothers! Shall all our sorrows be in vain? Have we been afflicted for nothing and shall we give birth to panic? HaShem is righteous, a lover of righteous deeds, and there is no end to his mercy. That which he has said he will do, and he will surely have compassion just as he said. HaShem is near to all who call upon him in truth.

Please, my beloved brothers, be mindful of all your days and nights. Indeed our Beloved has extended his hand through the opening. The days of repentance are days of benevolence and favor. Let us also call out, "I am my Beloved's." Let us make the Word of HaShem a lamp for our feet, and let us walk on the path. Let truth, life, and salvation speedily come.

> "Behold, I belong to my Beloved,"
>> Says the people of Israel.
> "He is my splendor and my glory,
>> And in his kindness I am redeemed from trouble."
> And our Master will answer from the heights:
>> "I have chosen you, O Israel.
> If your feelings are aroused for me,
>> I will come to you and redeem you."

THE SEVENTH MONTH:
THE MONTH OF ETHANIM

Volume V Issue 1, Tishrei 5958 (1898) pgs. 1–8

The first day of this month is Rosh HaShanah—the new year—for all the Jewish people in all their towns and dwellings. This is the seventh month from the month that marks Israel's exodus from Egypt. It used to be called "The Month of Ethanim."[323] Perhaps it was called by this name because there was no rain during this month in Canaan and Palestine except for the water that came from the ever-flowing streams,[324] which never dried up throughout the whole year, or perhaps because through these streams, and during this month, the everlasting foundations of the earth were created. The meaning of this name is actually "the month in which the heavens and the earth were created."[325]

When the children of Israel returned from Babylon they changed the name of this month to "Tishrei."[326] From that day until now, the

---

323 1 Kings 8:2.

324 This word ethanim, or *eitanim*, appears in Exodus 14:27, Amos 5:24, and Psalm 74:15. However, it does not only refer to rivers and streams. In and of itself the word means "strong" and "durable," as in something that is eternal and indestructible. Even though it is most commonly used in reference to waters, the prophets also use it in reference to the foundations of the earth. See Micah 6:2. Job also uses it when speaking of strong and important people (Job 12:19).

325 According to Rabbi Eliezer, who says that in the month of Tishrei HaShem created the world (b.*Rosh HaShanah* 11a).

326 *Leviticus Rabbah* 48.

Jewish people have called the seventh month by the name Tishrei, which is the same name for this month in the Syrian language.[327] According to the great linguists, the interpretation of this word is "beginning" or "commencement." And so it is. Even in ancient times this month was the new year for the people of Israel.[328]

Our forefathers were farmers and vintners and they worked the ground that HaShem gave them: they plowed it, sowed it, and reaped it. And because their work was completed by this month, the month of Tishrei was considered the first month of the [agricultural] year. In the month of Elul the fieldwork ended, the harvest was gathered to the threshing floor, and the vintage to the wine press. When this period ends a new one begins, and a new year is ushered in.

THE NEW YEAR FOR YEARS

The month of Ethanim is the beginning of the new year. The month of Aviv (or Nisan) is the new year for the pilgrimage festivals and for kings,[329] as well as the birth of the nation of Israel,[330] and there are those who say that it is also the new year for renting houses.[331] But the month of Ethanim is the new year for years, the *shemittah* cycle,[332] the Jubilee cycles, agriculture,[333] and the beginning of the synagogue worship cycle.[334] If HaShem had not commanded that the children of Israel celebrate Sukkot on the fifteenth of Tishrei, they might have celebrated the harvest festival at the end of Elul or on the first day of Tishrei.[335] HaShem had a different idea.

---

327 In Syrian it is called "Tishrin."

328 It was the custom of all Semitic peoples—Syrians, Ashkelonites, etc.—to begin the new year in the fall.

329 b.*Rosh HaShanah* 1a.

330 For when the Israelites left Egypt they truly became a nation.

331 b.*Rosh HaShanah* 7a.

332 The years of debt release.

333 b.*Rosh HaShanah* 1a.

334 And so it is the case today that in the month of Tishrei we restart the Torah cycle beginning with Genesis.

335 This is merely my opinion, for it would stand to reason that the new year would commence at the very end of the harvest.

HaShem singled out the month of Tishrei and set three appointed times within it. The first day is a day of complete rest, remembrance, and trumpet blasts. It is a holy occasion on which no form of work may be done: it is Yom Teruah.[336] The tenth of the month is Yom Kippur, a holy occasion, a Sabbath of complete rest. Finally, on the fifteenth is Sukkot, a festival lasting for seven days.[337] These are the appointed times of HaShem that are called holy occasions.

YOM TERUAH IN THE TIME OF EZRA

In ancient days they did not call Rosh HaShanah a festival,[338] for only the three pilgrimage festivals are called festivals [Passover, Shavuot, and Sukkot].[339] On Rosh HaShanah people would not make pilgrimages to Jerusalem, nor would they celebrate together en masse. What did the ancient generations do on Rosh HaShanah? Our forefathers did not relate the customs of the ancients for Rosh HaShanah. The Torah merely commands that an offering of fire be brought as a pleasing odor to HaShem along with the offering for the beginning of the month and the continual offering, etc., and to sound trumpet blasts. We are not told anything beyond what the Torah of Moses says.

The prophets and seers also did not tell us anything about Yom Teruah. Even the Prophet Ezekiel tells us nothing.[340] It was only in the

---

336 ["The day of trumpet blasts." This is the first day of the seventh month, which is also called Rosh HaShanah. Lucky uses these two titles interchangeably.]

337 Leviticus 23:23–44 and Numbers 29, the whole chapter.

338 In the Torah neither Rosh HaShanah nor Yom Kippur are called a festival (*chag*).

339 See Exodus 34:18–26; Leviticus 23; Numbers 29; Deuteronomy 16.

340 From Ezekiel 40:1 we can determine that during the exile, or shortly beforehand, they called the month of Tishrei the new year. In those days the months were named according to their sequential order (first month, second month, etc.) and the month of Tishrei was the seventh month. And Ezekiel, the prophet of the exile, saw a vision on the tenth of this month of the new year. And what was his vision? The building of the Temple, etc. Therefore it occurs to me that there possibly was no "Rosh HaShanah," rather just the beginning of the month of Tishrei, and on the tenth of the month was Yom Kippur, which is when he saw his vision. He was a priest, therefore he was contemplating and remembering the priestly duties on that day. It was then that HaShem comforted him and showed him a vision of the building of the Third Temple.

days of Ezra, after they returned from Babylon, that the people were gathered on the first of the seventh month. Ezra the priest brought out the Torah and read it in front of the congregation from sunrise to sunset; he blessed HaShem the great God, and all the people answered, "Amen, amen," bowing and prostrating themselves before HaShem. Everyone wept when they heard the words of the Torah, and Ezra comforted them by telling them, "Go, eat choice foods and drink sweet wines and send portions to those who have not prepared anything, for this day is holy to our Master. Do not be sad, for the joy of HaShem is the source of your strength."[341]

In the days of Ezra they began sanctifying Yom Teruah more so than the previous generations. Our sages of blessed memory understood the Scriptures and sought commandments concerning Yom Teruah. Although they lived in the days after prophecies had ceased, those scribes were disciples of Ezra and his disciples; they were holy men clothed in a spirit of piety. They saw that Yom Teruah was a day of complete remembrance, request, supplication, and prayer. For it is written, "It will serve as a remembrance for you before HaShem your God, and you will be remembered before HaShem your God, and you will be saved from your enemies."[342]

REMEMBRANCE AND REPENTANCE

The trumpet blast symbolizes the breaking of the human heart and the emotions of grief within the heart.[343] This is how our sages of blessed memory—pious scribes—understood it. Yom Teruah was a day of a memorial trumpet blast before HaShem. Our sages continued to study the Scriptures, surmising that "a day of remembrance" means "a day of repentance." They deemed it a day for the children of Israel to stand before HaShem, calling to him and supplicating before him, remembering his greatness, enthroning him as king, and requesting compassion and pardon of sins from him.

---

341 See Nehemiah 8.

342 Numbers 10:9–10.

343 The word *teruah* ("trumpet blast," תרועה) can be translated as "whine," "cry," or "scream."

We have sinned before HaShem; we have all sinned. Yom Teruah is like a messenger sent to announce the good news of Yom Kippur, and Yom Teruah prepares the way for it. Yom Teruah is a day of remembrance, and every male[344] comes before HaShem for a day of judgment. With the sound of the shofar God became King over us. He granted us instruction, judgment, and law so that Israel would be holy, for HaShem is holy and only holy ones are permitted to come before him.

HaShem, in his great mercy, looks upon us longingly and favorably from the beginning of the year until the end, and he commands his angels to guard us for every one of those days. This day is the beginning of the year. In his mercy and faithfulness, HaShem renews it for us, for we are evil sinners. Therefore, it is our duty to return to HaShem in true repentance, to come before him with a shofar[345] in order to improve our deeds,[346] to renew our actions,[347] to request that he rule over the entire world in his glory, to appear in his splendorous majesty, to extend salvation and mercy from the eternal heavens, and to remember the covenant of kindness and compassion to our favor.

ROSH HASHANAH IN THE TIME OF YESHUA

On this Yom Teruah all our energy is spent sitting in the synagogues praying to HaShem our God, and we sound the shofar to crown him as King. With sounds of sighing, brokenness, and howling we sing psalms and hymns until dusk. We who are disciples of Yeshua the Messiah also sit there in the synagogues on Rosh HaShanah—Yom

---

344 [Lucky is making a correlation with the terms *zikaron* ("remembrance" זכרון) and *zachar* ("male," זכר), as they contain the same Hebrew root. His point is obscure.]

345 The Torah does not specifically indicate what to use to sound the blasts. HaShem only commanded that they blast on trumpets, which is a generic word in Hebrew (Numbers 10). However, our sages said that the commandment for this day refers to the shofar (b.*Rosh HaShanah* 26a).

346 [The Hebrew verb used for "improve" (*le-shaper*, לשפר) has the same root as the word *shofar* (שופר). Lucky is drawing a parallel between the two words and subtly explaining why the shofar is the instrument used for the trumpet blasts.]

347 The words "to renew" (*le-chadesh*, לחדש) and "month" (*chodesh*, חודש) share the same root. This is because HaShem renews man's deeds every month, pardoning him and giving him opportunities to repent.

Teruah—and we sound the blasts and shout praises to HaShem our Heavenly Father. We also sanctify him and crown him King through the sound of the shofar. For we observe the decrees of Yeshua our Master,[348] therefore we do not change the words of the sages, the scribes, and the Pharisees, and we will not deviate from anything they taught us.

While the Son of God was still walking the earth he observed this day according to the Jewish religion and customs of his day. Unfortunately, the gospel writers did not relate those customs; even Matthew told us nothing of them. Yet, if Yeshua our Master had not observed all the customs of his day, the gospel writers would not have hesitated to tell us, for they always alerted us when he deviated from the customary path even slightly.

Perhaps the Jewish customs for Rosh HaShanah were very different from what they are today. If my assumptions are correct, then the wondrous sign that our Master performed as recounted to us by Matthew (15:32–39)[349] occurred right after Yom Teruah. Perhaps the people went with him to the Sea of Galilee in order to be with him on Rosh HaShanah so as to receive his abundant blessing and to hear Torah from his lips. Or perhaps our Master was in Jerusalem on Yom Teruah and afterward went to the Sea of Galilee accompanied by the people who dropped everything when they saw him.

When they had no bread, Yeshua our Master satiated them with seven loaves of bread and a few small fish. The Pharisees and Sadducees who approached him in order to test him[350] asked him for a sign. They wanted to see if Yeshua the Messiah was aware of the sayings concerning signs that occurred on the first of the year, for it was taught that if the first day of the year was warm then the rest of the year would be warm, etc.[351] Because of this our Master became incensed with them and called them "hypocrites," saying, "An evil and adulterous generation

---

348 Matthew 23:2, where Yeshua commands his disciples to listen to the Pharisees who sit in the seat of Moses.

349 [The feeding of the four thousand.]

350 Matthew 16:1 and on.

351 See b.*Bava Batra* 147a.

requests a sign, yet a sign will not be given to it except the sign of the Prophet Jonah."

Even though our Master had said this before when they asked for a sign,[352] this time the reason that he called them "an evil and adulterous generation" and referenced the "sign of Jonah" was because he was already thinking about the order of service on Yom Kippur. In his day, just as in ours, Leviticus 18 (in Parashat Acharei-Mot) was read in the afternoon, and then they read the book of Jonah afterward. This is where our Master derived his analogies. He likened them to a generation that was defiling the land, and that the sign of Jonah would be given to them in that HaShem, who has compassion on all his creation, changes the laws of nature so that his creatures might live.[353]

SON OF JONAH

When Yeshua came to the area of Caesarea Philippi he asked his disciples, "What do people say about me? Who is the son of man? Who am I?" Shimon the apostle said, "You are the Messiah, the son of the Living God!"[354] Shimon the fisherman was the only apostle who responded with words such as these. He was a son of Jonah,[355] yet he was not awaiting the sign of Jonah. Our Heavenly Father revealed to him that Yeshua was the Messiah, and Yeshua our Master said to him, "O how exceedingly happy are you, Shimon, who are a son of Jonah son of Amittai,[356] for the truth[357] has been revealed to you.

---

352 Matthew 12:39.

353 [Meaning that HaShem commanded the large fish to spew Jonah out of its mouth and he did not allow the destruction to occur to Nineveh. In these instances, the laws of nature and the laws of cause and effect were suspended and changed by HaShem in order to spare the lives of his creation.]

354 Matthew 16:15–16.

355 [While Shimon was a son of a different Jonah (elsewhere John), Lucky is suggesting that Shimon was also a direct descendant of the Prophet Jonah— both spiritually and physically—and that Yeshua was referencing this when responding to Shimon's revelatory answer.]

356 [Yeshua is naming the Prophet Jonah, not Shimon's father. See Jonah 1:1.]

357 [Lucky is drawing from the Hebrew root of the name of Jonah's father: Amittai. The root of this name is the Hebrew word *emet*, which means "truth." Thus Jonah—and also in this case Shimon—is a "son of truth."]

Therefore, you are Keifa, a rock, one of the strong[358] foundations of the earth, and upon you I will build my congregation.[359] In the month of Ethanim I will set it upon the foundation stone, on Rosh HaShanah I will establish it, and the gates of Sheol will not overcome it.[360] Satan and all his angels who perform his desire will wage war against it, but every weapon formed by them will not prosper."

THE CUSTOMS OF MESSIAH'S ASSEMBLY

I speculate that all this occurred on Rosh HaShanah or a few days before Yom Kippur. And even if my speculations are incorrect, it does not change the fact that everything attests to our Master Yeshua having observed Yom Teruah according to the Israelite customs of his day. The early generations of Yeshua's disciples also sat in the synagogues and offered prayers and supplications; they considered the wonderful works of HaShem and his kindness, and they read the Holy Writings. The writers in the early days of Messiah's assembly attest to this.

This is who we are today. We are the disciples of those early generations who belonged to Messiah's original assembly. We sit in the synagogues where Jews gather to pray and pour out their hearts like water before HaShem. Together with them we blow the shofar and sanctify the first day of the year, for we agree with Rabbi Yosei that mankind is judged every day, and we agree with Rabbi Nathan, that mankind is

---

358 [The Hebrew word used here for "strong" is *eitanei*, a form of the word *eitanim*, and the name of this seventh month.]

359 Similar to this Rabbi Eliezer said that on Rosh HaShanah the patriarchs were created (b.*Rosh HaShanah* 11a), meaning that the foundation of Israel's Torah was established on Rosh HaShanah, and the patriarchs are that foundation. The Torah is the intimate knowledge of HaShem that he revealed to those who had faith, first to Abraham, then Isaac, etc. Yeshua also raised up a foundational stone (*keifa*) on Rosh HaShanah.

360 Perhaps Yeshua's words are referencing the Midrash and the Targum, which interpret "And on that day" (Job 2:1) as "this is Rosh HaShanah." Satan wanted to destroy everyone, and on Rosh HaShanah he came to accuse, because he saw that Israel was repenting. He was angered even more when he saw the Jewish people believing in Yeshua, for he then knew that his end was near. Therefore, he came to accuse ten-fold, but he did not succeed.

judged in every hour.[361] We are in HaShem's hand and he may do with us as he pleases. Rosh HaShanah is a day in which we stand before HaShem the Living God to be judged. On this day we look behind us at the past year, and we ask ourselves if we have upheld HaShem's commandments, and if we are worthy to be redeemed or rejected before HaShem and his Messiah.

How numerous are the cries of our hearts! How great is our howling! Do we have any justice or righteousness to present before HaShem deserving of his kindness? From the soles of our feet to the tops of our heads we do not have one uninjured limb.[362] Yet in this we find comfort, for he is our strength. This King is adorned in majesty with a helmet of salvation upon his head, sitting on his holy throne. He is a King who judges righteously and who is girded in might. His name is made great through might, and his arm is mighty.[363] With the myriads of assemblies of the people we also come to give thanks and praise to the name of HaShem. We, the children of the King,[364] gather to crown him as King over us, the King of the kingdom of heaven, and we blast the shofar before HaShem the King.

THE SHOFAR BLAST

The shofar shakes and startles us so that we do not remain slumbering and sleeping. Why are we asleep? Let us arise and pray, for those who slumber are children of the night, children of darkness, and we are children of the light, children of the day. Therefore it is our duty to put on the armor of faith and love, and the helmet of hope and salvation, for HaShem has not decreed wrath for us, but rather that we should acquire salvation through Yeshua the Messiah, our Master.

When we blow the shofar we remember the outcast of Israel who still do not know the love of our King Yeshua the Messiah. Our hearts cry out to our Heavenly Father, beseeching him to hasten the day when their eyes will recognize the Messiah, the one whom their souls desire.

---

361 b.*Rosh HaShanah* 16a.

362 [Isaiah 1:6.]

363 See the *Machzor* for Rosh HaShanah.

364 Matthew 17:25–26.

Then they will bow to him, and, on that day, there will be a great shofar blast, and all those who are lost and outcast will come to worship HaShem on the holy mountain.

The shofar reminds us of the day of HaShem,[365] which is close and quickly approaching, the day of trumpet blasts, the day in which our Master will come to judge the earth and all within it. The day of HaShem is a day when the heavens will disappear through fire and the foundations of the earth will burn and melt.[366]

The shofar reminds us of the resurrection of the dead. For the Master of the universe will descend from heaven with a shout from the prince of the legions of angels and a blast from the shofar of God, and the dead in Messiah will arise first. Afterward, we the living and remaining ones will be taken and will ascend with them in the clouds to the heavenly expanses.[367]

In the place of the festival's additional offering [*mussaf*] we offer a sacrifice of thanksgiving to God, which is the fruit of our lips that render praise unto his name. From the innermost place of our hearts we offer prayers, saying:

> May your name be sanctified upon Israel and Jerusalem! Cause all your works to fear you, and everything created in your likeness to worship you. May they perform your will with pure hearts and as a single being. May they sound the shofar before you and bless your holy name, and may they tell of your righteousness to the remote islands, and may the peoples who did not know you seek after you. May they abandon their idols and bend down to serve you. May they fear you as long as the sun shines and accept upon themselves the yoke of your kingdom, for your yoke is light and your

---

365 The prophets said "the day of HaShem" would come, the day when HaShem would bring the earth and all within it to judgment (Isaiah 2:12; Joel 1:15; Amos 5:18, etc.). Malachi even ended his prophecy with the words "the great and fearful day of HaShem" (3:24). When the prophets said "the day of HaShem," their listeners knew that they were speaking of the day of judgment. John also saw this day in his vision (Revelation 1:10).

366 See 2 Peter 3:10.

367 1 Thessalonians 4:16–17.

burden is pleasant. May those who are far off hear, that they may come and crown you, and may you alone reign over all the works of your hands. For you are the God of truth; your word is entirely truth[368] and it will endure forever.

THE KINGDOM, REPENTANCE, AND SHOFARS

We say that blasts are sounded in honor of the kingdom, remembrance, and shofars,[369] paralleling the three priestly functions carried by Yeshua our Master. He was king, priest, and prophet, therefore we say "kingdom" first to correspond to his kingship. Then we say "remembrance" to correspond to his priesthood, for the priest's job is to bring a remembrance of us before our Heavenly Father. We have a very worthy high priest: Yeshua, Son of God, who crossed through heaven and who is the Eternal Priest in the order of Melchizedek. Because of this he is able to save all those who approach God through him with an everlasting salvation. Instead of the binding of Isaac, which was a foreshadowing and a sign, we explicitly say, "Remember today in mercy the offspring of the Passover Lamb, that was offered for our sake,[370] for you are the God who remembers the covenant."

Lastly, we say "shofars" corresponding to his role as a prophet, for the voice of the prophet is like the sound of a shofar, warning the people. Our Master is the Prophet of Consolation, and he blasts the shofar to gather the scattered and the dispersed throughout all the earth. HaShem, God of Hosts, will appear and protect them, and he

---

368 One night before Passover, the day he was to be offered as a sacrifice, Yeshua the Messiah prayed to our Heavenly Father, saying, "Sanctify them with your truth, *for your word is entirely truth*." The spirit of his prayer was praying the same words that all Israel says together on Rosh HaShanah and Yom Kippur.

369 [A total number of one hundred shofar blasts are sounded on Rosh HaShanah. The number of blasts increased from nine to one hundred over the centuries. According to the synagogue liturgy, thirty of these trumpet blasts were added for the sake of "kingdom, remembrance, and shofars."]

370 The binding of Isaac is a foreshadowing of the Messiah. When it was the appropriate time the Messiah would come and be bound to the wood on which they crucified him.

will bring them to his holy mount. He will gladden them in his house of prayer, for his house will be called a house of prayer for all peoples.

May HaShem allow it to be so speedily and soon in our days. Amen.

THE MEDITATIONS OF MY HEART ON ROSH HASHANAH

(TO MY JEWISH BROTHERS WHO OBSERVE THE TORAH OF MOSES AND THE TESTIMONY OF YESHUA)

Volume V Issue 1, 5658 (1898) pgs. 18–24

B rothers and fellow Jewish believers in the Messiah! On Rosh HaShanah, while I was sitting in the house of prayer in the Great Synagogue of Lvov and pleading before the God who gives me life, whispers of hope and feelings of sorrow flooded my heart simultaneously, and tens of thousands of questions disturbed my heart and began a conversation within my spirit. Can this only be happening to me?

I felt certain that you, my dear brothers, also experienced the same thing. Joy and horror and hope and sorrow must have arisen together and inspired the same conversation within your hearts as well. Since you are all human beings, surely you have also heard these mortal whispers, these whispers of the heart. It is difficult for a mortal to depart from something that is part of him—it sickens the heart. The sickness of his heart grows sevenfold if he must depart from something precious, beloved, and pleasing to him. And what is most precious in life to mankind?

Rosh HaShanah is a difficult day for us because our eyes see one year—one small portion of our lives—turning away from us, departing from us, wandering away from our tent, and surrendering its place to the subsequent year.

Even this year is walking away from us at an incredible speed, finishing its course and now leaving. Its hustle and bustle has all but vanished, and we scarcely noticed it. How abundant were the goodnesses that we derived from it in such large quantities! The loving-kindness and truth that HaShem showed to us during this year was no less significant. There were so many brothers and neighbors that we loved, and they reciprocated that love to us. Brotherly love is the cornerstone and foundation of life. While this year departs from us, perhaps many brothers will depart from this physical reality and go to a land that no human eye has yet seen, and that can be seen only through the Holy Spirit.

There were many moments—precious moments—in which we were able to spread goodness and loving-kindness to all men who are created in our image and likeness. A year consists of twelve months, and a month of thirty days, and a day of twenty-four hours, and every single hour consists of sixty of these "moments." Now recount all these moments to me. What a great story you have! And now, all the moments have passed and are no longer there. There is not even one of which we can say, "You belong to us."

THE WHEEL OF LIFE

There is a large and awesome wheel before our eyes, and it takes up a large area, immeasurable by created beings. This wheel turns and turns unendingly. What wind powers this wheel? What force has set this wheel spinning? Where is the hand that set it in motion? No mortal eye has yet seen it. It spins and jerks and spins and turns quickly. It does not stand still. No man or anything on earth can halt it. Every time the wheel turns, it brings new things. One moment it brings us joy and gladness, and the next sadness and grief.

We do not have the ability to halt the spinning wheel, yet we do have the ability to steer and tilt it into its proper place. At times it descends spinning in the mud, marsh, and slime, kicking up clay and stones that strike us. As it rises, it turns faster and faster. Winds blow and beat it to no avail. Happy is the man who knows how to steer the wheel and keep it upright.

My brothers! You all stand upon this wheel. It turns you; because of you it spins. The name of this wheel is "The Wheel of Life." Poets and wordsmiths call it, "The Wheel of Time." Even during the year, which quickly passes away, the wheel does not rest from turning or cease from spinning. During the course of the year, things of little interest have occurred for us, and many things that we hold dear have departed from us. We have also glimpsed many things from afar that have not yet reached us. There is not one of you to whom this Wheel of Life has not brought some fortune, whether good or bad, whether the rod of punishment or grace.

WERE WE PAYING ATTENTION?

And what have we done? Were we awake? Were our eyes wide open to watch as life rushes only to flee from us, never to return again? Or were we slumbering? Were our eyes closed while we rested our heads? Were we spared from the destruction that this departing year left in its wake? Have we received its good gifts as those who are wise? Have we patiently borne the chains with which it shackled our feet? Come; let each man among us honestly and truthfully examine his own heart.

Our sages of blessed memory spoke wisdom when they said that on Rosh HaShanah all those who come into the world must pass before HaShem. He who created them also created their hearts, and he scrutinizes their deeds with understanding. Mankind has sinned, becoming corrupt and loathsome, not choosing HaShem's ways.

Three books are opened on Rosh HaShanah, for it is a day of judgment for us. The books represent the life that is departing from us, and within them are written all the deeds we have done, whether evil or good. On this day of judgment, HaShem visits his creations—every single soul and spirit—and requires an accounting for all their deeds. Nothing is hidden from his eyes.

OUR DAYS ARE LIKE GRASS

And what about us? Man's origin is from dust, and to dust he shall return. He will dry up and be blown away like a blade of grass. He vanishes like a passing shadow, a dissipating cloud, a gust of wind, and a fleeting dream. The pure soul that HaShem granted to us returns alone to its source—the source of light and eternal life—if we have made the Rock our fortress and if we have taken refuge in the shadow of Yeshua, who has become our ransom, salvation, and righteousness.

For this reason, my fellow brothers, my spirit utters the words of the psalmist who sings HaShem's praises with a lament upon his lips: "Man's days are like those of grass; he blooms like a flower of the field; a wind passes by and it is no more, its own place no longer knows it" (Psalm 103:15). Yet there is also a voice of exaltation and salvation on his lips as he sings: "But HaShem's kindness is for all eternity to those who fear him, and his righteousness to the children's children of those who observe his commandments and remember to faithfully perform his decrees" (Psalm 103:17–18).

Behold, this psalmist was a man just like us. The whispers of his heart are many and varied. This time he desired to wrap his spirit in songs of thanksgiving and praise to the gracious God, whose grace is for all eternity. However, sorrow and grief also arose within his heart. He recalled the goodness and the kindness that HaShem did for his people, and he recalled the weeks and months that had passed and were no longer. His heart mourned, sighing bitterly: "Man's days are like those of grass, etc."

Are not these whispers of the psalmist the same whispers of our own hearts? He speaks as one of us, weeping about life that is fleeting quickly. Nevertheless, his lips mingle words of comfort with his words of grief. There is healing in the wings of his song. Righteousness can be gleaned from it. Therefore, come now and let us examine together and plummet into the depths of his words!

I.

Time goes ahead of us quickly. Hastily it runs. Frantically it goes on its way! This is the example of the wheel. God of gods! How swiftly life passes! How quickly it flees! Will you lengthen the time before the blossom withers? Will you add to the lifespan of the grass?

Our life is like grass. Look behind you, my brothers, think of the days of your infancy, think about the days of your childhood, and remember the days of your youthful vigor. Where are they now? They have fled. When we began to walk the path of life we looked ahead and saw that the road was long, extending beyond the horizon. We thought that the race would extend for endless days and years.

Now we are closer to the goal and in just a little while we will have reached the end of the race. We look behind us at the road that we have run and behold just how short it was! How quickly we ran its course! How quickly we traveled over this path! Moses our teacher, peace be upon him, was eighty years old when he sang: "HaShem you have been our refuge in every single generation" (Psalm 90:1). Then he looked behind him at his path—the fleeting path of his life—and whispers of sadness came to him: "We spend our years like a sigh ... they pass by speedily and we are in darkness" (Psalm 90:9–10).

Life passes by swiftly, carrying us quickly along with it like a shadow that no longer knows where it started. Our life is like the day of tomorrow when it has already passed. As we advance in years, the whispers of the heart of Moses our teacher, peace be upon him, whisper in our own hearts.

THE FLEETING PRESENT, VANISHING PAST, AND IMPERCEPTIBLE FUTURE

My brothers! These years that we have all known, have they not vanished like a dream? What is it to you, O life, that you flee so hastily? What is it to you, O time, that you pass by so quickly? It is a riddle that has no solution. All of life is a riddle without a solution: the bud blossoms and the blossom blows away. What is the force that makes it blossom, and what is the reason that it blows away? This moment whose name is "present" or "now," what is it? Can we comprehend it? Can we understand ourselves by it? When we open our eyes to look at it, the moment has already passed by and gone. It is already behind us.

What of the times and ages that have already gone, vanished, and passed away? What of the hours, days, months, and years, which we have named the past? Does it profit us to understand them as they are running their course? Can we see them now? Their feet have hit the ground and they have walked off. They have departed even from our memories. And that which will occur in the future, has it been revealed to us? Are we able to interpret the signs of the past and predict what is yet to happen?

Nothing has been revealed to us about that which is to come. The future is darkness enshrouded in fog. Even if some sort of vision were shown to us, how could we perceive it through such a thick fog? We could not see enough to understand it. Even if it were to come near enough to touch, could we grasp it tightly enough so that it would not be torn away from our hands? Perhaps it will never even come near us.

FOOLISH ENDEAVORS

My brothers, perhaps you imagine and say in your hearts: "My life and my time is in my hands, within my control. If I forbid the wings of time to beat, they will surely stand still. If I permit them, they will surely fly away." How could you think such foolishness? The reality is quite the opposite! There is no stopping life as it is fleeting. "The wind passes by him and he is no more."[371] The wind blows and you listen to its voice and yet you do not know from whence it comes or to where it goes. Such is life.

Go ahead and try it, my brothers. Look into it, my brothers. Squander all your wealth and capital. Sacrifice your reputation and all the precious glory for which men honor you. Come with your wisdom and with the sweet nectar of your loquacious lips. Perhaps you will be able to halt one day. Perhaps you will slow down the passing of one hour. Perhaps you will entice a single minute to heed you when you say, "Stand still." Perhaps it will stand still.

You will not succeed. You cannot stop the sun from performing its duty, nor can you grasp the moment before it evades you. The moments,

---

371 [Psalm 103:16.]

and all the joy that follows them, all the sufferings and troubles that are loaded upon your shoulders to carry, all the activity that you accomplished through them, all the intricate webs that were spun through them, and all the amusing things that your hands have done, all of them have ended, concluded, finished, left, and are no more. They did not want to remain with you.

Do not say in your hearts: "I will return to the days that left me. I will turn the wheel backward and I will spin it to the spot where they left me. The bud will blossom again a second and third time, even a tenth time." Do not say this. You possess one second. Indeed, the bud will blossom next year, and a flower will adorn your garden a second time. However, the bud no longer exists; next year you will not see the actual bud that blossomed in your garden this year. The wheel of life continues on and turns, yet while the wheel turns before you, it will not turn backward. The life that you lived you will never see again. The psalmist, a prophet of HaShem, says: "Its own place no longer knows it;" and Yochanan the holy Chasid says: "The universe will surely pass away and all its desires with it."

OUR DEEDS SHALL FOREVER ENDURE

Life passes by and all its desires with it. It has already decided our sentence, whether it be punishment or grace. It will not return with that which it has fleetingly taken. The delights and amusements that we once enjoyed have gone, never to return. Even the sadness, mourning, sighs, and tears that melted our eyes and embittered our hearts have fled and passed away, never to return. However, the deeds that we have done while still living will always remain, whether good or evil.

Our malice and error, through which we shamed ourselves, still endure. The good deeds that we neglected to perform are engraved upon tablets as a remembrance. We can see how we hated discipline. The knowledge with which our hearts conducted us, all the good deeds that we did, and the grace that we showed to our neighbors—or the grace that we withheld from them—all of these things are written in a book of remembrance, and like marble tombstones they stand before us. Our sentence will be decreed by what is engraved upon them. Woe to us if we merit a harsh inscription. He who does the will of God will dwell securely forever.

II.

O Holy Truth! Your voice is a voice of warning that causes the heart and the innermost parts to tremble! You grasp tightly onto the corners of our minds and compel us, even if our hearts are unwilling, to hear the words of comfort and the counsel that the holy psalmist speaks to us.

My fellow brothers! See how life quickly flees from us! Therefore, you must also be quick to do your deeds. Wake up! Get up! Awaken your senses, for in just a little while the day will change. Be careful not to act like fools, rather like wise people. Appreciate the hour while it is still with you and see what benefit it can be to you. Do not be lazy and do not fall asleep, for you will swiftly pass away.

Remember the commandments of HaShem, your Creator and Molder. My brothers, place them before your eyes always, and let them be a remembrance to you to obey them and perform them. Do not say: "I am exhausted. I am tired. My soul has grown weary." Do not slack in doing what is before you; while you are still alive you must do them.

Behold, now is a time of favor. Now is a time of salvation. Today, if you hear my voice! Do your good deeds while it is still day and work your good works before the sun darkens. For morning will come, and so will the night. Night will come and then you will not be able to do anything. Life is wrapped in a thick blanket of difficult riddles that have no solution. Therefore, why do you contemplate them, talk about them, or think about things over which you have no control—things that you have no power to move or change?

CREATED FOR A HOLY PURPOSE

Abandon all frivolous chatter. HaShem erected boundaries in order to test you and he said, "You may come this far, but no further."[372] Even if you spend the whole year contemplating life's difficult riddles day

---

372 Job 38:11.

and night, you will find no solutions. HaShem, who created you, knows all. He who gives life to every living thing, perceives everything. He possesses the solutions you seek. Trust in him, for he does no injustice. You have a safe refuge under his wings. Why would you fear any evil that has not yet come? Why would you inflict your soul with unending pain? Look at what is in front of you: the future.

Darkness spreads over it. The hour is given to you: do what you must do. Behold, HaShem made a covenant with you saying, "I have formed you to be holy for me; I have created you to do my will." In every dark period in life, it is as clear to us as the afternoon sun that we were created for a holy purpose. And you shall love HaShem, your God, with all your heart, with all your soul, with all your might, and with all your understanding, and you shall love your neighbor as yourself. The sin of the first man became like a wall between us and HaShem. Yet HaShem took pity on us, for HaShem is love. And he has loved us with a mighty love and he has given us Yeshua to be a salvation for us, to demolish the dividing wall, and to open up for us the gate to the holy of holies.

Therefore my brothers, it is your duty to sanctify your souls and to submit your bodies as a living sacrifice, holy and acceptable to God. This is how you should love HaShem. Now give your neighbor godly advice, for it is your duty to lead him down the straight path. You must be like an angel of goodness to him, guarding him in all his ways, for this is the commandment of love.

PURSUE HIS MIGHTY LOVE

Life is quickly fleeting and there is nothing to stop it. If that is so, then why do you strive to obtain possessions that will vanish as though they had never existed. Turn your eyes away from them and turn to something that will endure for generations to come. The kindness of HaShem is forever and ever.

Oh how great are the kindnesses of HaShem that he has bestowed upon you in his great compassion and in his mighty love with which he loves you! He has revealed to you his desire and his will, and he has sent you his word through the prophets, and he has given you a heart with which to understand and ears with which to hear so that you will be able to search and to choose, and so that you will guard all your ways. In the last days he sent his only son from heaven, Yeshua the Messiah, so that you would perceive his mighty love.

Yeshua is the grace of HaShem. He is grace and truth. Through him you acquire HaShem as an eternal inheritance, and through this grace you will be able to come before HaShem your God. He is the solution to all riddles; he is the one possession that will never pass away.

Life flees from you, and there is no way to make it return. If this is so, then why do you weep over the troubles that come upon you and over the suffering that you must bear? Even your troubles must also pass away, never to return. Why are you boasting in the wealth that you have acquired? Why grow haughty over delights and amusements? They will all pass away and will never be remembered again.

FULFILL ALL OBLIGATIONS

Weep and wail over all the goodness that you could have done for both yourself and your neighbor (who was created in the image of God, just as you were) and yet you did not do. HaShem has given you a family; our Heavenly Father has granted you sons and daughters. Have you done all that you must do for your lifelong companion, your covenanted wife? Have you honored her as you want to be honored? Have you worried about her and about your sons and daughters as you are obligated? Have you offered up a single prayer on her behalf and on behalf of your offspring?

And your servants and employees, have you done to them in accordance with the heart of HaShem? You are also a citizen of your town and country; have you done your duty to your town and country? You are a member of a small community, a community of Torah and the testimony of Messiah; have you done all that is required of you for your community? Suppose evil befell all of these; would you sacrifice your life for them? Then weep, mourn, and bitterly cry out. For the cries of the children of your household, and the shouts of your fellow countrymen and congregants rise up to heaven and remain there awaiting your arrival before the judgment seat.

Rejoice if you have conquered your lusts, if you have mastered your desires, if you have planted pure and righteous thoughts in your mind. Rejoice if you have been a blessing to others of your generation who dwell alongside you, if you have shown kindness and goodness to them, and if you have given your body over as a pure sacrifice on their behalf in order to benefit them. Be happy, rejoice, and exult, for your deeds will never be forgotten. They will remain even when the generation after you has come and gone.

ANSWERING THE RIGHTEOUS JUDGE

Life is fleeting. Therefore do not cease the pursuit of what is necessary. Seek out the kingdom of God and his righteousness, and do not forget that you, too, will come to an end. In the dawn of the new life—true eternal life in the world that is made up entirely of truth, kindness, and life—you will stand before the throne of HaShem, and the Righteous Judge will surely ask you:

> Behold, I have given you life and I have lengthened your days; what did you do with them? I gave you status amongst your peers; what good did you work among them? I have given you many gifts, talents, and advantages, and I have entrusted five talents of gold to you; what have you earned with them? What have you purchased? Give me back my investment with interest, for I have given you grace and truth; what will you give in return for all the things I have lavished upon you? I have called you to be holy for me; have you sanctified and dedicated your life to me? I descended to earth in order to take you out of slavery to sin and to bring you under the hand of grace; have you served HaShem as he desires? Have you walked in the ways of the Torah of grace, or have you merely performed the commandments of men externally and not in accordance with my Spirit?

If the One seated in judgment asks you these things, how happy you will be if you can answer:

I have fought the good fight and I have guarded the faith. I have no righteousness or merits, yet through Yeshua I am made righteous and he is my refuge, and I take shelter in the shadow of his wings.

If you pursue the righteousness of the Messiah, if you guard the faith, and if you trust in the intercessor whose blood purifies you from all sin, you need not fear life's swiftly fleeting nature. For your blossom will never wither, your life will not end, and your days will be everlasting, for HaShem's kindness is for all eternity to those who fear him.

YOM KIPPUR

Volume 5 Issue 1, pgs. 8–13

The second appointed time that occurs during Tishrei, the month of Ethanim, occurs on the tenth day. Its name is "Day of Atonement" (Yom HaKippurim), "Sabbath of Complete Rest,"[373] and "the Fast."[374] The Jews who spoke Greek called it "Day of Complete Fasting," "The Holiday of Fasting," and "The Great Holiday."[375] The Israelite scribes who lived in Babylon called it "The Day," or "The Great Day." Today the Jewish people call it "Yom Kippur."

Yom Kippur is neither a festive nor happy day. It does not commemorate the exodus of the children of Israel from Egypt. Rather, like Rosh HaShanah, it is a day of remembrance before HaShem.[376] Rosh HaShanah paves the way to Yom Kippur. It is a day of remembrance and the voice of the shofar blast warns the children of Israel, saying, "Repent, purify, and sanctify yourselves, for the day of reckoning is coming; the day of repentance is here—the day in which the high priest makes atonement for the children of Israel to purify them from all their sins once a year so that they may be spotless before HaShem."

Indeed every man is a sinner; there is no one who is righteous, does what is good, and does not sin. He is ritually unclean and impure.

---

373 Leviticus 23:27, 31.

374 Isaiah 58:3.

375 According to Philo.

376 [Day of Trumpet Blasts.]

HaShem is holy, and the ritually unclean cannot access his presence. Therefore, in his mercy on all his creation, HaShem made a way for his children to come before him, and he taught them this path of repentance.

ATONEMENT THROUGH BLOOD

In the beginning HaShem commanded them to offer the blood of bulls and sheep in order to atone for the sins of the Israelites. Blood atones and covers over the crimes of mankind, and HaShem erases them from his book, for he is a gracious and compassionate God. The blood of animals and birds is innocent blood, for they did not sin against HaShem, and it atones for the sins of people who have sinned, committed crimes, and transgressed before our Heavenly Father.[377] This is what HaShem commanded.

For this reason Aaron came into the holy place with a bull for the sin offering and a ram for the burnt offering to atone for himself and his household, and two goats and a ram to atone for all Israel. He would cast lots for the two goats, one for HaShem and one for Azazel. The priest would slaughter the one whose lot fell to HaShem, and he would place his hands on the second goat—the one for Azazel—and he would confess all the sins of Israel, all their iniquities and crimes, and he would place them upon the head of the goat and send it away with an appointed man into the wilderness to a remote land to which the goat would carry away the iniquities of the children of Israel.[378]

The high priest comes once a year with the blood of goats and calves in order to make atonement, for there is no atonement without the shedding of blood.[379] Everything is purified by blood according to the Torah. It was incumbent upon the priest to perform this type of atonement work. In doing so he atoned for the entire nation. The blood

---

377 The greats in Israel—such as the Ramban, Abravanel, and others—have explained why HaShem commanded that it should be done this way. However, this is not the place to transcribe their words.

378 Leviticus 16.

379 b.*Yoma* 5a; b.*Zevachim* 6a; b.*Menachot* 93b.

of the sacrifices took away the sins of the people and Azazel's goat (i.e., the scapegoat) carried their sins to a remote land.

AN ACCEPTABLE FAST TO HASHEM

HaShem commanded the people to afflict their souls on Yom Kippur, to be saddened and mourn, and to sit with an embittered soul and broken, contrite heart because of the sins they committed liberally. This is the meaning of "you shall afflict your souls."[380] HaShem commanded them, "Lower your heads, humble your proud spirits, cause your hearts to mourn, surrender yourselves before me, for you are wicked and you are sinners. Turn from your wicked ways. Return to me!"

This was what HaShem intended: repentance, prayer, and righteousness; these three things are the lovely treasures of Yom Kippur. Every one of the children of Israel must come before HaShem in repentance and with prayer, and HaShem will give them everlasting righteousness, for HaShem himself will provide a ram for the burnt offering. HaShem himself will choose the goat that will carry the sins of his people. This was HaShem's intention.

The entire sacrificial system was a shadow of the good things to come, the good things that HaShem intended to give to his people and to everyone who bore the name "human being." Did the early generations plumb the depths of HaShem's thoughts? No, for all his thoughts have not been made known to us.

If we judge based on the words of Isaiah then we will reach the conclusion that in the outer courts of the kingdom of heaven we still do not understand what HaShem is asking of us. They interpreted the words "you shall afflict" to mean "fasting." Yom Kippur was a day of fasting, and on this day every single year the children of Israel have refrained from eating and drinking. They have mourned, bowed their heads, and put on sackcloth and ashes. Yet they devised and carried out devious plots on a day of fasting, and HaShem said to Isaiah:

---

380 [Leviticus 23:27.]

Cry out loudly, do not hold back! Raise your voice like a shofar, like the shofar that they are blasting! So too, raise your voice and recount to my people their crimes, and to the house of Jacob their sins. Indeed, on a fast day they see to their affairs and oppress their workers. They fast for contention and strife, and they strike with a fist of wickedness. Is this the fast that I have chosen? Is this what they call a fast and an acceptable day to HaShem? Is this not the fast that I have chosen: to loose the fetters of wickedness, to undo the bands of the yoke? Is it not to share your bread with the hungry? Then will your light break out like the dawn and your healing shall spring forth speedily, and your righteousness will go before you and the glory of HaShem shall be your rearguard.[381]

If Israel repents with a pure heart, if they afflict themselves on a fast day, mourn over their sins and seek HaShem their God and David their king, then HaShem will cause the daylight to dawn and the glory of HaShem—which is the Messiah—will be their rearguard. They will no longer stand in the courtyard of the kingdom, rather, they shall go into the inner sanctuary, into the holy of holies, and then they will see all matters of truth and holiness through the Holy Spirit.

A NEW ORDER

All the days that the Temple stood in place, the priest performed his duty on Yom Kippur. When the Israelites went into exile in Babylon the Yom Kippur service ceased for seventy years, and Ezekiel, the prophet of exile, saw actual visions of God on Yom Kippur, for the hand of HaShem was upon him. HaShem showed him the form of the Third Temple and all the utensils and accessories that would be in it. Yet Ezekiel did not see a vision of Yom Kippur itself, for there will be a new order in the Third Temple.

HaShem had compassion upon his people who were in exile in Babylon. He brought them out of there and gave them prophets and leaders. Ezra the scribe set his heart upon explaining the Torah of

---

381 [Isaiah 58:1–8.]

HaShem, performing it, and teaching law and statute in Israel. He repeated all the words concerning the appointed times and he established Yom Teruah (Rosh HaShanah) on the first day of the seventh month.

Yet they did not observe Yom Kippur anymore, for the Temple was no longer standing. When the Second Temple was rebuilt the priests offered sacrifices and performed their duties on Yom Kippur every single year, and the people afflicted themselves through fasting, refraining from all eating and drinking. The order of the service changed some.

According to the words of our sages the children of Israel were gathered together when the high priest confessed their sins upon the goat, and they answered, "Blessed be his glorious name; his kingdom is eternal." There were also many pools for immersion that were not present during the First Temple. The people still stood outside and the high priest entered alone into the holy of holies, and the meaning of this day was not yet apparent to every member of the nation. Offering and sacrifice cannot make the heart of the worshiper perfect and innocent, for offerings, libations, and various immersions deal with the body, purifying the flesh of the ritually unclean person and the sinner. They do not purify the *heart* of the sinner from works of death.

CELEBRATION ON YOM KIPPUR

There was never such celebration as there was during Yom Kippur, when the maidens of Israel would go out dancing in the vineyards with young men accompanying them. A virgin would find herself a husband on this day, and a young man would find himself a bride.[382]

In the Temple the priest would atone for the sins of the Israelites. Many of the people would be with him, and outside the Temple young men and maidens would be dancing. This was a day of complete rest, and they did not do any form of labor. Yom Kippur was holy day of celebration in Israel, even though they were fasting.

---

382 [m.*Ta'anit* 4:8].

ANOTHER CHANGE IN ORDER

At the end of days the righteous Messiah will be revealed in order to bring transgression and iniquity to an end by sacrificing himself. The high priest to whom no one can compare, the high priest who is pious, perfect, pure, who is separated from sin, and who has come from heaven will come one time into the inner holy place with his own blood and he will find eternal redemption. Then the morning light shall dawn. For on the day that Yeshua the Messiah offered up his own blood, one offering for all sins, the curtain covering the entrance to the holy of holies was torn in two, from top to bottom, and the Sanctuary was opened to all who return to HaShem with a pure heart.

About forty years after Yeshua offered himself on our behalf the priests were still offering sacrifices in the Temple. Afterward, foreign enemies came and destroyed the Temple, and now we have no priest and no sacrifice, no altar and no grain offering. Now Yom Kippur takes on another form. Our sages of blessed memory, who lived up until 200 CE, changed the way it looked. The teachings of Yeshua and his disciples greatly influenced them, even though they rejected those teachings.

On Yom Kippur, when Yeshua's disciples were gathered around him, he began to tell them that he would suffer at the hands of the elders, leading priests, and scribes, and that they would surely put him to death, yet on the third day he would rise. Just as Moses raised up the serpent on the standard in the wilderness and all who were bitten and looked upon it lived, so too, would the son of man be lifted up and all who believed in him would find eternal life. HaShem would forgive that person all his sins. Yeshua revealed to his disciples that he was the lamb who would bear the sins of the world, that he was the sacrifice that would sanctify all who return to HaShem with a pure heart.

Those who hated Yeshua did not heed his words. Yet they did not realize that Yeshua's words entered their hearts slowly but surely, little by little, and when the Second Temple was destroyed our sages taught that there is atonement even without the blood of bulls and goats, and that there is no atonement without repentance. Great is repentance, for it reaches the throne of glory![383]

---

383   b. *Yoma* 86a.

Now the children of Israel dwell in sorrow and grief, in mourning and bitterness, weeping, afflicting themselves, and confessing their sins in synagogues. Yom Kippur is a day of repentance; Yom Kippur is a day of sanctifying the soul, a day in which a person abandons the path of sin and wickedness and returns to HaShem his God.

A RESCUED PEOPLE

It ails the heart to see the children of Israel returning to HaShem while they are still groping at walls like blind people. Their eyes are still closed and they still do not see, even now, Yeshua the Messiah sitting on the throne of glory to the right of HaShem. We who are disciples of Yeshua, we who are children of Israel ourselves, who observe the Torah of Moses and the Testimony of Yeshua, we, too, sit in synagogues fasting, afflicting ourselves, and confessing our sins. We have all sinned greatly and there is never a moment in which we are not causing offense.

We also pray, "Yes, it is true. The evil inclination is within us; within him there is righteousness, abundant righteousness, and he will answer us ... and he will wipe away the crimes and wickedness from the children of the covenant,"[384] for we are children of the covenant of Yeshua. HaShem our God made a covenant with us through his own blood, for his blood atones for all sin, and behold, by means of it, we are a delivered people and we possess an eternal salvation.

Therefore we can say, "Wipe away all the crimes from your delivered people," and he responds, "I have pardoned you." We, too, pray with the entire congregation of Israel, saying:

> Cause our inclination to be subservient to you. Cause us to
> return to you in truth and with a pure and renewed heart.
> Cause us to guard your ordinances in our spirits and cir-
> cumcise our hearts to love your name. Confound our evil
> inclination that has been present with us since our youth
> and which has ensnared us. Not in the merit of our righ-

---

384 [From the prayer *Omnam Ken* which is recited on Erev Yom Kippur after *Kol Nidrei*.]

teousness do we cast our supplications before you, for we have no righteousness of our own, but in the merit of the righteousness of the Messiah, whom you gave us in your great mercy, do we rely.

Repentance and prayer are what we do on Yom Kippur. We afflict ourselves on this day because our sins and our transgressions were the reason Yeshua the Messiah was put to death. In his great mercy HaShem gave his only son as an offering so that we could live purely, cleansed from every sin and crime. If we had not sinned the Messiah would not have needed to be an offering.

WE HAVE NOT WITHSTOOD SIN

We afflict ourselves and we weep bitterly because up until now we have not withstood nor fought to the death against sin. We afflict ourselves and sit in mourning and sadness over the fact that we have still not clothed ourselves in the love that is gilded in perfection. We are still not perfect in the uprightness and fullness of Messiah, and we are still like children dispersed and scattered in every direction by the decrees of men who devise plots against us. There are surely many sins to weep over. Our inner being is still weak and has not strengthened itself in the might of the Spirit of HaShem.

Thus on this day we sit and afflict ourselves, for this day is a day of repentance and atonement. It is also a day of atonement for us, for HaShem has distinguished it from all the other days of the year to be a day of repentance and prayer. Repentance, prayer, and righteousness of the Messiah are a part of our everyday lives, but they are a part of this day even more so. This day is holy, because HaShem sanctified it, and that which HaShem commanded we shall observe and perform. It is good for us to do all that HaShem has commanded.

Happy is the man who observes this day. Happy is the man who sets the beginning of the year aside for repentance and prayer, and who sanctifies his body as a living offering that is holy and pleasing to God. Happy is the man who sets his heart every single day to renewing and changing himself into a new man, always discerning what the good and perfect will of God is. And happy is the man who does this sevenfold on the tenth of the seventh month, the month of Tishrei, on the day that HaShem has designated as the day of repentance. One who does this is truly learned in the faith and service of HaShem.

SUKKOT

Volume V Issue 1, Tishrei 5958 (1898) pgs. 13–17

O n the fifteenth day of Tishrei is the third of HaShem's appointed times that occur during this month. Sukkot is a seven-day festival to HaShem. The first day is a day of complete rest, a holy occasion, and no form of work may be done on it. The eighth day is a day of complete rest, it is the conclusion[385] to the holiday, and it is also a holy occasion on which no form of work may be done. Every day between the first day and the eighth day is called *chol ha-mo'ed* (secular day of the holiday). On Sukkot, every citizen of Israel dwells in a *sukkah* (booth) for seven days so that everyone who sees them will know that they are dwelling in the *sukkot* with which HaShem housed the Israelites when he brought them out of Egypt with a strong hand and an outstretched arm, and through signs and wonders, which he performed for no other nation.[386]

This holiday is a remembrance of the Israelite exodus from Egypt, of Israel's history, and of the wondrous events that HaShem miraculously performed for Israel, just like he did during Passover and Shavuot. Like

---

385 [Lucky is interpreting the word *atzeret* (as in the title of the holiday, *Shemini Atzeret*) to mean "conclusion," basing his interpretation from the Hebrew root *atzar* ("to stop"). Other translations render the word *atzeret* as "gathering" or "assembly," but this word does not have a definitive translation into English. Lucky agrees that this is a day of gathering and assembly, but he nevertheless interprets this word as "conclusion," and calls it the conclusion to the Sukkot holiday.]

386 Leviticus 23:33–44.

these other holidays, every Israelite male would go up to worship and appear before HaShem in Jerusalem.

Sukkot is one of the appointed times called a "festival" (*chag*) in the Torah, for the children of Israel celebrated it as a "festival of worship" and a "festival of joy" before HaShem. This holiday belongs both to the Jews and to HaShem. Israel was the people of HaShem, Judah was consecrated to govern Israel, and Israel was a kingdom of priests and a holy nation. Israel was like the courtyard of the kingdom of heaven, for HaShem made himself known in Israel first, and Israel built the Temple of HaShem. All of Israel's deeds, even his holidays and celebrations, were times to worship HaShem.

"THE FESTIVAL"

Even though the Torah does not delineate how they should be celebrated, the name "festival" tells us that there was great dancing, and that they would go out en masse to the village streets. The festival days are days of joy and exultation. The shofar blasts of Yom Teruah have passed along with the days of crying, fasting, and mourning. Yom Kippur is no longer here and HaShem has made atonement for his people. The days of Sukkot come as days of rejoicing and celebration for us.

Sukkot is by far the greatest of the three appointed times that occur this month, and its celebration is even greater than that of Passover or Shavuot. Therefore, Sukkot is merely called the *chag* ("the festival"), and everyone knows that when someone is talking about the *chag* they are referring to Sukkot.[387] There is no festival like this one.

A HOLIDAY OF JOY

The Festival of Sukkot is also a festival of ingathering, thanksgiving, joy, and praise to HaShem for blessing our fields and vineyards. HaShem commanded through Moses:

---

387 This occurs frequently in the Gemara, and every time they simply say *the chag*, they are talking about Sukkot.

When you gather your crop from your field, when you gather the yield of the land, when you gather from your threshing floor and from your vat, you will celebrate a festival to me for seven days and you will rejoice before me: you and your son, your daughter, your manservant, maidservant, the Levite, the stranger, the widow, and the orphan that are in your gates, and you will be happy. For HaShem your God will bless you in all your yield and in all the works of your hands, and you will take the fruit of the splendid tree,[388] branches of palm trees, boughs of leafy trees, and willows of the brook, and you will rejoice before HaShem your God.[389]

Sukkot is a holiday of the joy of life and of blessing. It is a holiday for the entire people, for every single person—a family and household holiday. How lovely is Sukkot! In the house of the Israelite citizen it is a day of complete rest, the children of the house sit around the table in the sukkah and the table is filled with generous amounts of food and drink. The Levite, the stranger, the widow, and the orphan are also there rejoicing and in good cheer. In the Temple of HaShem all the males appear before HaShem with the four species in their hands, rejoicing and bringing sacrifices and offerings.

SECOND TEMPLE CUSTOMS

In the First Temple Period Solomon hosted the festival.[390] Zechariah prophesied that every year there would be those who would come up to Jerusalem to celebrate Sukkot,[391] for the festival of Sukkot would never be forgotten.[392] During the time of Second Temple that Nehemiah son of Hacaliah built, the Israelites significantly increased the

---

388 [Also rendered as the *hadar* tree, and interpreted as referring to the citron.]

389 See Leviticus 23:39–44 and Deuteronomy 16:13–15.

390 1 Kings 8:2. There it just says "the festival," but as we have already mentioned, this refers to Sukkot. Also see 2 Chronicles 7:8–10.

391 Zechariah 14:16–19.

392 Nehemiah 8:14–18.

joy of this celebration and they added things that were not there during the First Temple Period.

During the Second Temple Era, they poured out a water libation upon the continual offering during *shacharit*. They drew water from the pool of Siloam with silver lavers and poured it onto the altar, onto the continual offering, and they accompanied the libation with shofar blasts and shouts of praise. This ritual was done so that the land would receive the blessing of rain. They also adorned the altar with willow branches, and every single day during the festival they would circle the altar once and say, "Please, HaShem, save us! Please, HaShem, prosper us!" On the seventh day they would circle the altar seven times.

They performed the joyous celebration of the water drawing ceremony with their lamps and lights aglow, and there was no corner of Jerusalem that was not illuminated. Pious people of good repute danced with torches in their hands singing, "Hallelujah!" The Levites played on the harps, lutes, symbols, trumpets, and countless other instruments. This happened every evening after the continual offering during the interim days of the holiday and they sounded the shofar and shouted praises. Who can describe the joy of the water drawing ceremony? Our rabbis informed us that anyone who had not seen the water drawing ceremony had never seen joy in his life.[393]

Many from the families of the nations came to see what Israel did during this holiday. The nations also had holidays, and they celebrated a great festival of dancing to the god Tammuz. It was an important holiday to them, and they thought that Israel also celebrated this festival to Tammuz. However, the celebrations of the Gentiles were not like those of the Jews, for in Israel they created a partition, separating the women from the men, so that the men would not fall into temptation and give in to their desires during their festivities. This is not how it was with the Gentiles.

---

393 b.*Sukkah* 48–49.

AMONGST THE FESTIVITIES SORROW AWAITS

In everything they did the Israelites feared sin. There were those among them who would say, "Happy is our youth, for it has not brought disgrace upon our old age," and others would say, "Happy is our old age, for it has atoned for our youth"; yet everyone says, "Happy is anyone who has not sinned, and whoever has sinned can repent and be forgiven." The Israelites learned the path of HaShem—the path of repentance. For the hand of HaShem is always ready to receive those returning to him in truth and with a pure heart.

Nevertheless, no matter how great Israel's rejoicing was, pain and grief lay hidden in their midst, for the people of Israel were divided. They had many different sects and factions. A great conflict arose between all those sects, and the peace amongst the people was destroyed.[394] The hand of the enemy was upon the land of Judah and upon the Holy City, and the Gentiles trampled the glory of Israel. But in those days the Redeeming Messiah of whom the prophets spoke appeared, and he went all throughout Jerusalem to proclaim repentance to sinners.

LIGHT OF THE WORLD AND FOUNT OF SALVATION

At the end of the first day of Sukkot, Yeshua the Messiah took his disciples Shimon Keifa,[395] Yaakov,[396] and his brother Yochanan, and they ascended a high mountain. There he transformed before their eyes. His face glowed like the sun and his clothes became radiantly white. He was the light of the world, wrapped in light like a garment. This is how he revealed himself before his disciples. They saw a light greater than that of the water drawing ceremony, and this light did not come from golden menorahs, golden lamps, or oil.

Yeshua brought his three disciples on a high mountain in order to establish the celebration of the water drawing ceremony for them, and to impart knowledge to them, so that they would understand the words

---

394 The conflict was between the Pharisees and the Sadducees.

395 [Simon Peter. In the ensuing narrative, Lucky suggests that the transfiguration occurred during the Festival of Sukkot.]

396 [James.]

of the Prophet Isaiah in his small twelfth chapter. It was not concerning the water libation or the light of the ceremony that HaShem said, "And with joy you will draw water from the fountains of salvation."[397] Behold, the salvation of Israel has come, and Yeshua is his name, for he will save his people Israel from all their sins.

LOOK AND SEE; LISTEN AND HEAR; ARISE AND SHINE

"Shout for joy, you who dwell in Zion, for great in your midst is the Holy One of Israel."[398] O pious people and men of good repute! Why do you dance like idol worshipers before the altar? Lift up your eyes and see that your salvation comes. Arise and shine because your light is coming. See how his face glows like the sun and how stunningly white his clothes are. Look and see!

Look, Moses and Elijah are also coming! Yeshua's disciples saw them. And look how Moses and Elijah are speaking with Yeshua. Cast aside your torches that you are holding and ascend the mountain. Listen to what Shimon Keifa is saying, "My Master! It is good for us to stay here, and if you desire it, I will make three *sukkot*: one for you, one for Moses, and one for Elijah."[399]

Remain for a little while longer and listen. A voice calling from within the cloud that covered them said, "This is my Son, my beloved one, in whom my soul finds favor." Israel did not hear the voice that was calling out from the cloud. Only others heard. Then Judah went into exile. Now it has been eighteen centuries that he has been dispersed and scattered among the peoples; however, Judah still dwells in booths during Sukkot, even to this day.

But the festival has ceased to be what it was back in those ancient days. It is no longer a harvest festival, and we no longer have a Temple to go to where we can bow down and appear before HaShem. The joy of the water drawing ceremony and the water libation has passed. Yet it still remains a holiday of thanksgiving and praise, and the children of Israel sanctify this day, calling it "the time of our rejoicing."

---

397 Isaiah 12:3.

398 Isaiah 12:6.

399 Matthew 17:1–8.

They live in the sukkah for seven days, leaving their permanent houses and apartments, and they reside in a structure that is not permanent.[400] On each of the seven days they shake the four species in their hands and encircle the bimah[401] upon which the Torah is read, and they cry out "Save us! (*hosha-na*):[402] In accordance with your faithfulness, *save us!* In accordance with your covenant, *save us!*" On the seventh day they encircle the bimah seven times and sing the Hoshana Rabbah petitions.

ISRAEL AWAKENS AND THE GENTILES ASCEND

Those of us who are disciples of the Messiah, who observe the Torah of Moses and the Testimony of Yeshua, also do as our Jewish brothers do. We, too, sit in booths for seven days with the rest of the Israel. We keep the festival on account of the clouds of glory that surrounded our forefathers in the wilderness so that the excruciating heat would not strike them, because HaShem made our forefathers dwell in booths when they left Egypt, and because HaShem will yet raise up the fallen sukkah of David, and the rest of mankind and all the nations that bear the name of HaShem will seek out God.

The hearts of our brothers are still as hard as stone and they still reject the Messiah our Master. Yet behold, the wind is beginning to blow upon the flesh of the dead bodies of these murder victims, a sign to us that these dry bones will live again. Israel is awakening now, and HaShem will have compassion and turn his heart to him so that Judah can hear the voice that is calling out to him, "Return now to HaShem your God."[403] And it will be that at evening time there will be light and all the families of the Gentiles will come up to Jerusalem to bow down to the King—HaShem of Hosts—every year, to celebrate Sukkot, and sin will vanish from the Gentiles. They will all be pure, and even on the

---

400 b.*Sukkah* 2a. See the words of Rabba.

401 [Podium or pulpit.]

402 [Or Hosanna. This is what the crowd called out when Yeshua entered Jerusalem.]

403 [Hosea 14:2.]

bells of their horses the words "Holy to HaShem" will be inscribed.[404] Behold, the day on which HaShem will do all these things is quickly approaching.

We disciples of Yeshua also sit in the sukkot because HaShem has administered his *Shechinah* among us. The Torah was clothed in flesh and resided among us, made a tabernacle within our hearts, and Yeshua the Messiah is the Torah clothed in the flesh of a body, yet whose glory is like the glory of a father's only and unique son, full of kindness and truth. He is the one HaShem sent among us to spread his sukkah of true, heartfelt peace over us, a peace that transcends all understanding. No one can truly grasp it. Therefore, we sit in the sukkah and the Spirit of HaShem and his Messiah are with us, our hearts are filled with the joy and gladness of HaShem, and the spirits of all the righteous in the world whisper to us, strengthening our hearts.[405]

CELEBRATING WITH ALL ISRAEL

We sit in the sukkah with the rest of Israel, and we sit with them in the synagogues and pray along with the rest of Israel, "O Good and Benevolent One, who requires us to build your House as in the beginning so that every Israelite male may appear before you." We, too, end our prayers with the *Hallel*.

We also sanctify the seventh day—Hoshana Rabbah—for we also consider this interim day of the festival to be holy. And on this day, on the twenty-first of the month of Tishrei, the word of HaShem came through the Prophet Haggai, saying, "In a little while I will shake the heavens and the earth ... and they will come with the wealth of the nations ... and in that place I will grant peace."[406]

Behold, the Prince of Peace has come! The glory of the latter House was greater than that of the first. The Messiah came into it. Behold, our King came, poor and riding on the foal of a donkey, and we laid palm

---

404 Zechariah 14:20.

405 These are our seven holy guests (*ushpizin ila'in*)—Abraham, Isaac, Jacob, Joseph, Moses, Aaron, and David—whom we only invite to come when the gladness of HaShem is present.

406 Haggai 2.

branches on the road and called out, "*Hosha-na* to the son of David! Blessed is he who comes in the name of HaShem! *Hosha-na* in the highest heights; our eyes are fixed on HaShem!"

On the eighth day we bring the festival to a "conclusion" (*atzeret*) and we circle around the bimah seven times with the Torah scroll, saying, "For from Zion the Torah will go forth and the word of HaShem from Jerusalem." The Messiah came from Zion, and the word of HaShem went forth from Jerusalem clothed in the garments of flesh. We shout out words of love and praise for our Master to hear. We call him, "Mighty Redeemer," "Speaker of Righteousness," "Clothed in Splendor," "Guardian of the Covenant," "The Torah Clothed in Flesh," etc.

These are the appointed times of HaShem, holy occasions that occur during the seventh month, the month of Ethanim.

THIS IS HANUKKAH

Volume III Issues 2–3, Tevet-Shevat 5651 (1891) pgs. 37–50

The light of this day—this is Hanukkah. And it is now Saturday evening, which marks the conclusion of the holy Sabbath. I am sitting in prayer with my Siddur, sending the Sabbath off in song and exultation. The Hanukkah lights are lit—it is magical watching their blue and white flames flicker—and I sing songs of praise: "I extol you HaShem, for you have raised me up and have not caused my enemies to rejoice over me";[407] "Mighty Rock of my salvation, to praise you is a delight ... men of insight, eight days were established for song and exultation";[408] "May God have compassion on us and bless us ... that your way would be known in the earth, and your salvation among all the nations."[409] Yet this joy suddenly flees from me, and a great sorrow takes hold of my heart. What is this sorrow? It puzzles me, but there it is nonetheless.

FORGETTING THE EVENTS

I begin to contemplate, deeply pondering matters, and practical questions start assaulting me. What is all this that we are doing? These

---

407 [Psalm 30: "A song for the dedication (*chanukah*) of the Temple."]
408 [*Ma'oz Tzur.*]
409 [Psalm 67.]

candles that we kindle,[410] why do we kindle them? What does this holiday teach us? Why did the great songwriters of ancient days seem to forget about this holiday and not leave us any liturgical pieces or songs that we could recite or sing for the remaining days of the holiday? This astonishes me. Yes, we have the song *Ma'oz Tzur*, and it is a wonderful song. But should we say *dayenu*[411] ("it is enough for us") over this one song? This song gives praise and ascribes wonder to the miracle "that was wrought for the roses through the remnant of the flasks."[412] Is this miracle the whole reason why we celebrate this holiday?

While I was still asking myself these questions the candles began to fade into smoldering wicks. They went out, and their wondrous glow went with them; still my unease remained with me. The days of Hanukkah are days of song and exultation. I learned this in my childhood. I grew up on the knees of the righteous of our generation, and it is the custom of those righteous ones—those Chasidim—to have many meals and to sing songs, hymns, melodies, and psalms of praise for all the days of Hanukkah, and even to eat dairy products.[413] Jewish children are given vacation from school during these days so that they will also rejoice, and they play with a toy upon which four Hebrew letters are inscribed: *nun* (נ), *gimmel* (ג), *hey* (ה), and *shin* (ש). This teaches them that a great miracle happened there (*nes gadol hayah sham*, נס גדול היה שם).[414]

---

410 From the blessing recited all throughout Hanukkah: *Ha-Nerot Hallalu.*

411 [The title of one of the many liturgical pieces and songs during Passover.]

412 [Words that come from the song *Ma'oz Tzur*. "Roses" symbolizes the Jewish people and "remnant of the flasks" refers to the oil found to light the Temple menorah—the *ner tamid*—in rededication of the altar.]

413 This is a commemoration of the actions of Judith, who killed Holofernes, the general of the Assyrian army. Judith was also from the Hasmonean dynasty, thus on this holiday we commemorate everything that she did, even though these events did not take place during the same period as Hanukkah.

414 See *Megillat Antiochus*, also called *Megillat Beit Chashmonai* or *Megillat HaChashmonaim* (Scroll of the Hasmoneans), *Megillat Chanukkah*, or *Megillah Yevanit* (Greek Scroll). This work is different than the Book of Maccabees, as this was originally written in Aramaic with a Hebrew translation. In centuries past, some Jews had the custom of reading this scroll during Hanukkah, just as they would read the scroll of Esther for Purim.

However, my soul despaired to see that, apart from this miracle that was "wrought for the roses through the remnant of the flasks," most of our youth and our elderly know nothing else about this holiday. I also mourned when I saw that many have even given up on celebrating and commemorating this event. And why do our Jewish brothers who have found rest for their souls beneath the wings of Yeshua the Messiah abandon this holiday as if it held no meaning for them? Should they not rather be the leading celebrants of this holiday?

This is the day that HaShem made. This is not a man-made holiday nor were these miraculous events contrived by humans; rather, HaShem performed all of these. Therefore, I thought that it would be good to present a faithful response to the three questions that were posed to me. Even if my words are not new to you, my works will nevertheless not be in vain, for perhaps I will awaken some of you, and this will be my reward.

THE HISTORY OF HELLENIZATION

Question 1: "What are we even celebrating on this holiday?"

This holiday commemorates the mighty acts and salvations that HaShem performed for our forefathers during those days at this time. "Greeks gathered against me in the Hasmonean days." Those were evil days for our people. They dwelt without Torah, teacher, or king. Tyrannical rulers, idol worshipers, and men of evil composure subjugated Israel. The Greek rulers greatly oppressed our people, and the horn of Judah was ground to dust.

Judea stood on the border between east and west, between the banks of the Euphrates River and the crashing waves of the Mediterranean Sea. When Greek philosophy—western philosophy—went eastward, its sects also reached all of Judea. Alexander the Great, who triumphed over many peoples with his sword, humiliating and subduing them, later said that he would conquer nations not by the sword, but by Greek philosophy. He ensured that these nations would fall under the sway of Greek philosophy. The number of those slain by Greek philosophy was greater than those slain by the swords of all the kings of Greece put together.

Alexander intended to build a vast kingdom of many regions in which only one language would be spoken (Greek), and in which its citizens would unite in one lifestyle and custom. To this end he planted the seeds of western philosophy in the eastern lands of Media-Persia. The wealthy and the well respected studied Greek thought and integrated with the Greeks. New towns arose and Greeks settled them. Many of them resided in the old cities as well. Thus, Alexander spread the "fortress" of Greek thought throughout half of Asia so that he could occupy all that territory without extensive bloodshed. He accomplished his goal.

Ancient Asia was almost entirely clothed in Greek culture. Every social class—even leaders and nobility—embraced Greek culture and ethics, essentially becoming Greeks living in Asian lands. The peoples' cultures did not have the strength to withstand it, thus little by little they all fell to Greek philosophy. This happened in Asia Minor, and also in Palestine three hundred years before Rabbi Yehudah HaNasi composed the Mishnah. Many of the cities in Palestine became Hellenized through Alexander and his successors.

The city of Gaza was already a trading post with Greece even before Alexander's conquest, and when he saw the city's advantages, he fortified it and made it his arsenal. Ashkelon, Jaffa, Akko, and all the coastal cities became Hellenized. The Greeks also built settlements for themselves in Samaria, surrounding tiny Judea on all sides. Throughout all the known world Greek became the official *lingua franca* as well as the language of commerce; anyone who wanted to do business with Greeks needed to learn their language. They came to love the Greek tongue and customs. The infectious influence of Greek philosophy blinded the land of Israel; Israel did not have the strength to withstand it.

EZRA'S WALL

In Judea and Jerusalem disciples of Greek philosophy increased daily. The people divided into two major groups. The first group was the Chasidim:[415] those who observed the Torah and the commandments

---

415 [I.e., the Pious. They are also referred to as the Assideans or the Hasideans.]

therein. The second was the Hellenists:[416] they condemned, violated, and abandoned the holy covenant, breaching the laws of Torah.[417]

Ezra foresaw the developments and feared lest Israel fall into the hands of those who would destroy them. He erected a strong wall—the wall of religion—building enclosures and guard rails in order to protect the spirit of the nation of Israel. Ezra gave Israel a religious book of instruction in the worship of HaShem: the Torah. He passed down laws to the people, as if from heaven, concerning the structure of worship, and he instructed them in what to do and not do. He taught about the tithe and the offering that was incumbent upon them to bring and the manner in which to bring it. He sanctified the entire lives of the Jewish people to the worship of HaShem. Afterward, many people made the study of Torah their occupation and craft, paying attention to every tiny letter, vowel, and punctuation mark so that they would be able to observe the entire Torah, not overlooking anything as seemingly small and insignificant as a strand of hair.

These people became the Pharisees and the scribes. They grew and expanded the edifice that Ezra had erected, making it into an expansive castle. The allegiance of the people originally aligned with the Chasidim, and they did everything that the Pharisees and scribes instructed them.

The Chasidim were not mighty warriors or physically able to rise up against their enemies to overthrow them; therefore, the power of the second group grew—the Hellenists who violated the covenant and broke the Torah every single day. Those who loved Greek philosophy were strong like a powerful lion and the pious Chasidim appeared as a docile lamb. Who knows if through the passing of time the lion would have devoured the lamb had HaShem not intervened?

---

416 This is what they called the Jews who spoke Greek instead of Hebrew. In reality even this group divided into two separate subgroups. The first observed the Torah and the commandments but they spoke Greek, and the second spoke Greek and did not observe the Torah at all.

417 The prophecy of Daniel 11 fully concerns this period.

ANTIOCHUS IV EPIPHANES

These were wicked days. However, HaShem had compassion upon his people and, while this time he chose the enemy of Israel as the means of his discipline and the rod of his fury, he did so in order to destroy that enemy. When King Seleucus IV Philopator died by assassination, Antiochus IV—also called Antiochus Epiphanes—succeeded him and took the throne. Antiochus Epiphanes thought to himself: "This time I will finish the design of Alexander the Great of Macedonia and I will Hellenize Judea."

Had he not been so unstable like water, and had he not tried to accomplish this task with severity and oppression, who knows if he would have succeeded? Everything he did and said was barbarous and aggressive, and he continually transgressed laws, societal norms, and customs. He had some worthy attributes, but his evil greatly overshadowed them.

He was gracious to the Hellenist Jews who violated the covenant, and he gave them authority over the entire region. They acted liberally and went and demolished every Torah law. Then they said, let us overwhelm the Chasidim in number and make them do as we do. When the Chasidim who feared God did not obey the order of the covenant-breakers, the king became incensed and commanded that they be driven out, that the treasures in the Sanctuary be ransacked, and that all Israelite Temple worship be replaced with idol worship.

PURCHASING THE PRIESTHOOD

In that time Onias III, the leader of the covenant-keeping, faithful Chasidim, was the high priest in Jerusalem. Onias' brother Yeshua was the leader of the Hellenizers, the covenant-violators, and because of his great love for Greek philosophy and language he changed his name from Yeshua to Jason. Jason lavished the king with flatteries and promises of great amounts of silver, requesting that the high priesthood be removed from his brother and given to him. He asked the king for license to build gymnasiums in Jerusalem in accordance with Greek custom and he asked that his fellows, the leaders of the group of covenant-breakers in Jerusalem, be called citizens of Antioch.

The king's wealth had already started to deplete, so he was very pleased with the silver Jason promised to give him, so he did as Jason desired. The Hellenizers had influence on the upper echelons of government, and there was great unrest in Jerusalem. Gymnasiums were built in the capital city next to the Temple. Men and young boys would go there, and even priests would abandon their service in order to go and revel in the games. When removing their clothes to put on different garments in the gymnasium, they would cover their circumcision,[418] for they were ashamed of the religious customs of their forefathers. Those who abandoned the holy covenant grew daily, and the community of the Chasidim became embarrassingly small.

Jason served as priest for three years. One of his party members, whose name was Menelaus, envied Jason and went to the king, saying "If it seems good to the king, withdraw Jason from the high priesthood and appoint me instead. I will pay double the amount that Jason promised to pay the king." His words won the heart of the greedy Antiochus; he appointed Menelaus as high priest in place of Jason, and Menelaus did even more wicked things than Jason.

Menelaus sent men to capture Onias III, who had fled into hiding. They killed him after his capture. Then he proceeded to empty the Temple of all its treasures and send them to Antiochus. Jason conspired against him, and while Antiochus and his army were marching toward Egypt to siege it, conspirators ambushed Menelaus and his men and he fled Jerusalem. Jason's actions greatly provoked the king's wrath, and the king led his army against Jerusalem, massacring the inhabitants and spilling their blood like water. He plundered the city and took every treasure from HaShem's House to Antioch, including the incense altar, the menorah, and the table of the showbread. The children of Judah never drank the cup of agony until they took that chalice, and HaShem's hand was still outstretched, striking them.

---

418 In those days they had an instrument with which they would pull the foreskin down over the exposed member so that they would appear to be uncircumcised. This is the method that our sages of blessed memory are referring to every time they say "covering circumcision" in the Talmud.

HELLENIZING JERUSALEM AND THE ABOMINATION OF DESOLATION

Two years later Antiochus decided that he would finalize his rule over Jerusalem, and he did. His intent to conquer Egypt failed, for the rulers in Rome would not allow him, so he decided to play out his scheme in Judea. The inhabitants of Judea were destined for the sword. At first, he ordered that the wall of Jerusalem be demolished as well as the marble edifices in the City of David. He built a large palace from that marble. He told the Judeans that it was illegal to circumcise their sons, observe the Sabbath, and perform the commandments, and he built a large podium in the Temple and placed a graven image in the Sanctuary. He commanded everyone to bow down and worship it, and anyone who disobeyed one of his decrees was put to death.

When the inhabitants of Jerusalem did not heed his orders, they enraged the king, and he led a great massacre in Israel. The men were put to the sword and the women and small children were sold as slaves. Many left Jerusalem and fled the country. The king made decrees throughout all Judea in order to oppress the people and force them to bow down to the graven image. Every month the oppressive officials would visit Israelite houses. If they found the Holy Writings in anyone's house, the residents would be forced out, put to death, their remains discarded, and the house would be given to one of the Greeks. Anyone who circumcised their son would also be killed and their property seized.

On 15 Kislev circa 3593 (162 BCE) Antiochus erected the image of the abomination of desolation in the Sanctuary, and he consecrated the Temple to that image. On Kislev 25 in the same year, the Judeans who resided in Jerusalem brought the first burnt offering and sacrifice to that abomination, and from that day on came woe upon woe, blow upon blow, for wrath came upon the entire land. Many Judeans fell down and prostrated themselves to the abomination. The children of Israel even celebrated the festival that the Greeks made for their god Dionysus, singing songs and drinking to the point of extreme drunkenness. Those who feared God in Jerusalem saw this and mourned; they were rendered speechless.

HASHEM'S MIRACULOUS GIFT

Antiochus' laws were incredibly heavy. His yoke was tied tightly onto the shoulders of Israel and there was no repose. These were malicious times, but the spirit of the people of Israel arose and stood firm, and HaShem was their helper. A great miracle happened there, one unlike any other that is recorded in the history of our people. If we look at these things with human eyes we will not be able to correctly discern them; instead we would say that this was a matter of idiocy and madness to rise up against a powerful king, the leader of an enormous and mighty army, while the people of Judea were weak and small in number.

However, when trouble came and the Greek king rebelled against HaShem, attempting to expel the God of Israel from the land of Israel, the faith and resolve of Judea grew stronger. They believed in HaShem and trusted that he would not abandon them in this time of great calamity, and that the arm of HaShem was not too short to save. The flame of the people's faith procured a spirit of strength and fortitude within them, and they went out and fought the mighty lions and were victorious. Gradually, the might of Israel began to manifest its splendor through the seemingly insignificant priest in the order of Joarib whose name was Mattityahu[419] from the small town of Modin.

This is the sign that HaShem gave. From the time HaShem began to perform wonders for his people he would occasionally choose a man of small importance as the instrument of his miracles. He chose Moses who was slow of speech to bring his people out from under the hand of Egyptian oppression, and he took David from his shepherding to be king over Israel, choosing his seed to be King and Ruler of an everlasting kingdom—the kingdom of heaven—and to rule over his people Israel and all the nations of the earth. In every new era someone arises in Israel before our very eyes, someone who is small in people's estimation, and yet does mighty acts in Israel and among the peoples.

God desires to show the children of Adam and Eve that it is not humans who possess power and authority, kingship and rule, strength and might—rather all these things come from him. This time he chose Mattityahu the priest, son of Yochanan the priest, and formed him into

---

419 [I.e., Mattathias: "Gift of HaShem."]

a weapon in his hand in order to avenge his holy name against the Greek king and his army.

The king's officials went to the town of Modin, built an altar, and forced the people to sacrifice to the Greek gods. Mattityahu refused to obey them and said, "God forbid that I should do such a detestable deed! Even if the entire kingly tribe of Judah transgresses the faith and becomes lawless, my household and I will serve HaShem, and where I reside there shall be no man who will lift his finger to do such detestable things if he values his life." And when he saw a Judean attempting to present an offering on the defiled altar, he killed him right beside the altar. He also killed a royal official and completely destroyed the defiled altar. After this, he fled to the mountains along with his sons.

Not long thereafter he realized it was not good to have fled to the mountains. There is no refuge or haven for the people of Israel, and even if he preserved his own life, the lives of the people hung in the balance before him. Many Chasidim like him also fled and hid in desert caves. Assyrian soldiers found their hiding places and attacked them on the Sabbath, coming against them like wolves, and the Chasidim did not want to pick up a sword on the Sabbath, thus all of them fell by the sword: men, women, and children. Not one person survived.

Mattityahu heard about this and saw that during such evil days the concept of "sit and do not act"[420] does not apply, for he surmised that HaShem was requesting them to act in such a time as this. He decreed that they should wage war. He was very old and when he was about to die he called his sons, ordering them to attack their enemies and drive them out of the land and to rescue the remnant that the wicked Greeks left behind.

---

420 [*Shev ve-al ta'aseh* (שב ואל תעשה) is a talmudic concept referring to violating a Torah command. The matter is discussed in b.*Brachot* 19b–20a as to whether it is permissible to violate a Torah command or rabbinic decree regarding preservation of human dignity. Mattityahu decided that it is better to break a commandment (i.e., carry a sword and fight on Shabbat) than to be massacred.]

VICTORIOUS IN BATTLE

Mattityahu had five sons: Yochanan was the firstborn, Shimon was the second, Yehudah the third, Elazar the fourth, and Yonatan the fifth. Yehudah was the lion lying in wait, ready to be roused, and like a lion he longed to devour HaShem's enemies. He was a mighty warrior and a man of action. Mattityahu appointed him as the leader[421] and his brother Shimon as his advisor. Mattityahu cautioned his sons never to become enraged with each other; rather in unity, with one heart and mind, to fight HaShem's enemies and bring them to their end.

HaShem was with Mattityahu's sons. Even the Chasidim joined them after some time, for they, too, saw that it did not avail them to remain complacent. A new ordinance was issued from the scribes: It was permissible to desecrate the Sabbath in order to take vengeance on HaShem's enemies and fight them. Yehudah went throughout the land killing anyone he could find who sacrificed to Greek gods and violated the covenant. He circumcised every male in Israel that still had his foreskin. He called the survivors to join with him against the king, their enemy and persecutor.

Yehudah annihilated the Assyrian army, and Apollonius, the commander of the Assyrian army, fell. Yehudah took Apollonius' sword and he used it until his death, carrying it on his hip as a symbol of HaShem's salvation. When the king heard everything that had happened he was furious and sent a large army to Judea. The king's armies happily marched against Judea, for they thought they would conquer it very easily. They trusted in the Greek gods and the might of their own armies. However, he who sits in heaven laughed.

---

421 Because of his strength he was later called Yehudah [Judah] Maccabee, which means "Judah the Boulder-Shattering Hammer." Only they spelled the name "Maccabee" (מכבי) in Hebrew with a *kaf* (כ) and not a *kof* (ק) so that they could extrapolate many different meanings and allusions from this name. Many interpreted that the name was an acronym for "Who is like you, HaShem, among the gods?" (מי כמוך באלים יי), and many others said that it was an acronym for "Mattityahu the priest, son of Yochanan" (מתתיהו כהן בן יוחנן). However, I think it stands for "The priestly order of the sons of Joarib [Yoyariv]" (משמרת כהונת בני יויריב), because they desired to establish the name of this priestly order from which these mighty warriors descended.

The enemy encamped near Emmaus, which was to the west of Jerusalem, and Yehudah son of Mattityahu was just south with his army. Gorgias, the Assyrian-Seleucid general, took half of his army and marched toward the mountains to attack Yehudah's army from behind. When Yehudah realized this he left his encampment immediately and traveled that night toward the second half of the Assyrian army that was under Nicanor's command. Nicanor's army was unprepared, for they did not think Yehudah's forces could come against them. Yehudah's army did just as in the days of Joshua: They sounded shofars and trumpets with long blasts of war, and they converged upon Nicanor's army like ferocious lions. Fear gripped Nicanor's men, and they fled. Yehudah's men pursued them all the way to Ashdod.

Three thousand were put to the sword. Those who remained at the camp became Yehudah's prisoners of war, and Yehudah's men burned the tents of the Assyrians. When Gorgias arrived at the encampment of the Jews, he did not find Yehudah or his army, so he turned back to the mountains where his camp was, and he saw smoke rising from a distance. Fear of Yehudah fell upon him. He and his army abandoned their position; thus Yehudah acquired large portions of territory.

HaShem granted Israel six months of rest. After those six months, Lucius gathered an enormous army, marched toward Judea, and encamped at Beth-Zur. Yehudah had a very small army, for the people of Israel were small in number at that time, yet he had a resolute heart. The men of his army did not fear death, and HaShem was with them. Battle after battle ensued, and Yehudah's army triumphed over the Assyrian army. Now Jerusalem could rest and Judea dwelt securely without dread of the enemy.

DEDICATING THE TEMPLE AND THE MIRACLE OF HANUKKAH

When winter came Yehudah turned toward Jerusalem, and Menelaus, who was then the high priest in Jerusalem, was in dread. Even the Assyrian battalion encamped in Jerusalem was gripped with fear. However, Yehudah was not concerned about them, rather he was focused on the Temple Mount. How awful the Temple must have looked! How great a wasteland it was! This vision pierced his heart.

The Temple was disarrayed, the altar defiled, the gates were no more, for they had been burnt. Thorns, thistles, and weeds grew in the Temple courtyard; it looked like a barren wilderness. Yehudah's first act was to clean the courtyard and return the Temple to its original splendor. Then he dismantled the defiled altar and built a new altar in its place. He purified and cleansed the Temple in accordance with the necessary laws and prescriptions.

On the twenty-fifth day of Kislev the inhabitants of Jerusalem rededicated the Temple and, after three years without a sacrifice to HaShem, they offered up a burnt offering and sacrifice. The Chasidim in Jerusalem who feared God were overjoyed, for HaShem had wrought a great salvation. They established these eight days of Hanukkah[422] as a celebration for generations to come, that all the Israelites in every generation would know of the salvations and acts of power that HaShem performed for their forefathers during these days.

Yehudah's adversaries, the covenant-breakers, defiled all the oils so that when Yehudah and his men wanted to light the holy lamp in the Sanctuary, they were unable to find any undefiled oil. The priests and Chasidim mourned over this, but HaShem had compassion on them. They eventually found a single flask of oil that was sufficient to last for one day. They used this single flask of oil to light the menorah, and it lasted for eight days. This is Hanukkah, and this is why we celebrate it.

THE LIGHT OF LIFE OF THESE CANDLES

Question 2: "Why do we light these candles?"

Josephus stated that the Hanukkah lamps represented liberty and freedom, and that they are a symbol of power and might.[423] During that time everyone interpreted them thus. In celebrating this holiday they lit lamps everywhere, in their houses, even on their rooftops, commemorating the triumph over their enemies.

---

422 They established this holiday as eight days long in order to resemble Sukkot. It also took eight days to dedicate the first altar (see Leviticus 8:33–9:2).

423 *Antiquities of the Jews* 12:323–326/xii.7.

Darkness symbolizes evil and trouble, and light represents life and joy. Light is the source of life and strength to the human body, and it represents truth in the human soul. It is the crowning glory of the world. Where there is no light, there is no life. If the sun went dark for three days, everything would cease to grow, and every living thing would cease to exist. Light gladdens every soul, delights every broken and dejected heart, and expels all sorrow and grief.

When times of trouble and evil come upon us, darkness clouds our eyes, blinding us, but when HaShem gives us comfort and salvation, our eyes are illuminated. The Greek empire came and blinded the Israelites during those days and in that time, and they forced the Israelites to write on the horn of an ox, "We have no portion in the God of Israel,"[424] and there was darkness throughout the entire land of Israel. HaShem's compassions were aroused and he called out to them, saying, "Arise, Daughter of Zion; arise and shine. My light is in your hand and your light is in mine. For the commandments are the lamp and the Torah is the light, and if you observe the Torah and the commandments you will have life, joy, and light!"[425]

When Yehudah dedicated the Temple, and when all the people of Jerusalem congregated together, they decreed that this dedication be celebrated every single year throughout all the generations with songs of rejoicing and thanks.[426] They lit the menorah in the Temple, they sacrificed thanksgiving and peace offerings, and they sang psalms of David in Jerusalem. In other Judean cities they lit lamps in their houses, courtyards, and in communal buildings.

All Jews everywhere have upheld and accepted upon themselves and their offspring—and upon all who accompany them—the celebration of these days of Hanukkah by lighting lamps and illuminating their houses, setting the menorah as a monument remembering the power and might, and as a symbol of the freedom, life, and joy that HaShem gave us during those days at this time.

---

424 *Genesis Rabbah* 2:4.

425 *Deuteronomy Rabbah*, Parashat Re'eh.

426 1 Maccabees 4:59.

The scholars of the Talmud say that these lights we kindle make known the salvation that HaShem wrought for us and for all mankind, and this act reveals and popularizes the miracle. Therefore they affixed laws and regulations of where to light the menorah, when, and how many candles to light.

In the first century two main schools of thought—Beit Shammai and Beit Hillel—differed whether we light one candle on the first day, adding one more candle each day thereafter, or if we switch the order and light eight candles on the first day and subtract one candle each day thereafter.[427] Both of these schools of thought decreed that a total of thirty-six lamps be lit during the eight days of Hanukkah; they only disagreed about whether the number increases or decreases. Beit Hillel won out over Beit Shammai, and now halachah is in accordance with the ruling of Beit Hillel.

If we light these candles only in order to publicize the miracle of the oil, then the composer of the song "Ma'oz Tzur" was correct in only mentioning that miracle and nothing else: "Through the remnant of the flasks a miracle was wrought for the roses." These candles are not a remembrance of the salvations that occurred through Yehudah the Maccabee and his army, rather they recall the flask of oil that bore the seal of the high priest that was found in the Temple.[428] This is why we do not kindle lights on other holidays commemorating salvations and acts of power that HaShem wrought for our forefathers. We must celebrate the miracle done through a menorah with menorahs, candles, and light. But why thirty-six candles?

THE HIDDEN LIGHT OF MESSIAH

The Rokeach[429] said, "We light thirty-six candles to celebrate the first light that shone upon the first man for thirty-six hours, then afterward the Holy One, blessed be he, concealed it for the righteous. This is the Messiah who is hidden in the Torah, and to everyone who studies

---

427 b.*Shabbat* 21b and on.

428 Ibid.

429 [Rabbi Elazar Rokeach, a.k.a., Elazar of Worms.]

Torah with a pure heart, the hidden light—the light of Messiah—is revealed to him."[430]

Similarly, all the Gentiles who believe in the Messiah light many candles every twenty-fifth of their twelfth month (which for them is like the twenty-fifth of Kislev for us),[431] and they call this holiday "The Birth of the Light of Messiah" (Christmas), for the hidden light has now been revealed and the Holy One, blessed be he, is calling out: "Arise, my assembly; arise and shine, for your light has come." All those who believe respond and say, "By your light do I see light. I have only awaited your light, and here it is."[432] Thus with lights we honor HaShem during these days.

HELLENIZATION CONTINUES

Question 3: "What does this holiday teach us?"

Greeks gathered against us during those Hasmonean days, and "Greeks" have gathered against us even in this generation. Those who hate Israel and Judah have not ceased; Hellenizers and covenant-violators multiply daily. Jews of Germany and France say, "We are Germans; we are Frenchman," and if this continues, Israel will cease to be a nation and no longer survive. We hear it even in this land and it terrifies us, for the Jews in this country also say, "We are Polish."

Everyone who loves their people will surely say, "I am wasting away! Woe to me, for my people do not understand the ways of truth! The betrayers have betrayed, and the cheaters who have cheated have been cheated."[433] Yet this is what this holiday teaches us: Every weapon formed against us in order to wipe our nation from the earth will not succeed.

---

430 See *Sefer HaRokeach* and *Sefer Benei Yissachar*.

431 They call their twelfth month "December." The custom to celebrate the revelation of the Messiah's light as we know it originated in Germany. Nevertheless, evidence can be found that this holiday was celebrated in the third century CE.

432 See *Yalkut Shimoni* to Isaiah 60.

433 [Isaiah 24:16.]

The hand of HaShem is strong, he is the Almighty God, and everything that he says will come to pass. HaShem said that there would be a nation in the land, and so there was. He decided to make us a great people, and who could overrule him? HaShem desired to make us his treasured people, his holy nation, and his will shall be accomplished on earth as it is in heaven.

HaShem has many emissaries. Behold, he will send hornets[434] and fiery serpents[435] among us and they will bite and sting us. Many from among us will perish. Yet it will be in our troubles that we cry out to HaShem and he will save us from our adversities. He will raise up a lowly man from among us, he will awaken a Judah, a Jephthah, or a Gideon. Or he will call out to Deborah from underneath the palm tree and she will call Barak, and by a woman's hand HaShem will subdue all our enemies and Israel will repent from their evil ways.

Then Israel will forget to say, "I am the son of a German," or "I am the son of a Frenchman," because he will say, "I am a son of Judah." Mighty Rock of my salvation, to praise you is a delight!

JOSEPH'S EXAMPLE

As for those of us who belong to the tiny community of the Testimony, this holiday teaches us not to be frightened or worried when we see how small our numbers are. Even then there were not many in Israel who were flying the banner of Yehudah's forces. There were many more covenant-breakers than covenant-keepers. HaShem chose those the world esteemed as small and the weak to be the instruments of mighty acts of valor.

Indeed, we are a small community, yet HaShem is our shield and the horn of our salvation, and no acts of power can overcome us. Our beginning may be humble, but our end will be glorious.

I find the story of Joseph, which is read in the synagogues during Hanukkah, exceedingly encouraging. His brothers called him "the dreamer" and they hated him, and before he came near to them they

---

434 [Exodus 23:28.]

435 [Numbers 21:6.]

conspired to kill him, but instead they sold him to Ishmaelites and Midianites, and Joseph was taken to Egypt. Yet HaShem was with him, and he was a successful man. Not long after arriving in Egypt, HaShem sent the wife of the chief steward, and Joseph was sent to prison. From prison Joseph grew in rank in the kingdom and became known by the name Zaphenath-Paneah. How wonderful and comforting this story is for us! HaShem chose us to raise up a remnant in Israel and to resurrect a greater remnant amongst our people. Why are you downcast, my soul, and why so disconsolate? Be comforted, for God has done this. The Word of HaShem will endure forever and he will do everything that he says.

In the synagogue today I heard what was read to us in the *haftarah*: "Shout for joy and rejoice, Daughter of Zion, for behold I come to dwell in your midst ... and HaShem has taken Judah as his portion in the Holy Land, and he will choose Jerusalem once more. All flesh be silent before HaShem ... for behold I am bringing my servant the Branch ... and I will remove that land's guilt in one day."[436] This is what HaShem has said to us through his prophet Zechariah, and just as he said so has he done.

Behold, days are coming when HaShem's good word that he spoke to the house of Israel and the house of Judah will be established, and in those days he will cause the Righteous Branch to sprout up, and he will cause justice and righteousness to reside in the earth. He came forth from Bethlehem Ephrathah to be a ruler in Israel, to proclaim a year of favor from HaShem, to be a covenant to the people and a light to the nations. And he was wounded because of our crimes and beaten because of our transgressions, for HaShem anointed him to proclaim good news to the humble and to bind up the broken-hearted. Therefore, all flesh be silent before HaShem, for the mouth of HaShem has spoken.

ADDING TO THE LIGHT

Why are you so disquieted, my soul? Rest and be still! Put your hope in God. Is HaShem's arm too short to save? We will yet be a large community. Let Hanukkah be a sign to us. For the halachah is in accordance with Beit Hillel. Just as candles are added, so too, will HaShem add

---

436 This is from the *haftarah* portion in Zechariah 2 for *Be-ha'alotcha*, which occurs on the Sabbath during Hanukkah.

to our numbers and the light of our testimony will become brighter. On the first night we light one candle, and every night after that we add another. Tonight we light eight candles. The light of Messiah has been born; he has been revealed first to the children of Judah, and now he is continuing to be a light to all the peoples. Many nations have come toward the light.

Our testimony will grow if we light according to the halachah and if we do not place the candles under a bushel measure. We must illuminate the entire house of Israel with the golden menorah. First we light one candle, then two, then three, and we must continue to add until we are in front of the menorah lighting all eight candles, for it is not by power nor by might, but by my Spirit, says HaShem of Hosts.

This is Hanukkah and this is its testimony. Therefore, I will conclude with a song, a hymn, and I will extend my prayer along with the composer of "Ma'oz Tzur" and say:

> Please, HaShem, reveal your holy arm to all the children of Israel, your people, and let all your children see your salvation and live. Then they will return to being your people just as they once were. For your mercy has not abandoned us, and your kindness has not ended. Your people will yet sing a pleasing song to you on the day of the dedication of the altar.

THE MONTH OF ADAR AND THE DAYS OF PURIM

Volume V Issue 3, Adar 5658 (1898) pgs. 41–49

This month, the month of Adar, comes twelve months after the month in which the Israelite exodus from Egypt occurred, and it is the sixth month of the year according to the Hebrew calendar. Its name is Adar. The Israelites brought this name from Babylon.[437] Expositors are confounded as they try to explain the meaning of this name. There are some who say it means "splendor" (*hadar*, הדר) because this is the month when trees blossom and flowers bloom in the eastern lands where our forefathers settled.

Even to us Jews who live in lands where this is not a luscious season, where trees do not blossom and flowers do not bud, Adar is still a month of delight. "When Adar enters, joy increases."[438] This is what our sages of blessed memory said when they were teaching Torah in Babylon. Indeed joy has increased in all Israelite settlements, and we who are Israelites and disciples of Yeshua, who observe the Torah of Moses and the Testimony of our Master, are also exceedingly joyful during this month.

---

437 *Leviticus Rabbah* 48.

438 b. *Ta'anit* 29a.

OBSERVING AND CONTESTING

We walk in the ways of our Jewish brothers, and we follow the commands of our sages who taught Torah in Babylon. Yet, if the sages erred in some matter, then we will say, "So-and-so teacher of Torah was in error when he said such-and-such." But if what they say is in line with the Torah, then we must observe and do it. We agree with Rabbi Yehudah son of Rabbi Shmuel who says that when Adar enters, joy increases. However, we disagree with Rav Papa[439] who claims that the luck associated with Adar ensures we are granted mercy. We do not believe in luck.

We also say to Rabbi Chanina that there is no reliance on luck in Israel,[440] and that it is forbidden to think that the stars decree good or evil for us. The stars are in HaShem's hands as well. God forbid that we should study the ways of the Gentiles. We will not be guided by signs from heaven. The Gentiles who did not yet know HaShem were intimidated and frightened by the stars. Those of us who know HaShem are not.[441] For we have all heard that HaShem's eyes are upon those who fear him and long for his kindness, and his ears are turned toward those who cry out to him. Even though he was a great sage of Torah, Rav Papa was mistaken, and we do not listen to him.

GIVING THE HALF-SHEKEL

The month of Adar commemorates joyous events that occurred in the history of Israel. Long ago, while our forefathers were still in their own land, the holy land that HaShem gave us as an everlasting portion, they would announce about the *shekalim* on the first of the month of Adar.[442] Emissaries went out to all the habitations of Israel, announcing

---

439 Ibid., 29b.

440 b.*Shabbat* 156a.

441 Ibid. This is what Rabbi Yochanan taught. See Jeremiah 10:2.

442 m.*Shekalim* 1:1. They would announce in all the land of Israel, and all its border cities, that everyone must bring the half-shekel that must be given in the Temple every single year, and from these shekels (*shekalim*) they would purchase public sacrifices that were continually offered throughout the year, from the month of Nisan until the month of Nisan the following year.

to the people that the time to bring the half-shekel contribution for the public offerings had come. They used the collection to purchase sacrifices that were to be brought before HaShem, and they used it to repair their roads[443] and eradicate all [forbidden] hybrid crops from their fields.[444]

ANCIENT MEMORIES

What beautiful memories those were! Our hearts overflow with joy when we remember that we once possessed the land of our inheritance. We once possessed all the fields and vineyards therein, and we were not like foreigners in lands belonging to strangers. Our joy multiplies seventy times seven when we remember that in Jerusalem, our holy city, HaShem, God of heaven and earth, caused his name and glory to reside. HaShem also received gifts there. He commanded us to bring the offering and to appear before him in the Sanctuary, in the place where he chose to sanctify his own name.

These memories gladden the heart and soul. Certainly we know that HaShem our God causes his name to be remembered in every land. We have even heard this from the mouth of Yeshua the Messiah. HaShem delights in those who worship him in spirit and truth, wherever they live. God is spirit, therefore those who worship him must worship him in spirit. And in every place where there are those who worship him in spirit, he considers that place holy.[445]

Yet, in those ancient days, when darkness still covered the land and fog still rested upon the peoples, the light of HaShem's Spirit shone only upon us. He also commanded us to build a House for his name's sake and to appear before him there. HaShem chose to cause his name to

---

443 For the good of the state and for the repairing of the world, and they were also told to repair the highways and the *mikva'ot* (pools for ritual immersion). Some say this was done for the sake of the Jews in the Diaspora coming to the land of Israel for the pilgrimage festivals.

444 m.*Shekalim* 1:1.

445 John 4:23–24. Here, our Master Yeshua is speaking with the Samaritan woman, and it seemed appropriate to him to explain what HaShem said through Moses (Exodus 20:21), "In every place where I cause my name to be remembered, I will come to you and bless you."

reside there in Jerusalem, and he greatly lavished his love upon our forefathers, choosing their descendants after them and giving them the Torah. He inclined his ears toward them, and he heard their pleas in that House for many days. Can our hearts not rejoice over this?

Indeed our hearts testify against us that, because of our sins, HaShem exiled us from our land and distanced us from our own soil. We are no longer able to ascend to worship him or appear before him in the Temple where his name once resided. Our forefathers sinned, transgressed, and committed crimes. They rebelled against HaShem and grieved his Spirit, and HaShem sent down fire upon the holy place, destroyed the Temple, the glory of the land faded away, and now we are in exile. Now there is no one to announce to us about the *shekalim,* no emissaries go forth to call for everyone to bring the half-shekel as a contribution to HaShem.

Our hearts testify against us that our priests and leaders rejected Yeshua, the Prince of Life, whom HaShem sent to be a public offering for the people of Israel and for all the peoples who repent from their evil ways and turn to HaShem. Our hearts testify that even the best among us did not see the light that was dawning, and they stretched out their hands against the Messiah of HaShem. Then HaShem destroyed his Temple, and the public offerings ceased.

Despite this sorrow, we delight in remembering the joy that once belonged to us. Moreover, hope captivates our hearts when we speak about how HaShem swore and will not relent. HaShem swore to return his scattered people, to raise up the tribes of Jacob, and to comfort the house of Israel. HaShem will keep his oath. Therefore, our joy is great!

YESHUA AND THE SHEKALIM

When we remember the *shekalim* we also remember the miraculous thing that our Master Yeshua the Messiah performed when he paid the half-shekel, and we remember what he said. When Yeshua and his disciples came to Capernaum, the collectors of the half-shekel approached Shimon Keifa, disciple of our Master, and said, "Does your rabbi not pay the half-shekel?"

Shimon answered, "He will pay it."

He went to the house where Yeshua was staying. When he came to the house, Yeshua greeted him, saying, "What is your opinion Shimon? From whom do the kings of the earth take their taxes? From their children or from strangers?"

Shimon answered, "From strangers."

Yeshua said, "Then the children are exempt. Nevertheless, in order that it will not be an obstacle to them, go to the sea and throw a fishhook in it, and take the first fish that you catch, and when you open its mouth, you will find a silver shekel. Go and pay it on my behalf and yours."[446]

I believe this story occurred during the month of Adar. Our Master and his disciples were in Capernaum, and the emissaries came to announce the *shekalim*. The collectors of the half-shekel wanted to hear what the Rabbi who teaches righteousness and truth thought about the *shekalim*. The name of our Master was great and renowned in Capernaum. He had many disciples who followed him and learned at his feet everywhere he went. News of our Master went out all through the land, for he taught with divine authority, unlike the teaching of the scribes.

The collectors of the half-shekel were not his adversaries, but neither were they his disciples yet. Perhaps they were also like Nicodemus who knew that our Master Yeshua came from God[447] and taught us like a great rabbi and teacher. They honored him as an instructor sent from HaShem. Because they honored him they did not desire to ask him if he would give the *shekalim*, so they asked his disciple instead.

In those days, many became disheartened because of the *shekalim*. Not everyone gave it happily or willfully.[448] There was no law among the people as to whether or not the priests had to pay the half-shekel; some thought yes, some no.[449] Thus the collectors approached Shimon Keifa to hear from his own mouth the decision of the Rabbi sent from HaShem. Perhaps they heard that our Master had laid his hands on

---

446 Matthew 17:24–27.

447 John 3:2.

448 Therefore, there were those who would weigh out the exact amount for those who did not want to give out of the goodness of their hearts (see m.*Shekalim* 1:3).

449 In the Mishnah (ibid.) it says that they did not collect the shekel from the priests for the sake of peace.

Shimon Keifa, giving him the keys to the gates of heaven, the authority to permit or forbid, and to teach legal matters and Torah,[450] and they thought that he also knew this decision.

Shimon answered them, "Have you not heard that our rabbi and teacher came to uphold the Torah and fulfill it, not violate it? Our Master came to fulfill all righteousness. He does not even violate the words of the scribes. Therefore, he will also give the half-shekel. And you have done well in believing that he would." Afterward Shimon Keifa went to the house to tell Yeshua about this.

THE COMMUNAL SACRIFICE

Our Master knew this matter before Shimon even told him, and he greeted him, saying:

> You spoke well in saying that we would give it. Let us surely pay the *shekalim* so that it will not be an obstacle to them. If I do not pay it, and if you, my disciple, do not pay it, they will surely erroneously say, "We do not need to give a contribution to the communal sacrifices because Yeshua and his disciples do not give the half-shekel," and they will not know why. Did HaShem not command for offerings to be brought? HaShem also sent me to be a communal sacrifice.
>
> You and all your fellows—my disciples—became grieved when I told you that it will not be very long before the Son of Man will be handed over to men who will surely kill him, and that on the third day he will rise. But know that I must be a communal sacrifice, an offering for every human being. The contribution of the half-shekel testifies about me. God forbid that we should put an obstacle before this people! Therefore you did well in saying that I would give it.
>
> However, it distresses me that you still do not understand this matter. You no longer look into it. From whom do the kings of the land take their taxes, from their children or from

---

450 Matthew 16:18.

strangers? Is it incumbent upon me to give the contribution to the communal sacrifice, even though I myself am the son of the Living God, the son of the kingdom?

So that we will not be an obstacle to the people, go to the sea and cast in a fishhook. Open the first fish that you bring up and within it you will find a silver shekel, enough to pay for the both of us. Even the king will not avoid paying the toll, and God forbid that he should! For this reason I came to earth to be an offering. I am not an offering for my own sake, for I am guiltless, innocent of any crime. There is no transgression in me. I came to be a communal sacrifice.

This is the decree of the King: The sin of the first man shall be atoned for. An atonement shall be given for the children of the first man in order to atone for his sin, which now has control over all his descendants. By the King's decree the blood of the offering must be shed in order to atone for this sin.

But the blood of bulls and sheep is not sufficiently valuable to atone for this sin. Thus my Father sent me to be an offering on behalf of everyone so that his decree may be enacted. My Father the King did not avoid paying the toll, and he offered me as an atonement for many. Therefore, everyone who desires to be purified from the sin of the first man must give his life and soul to me, presenting his body as a living, holy, favorable offering to God.

Please understand and perceive this matter, Shimon, so that you will be able to grasp the words I spoke to you and to all my disciples countless times. Do not be grieved anymore when you hear that I must be handed over to men who will surely kill me, for HaShem loves justice and hates theft in the burnt offering.[451]

---

451 Isaiah 61:8.

PRECIOUS MEMORIES

How precious is this memory! How wonderful it would have been if eloquent songwriters had arisen from among us to compose new liturgical songs for *Shabbat Shekalim*;[452] songs that are passionate and melodic; songs that recount the praises of HaShem for the kindness he showed us through our Master, Yeshua the Messiah, in giving him as the communal sacrifice!

We who observe the Torah and the Testimony keep the order of the four portions,[453] and on *Shabbat Shekalim* we recite *Yotzrot*.[454] These songs of *Yotzrot* may not be pleasing to everyone, but to us they are. We have precious memories for which to glorify and praise the name of HaShem and his Messiah, which go even beyond the words of these songs. How can we be silent? If we were, we would be found guilty.

DAYS OF PURIM

The days of Purim[455] also fall in this month. Purim is a joyous holiday for us just as the harvest festival was for our forefathers. In those days, when Israel was dwelling in their own land, and when their occupation was plowing and harvesting, Sukkot was the festival of joy of life and blessing. It was a festival of the people, a family and household holiday. Everyone celebrated it.

When the Second Temple was also destroyed and Israel went into exile, expelled from their own land by Roman armies, pilgrimages to Jerusalem ceased along with the harvest festival. Therefore, our sages of blessed memory transferred the celebration of the harvest festival

---

452 [The Sabbath when Exodus 30:11–16 is read.]

453 On each Shabbat in Adar, in addition to the regular Torah portion, we read four additional portions. Here are their names: *Parashat Shekalim*, *Parashat Zachor*, *Parashat Parah*, and *Parashat HaChodesh*.

454 The name given to the liturgical songs that are sung on all four Sabbaths mentioned above.

455 [While Purim is typically celebrated on the 14th of Adar, Jewish communities in Persia or in ancient walled cities (i.e., Jerusalem) also celebrate it a second day on the 15th.]

to Purim. The days of Mordechai[456] became days of drinking, celebration, joy, and gladness. They became an official holiday and festival.

The things that happened to the Israelites in Persia during the reign of Ahasuerus the Fool[457] were well known in the land of Israel, even during the early Second Temple Era.[458] Perhaps most of the people of Israel were aware of the book of Esther during those early days,[459] but they did not celebrate Purim in the land of Israel at that time.[460] In Persia they celebrated the holiday on the fourteenth and fifteenth of Adar, and perhaps there were also some people in the land of Israel who also celebrated it on these two days. However, the holiday of Purim had not yet been accepted by the entire people. They had not yet established the days of Mordechai as a holiday for drinking and joyful celebration.

PURIM IN THE FIRST CENTURY AND AFTER

By the time of the reign of Herod, the story of Purim was already well known in every Israelite home.[461] In those days Hillel the Elder rose in stature and established a school for Torah study; Shammai the Elder also established a school. But they never said anything about Purim, nor had they yet prescribed law or halachah for it. They did not celebrate it in the synagogues in Israel in those days. Thus, our Master Yeshua the Messiah would not have celebrated Purim, nor was it a day of drinking, joy, or celebration for him.

---

456 2 Maccabees 15:36. According to this passage Purim used to be called the "days of Mordechai."

457 [i.e., Xerxes.]

458 2 Maccabees testifies to this. Even the Jews who lived in Greece attested to this, for they celebrated this holiday even while Jews in Israel initially did not.

459 Perhaps. However, the language in that book suggests that it would not have been well known then. If we were to judge from the language, we would say that it was written roughly toward the end of the Second Temple Period.

460 This holiday is never mentioned in 1 Maccabees. According to the Jerusalem Talmud (y.*Megillot* 70:4) the sages and their sons would not establish Purim as a holiday in the land of Israel. Also, we cannot find anything said about Purim by even one sage that lived before the destruction of the Second Temple.

461 In his book *Antiquities of the Jews* 11:284–296/xi.3, Josephus attests to the fact that this holiday was already established in his day.

According to the book of John,[462] Yeshua went up to Jerusalem during Purim, but not to celebrate it. And Matthew never tells us anything about Purim, for Purim was not yet an official, accepted holiday. Even in our day there are still some who do not recite the *Hallel* at Purim.[463] Nevertheless, our sages who lived during the Second Temple Period and after established Purim as a holiday for all Israel. They decreed that the scroll of Esther should be read in the presence of the entire assembly, and that it was incumbent upon all Jews, even the women, to come and hear it. Today Purim is a halachically prescribed holiday for the entire people, but it is not like the other holidays of the Torah.

These sages prescribed many other rules and regulations: when to read the scroll, who can and cannot read it, and so on. This is because our sages were pious men who feared sin and observed the Torah and the commandments. They possessed a zeal for God, although that zeal was not always necessarily coupled with knowledge and understanding. Indeed, their eyes were blinded from seeing the light of HaShem that was dawning. They erred about Yeshua, the Prince of Life, and they did not recognize him. They rejected him and did not kneel before him.

Yet they observed the Torah and the commandments and were clothed in the spirit of piety. There were also many of them whose hearts did follow after Yeshua, even though they did not confess to it publicly before the assembly of Israel.

These sages saw that it was good for the Israelites in exile to celebrate Purim and read the scroll of Esther in synagogues. They attempted to make sure that everything Israel did was consecrated to HaShem.

Behold, Purim is well known in every Israelite home, and its celebrants dedicate this holiday to laughter, merriment, eating, and heavy drinking, even to the point of inebriation. Therefore, the sages established this holiday as a commandment so that it would be holy

---

462 John 5:1: "There was a festival for the Jews." This festival is Purim, for it is in the month of Adar, prior to the arrival of spring, that the waters of the Bethesda pool would be agitated. And in John 6:4 he says, "The appointed time of Passover is on the brink of arrival." This passage further supports that the festival spoken of in 5:1 is Purim.

463 [Psalms 113–118. The recitation of the *Hallel* signifies an established or sanctified Jewish holiday.]

to HaShem. They did so in order to prevent the Israelites from being foolhardy and reckless.

HAMAN IN EVERY GENERATION

These sages also found many words in this scroll that would serve to comfort the Israelites in all their troubles during their exile, for men like Haman can be found in every single generation. Such men suffer offense from one person and pour out their burning wrath on the entire people.

Mordechai had offended Haman by not kneeling or bowing down to him. Haman was a viceroy to the king, and everyone who saw him bowed. It is no surprise then that Haman felt enraged at Mordechai, so much so that he wanted to utterly destroy him and wipe him off the face of the earth. Yet how was the entire people of Israel guilty of sin? Only one Jew dared to incite the wrath of the king. Did they command him to do so? Did they encourage him to offend Haman? Did they tell Mordechai, "You should do this"? They probably had no idea what Mordechai was going to do. Even if they did know, perhaps they scolded and reprimanded him for doing such an offensive thing.

Haman did not weigh the matter in justice and righteousness. He did not seek the counsel of truthful people who loved righteousness. Instead he counseled himself and decided to give a bribe of ten thousand pieces of silver to the King's stewards to deposit into the royal treasury. He thereby purchased the authority to decree that every Israelite living in the provinces under Ahasuerus' rule was to be destroyed.

Are there not men like Haman in every generation? Many antagonists have risen up against us in order to wipe us off the face of the earth. Countless slanderers and adversaries have tried to bring all of us—our entire people—to an end: young and old, women and children alike. All this because one or two people offended them and caused their anger to flare up inside them.

WHAT WAS INTENDED FOR EVIL, HASHEM USED FOR GOOD

Yet HaShem in his abundant kindness and compassion overturned all this evil and used it for good. From the bitter has come the sweet, and from viciously angry bees has come delicate honey. From Mordechai came Haman's foaming rage upon us, and from the household of Mordechai came the remedy to heal the broken people. The foolish king who gave his ring to Haman to do whatever he saw fit to the Israelites transferred that same ring to Mordechai the Jew. In the name of the king Mordechai sent letters to the Israelites, calling them to assemble and defend themselves, destroying and killing all who came to murder them.

This account should bring comfort to all Israelites in the Diaspora. In his great mercy, HaShem always prepares the remedy before delivering the affliction, and the same means by which he afflicts his people he also heals them. There are certainly many good lessons in this book, and I do not need to belabor the point in order to prove it. For this reason the sages of the Mishnah established the reading of the scroll of Esther as law in Israel. They even decreed that this would be a holy day, a day of drinking and joyfulness, sending gifts to neighbors, and giving alms to the poor.

We who observe the Torah of Moses and the Testimony of Yeshua the Messiah also rejoice and celebrate during Purim. The days of Purim are a family and household holiday of joy for us as well. While we read the scroll we give thanks and worship God on high because of the goodness and kindness he showed to our people, rescuing them in every time of trouble and healing every affliction. We glorify his name for guarding Esther in all her ways, giving her the strength and courage to go before the king and request mercy for her people. This book testifies that Esther was a pious woman. Every daughter of Israel in every generation should learn from her.

Here in the Diaspora we pray to our Heavenly Father, pouring out words and supplications before him, asking him to remove every trouble and the hatred of our enemies so that we will not be forced to take vengeance upon them:

Vengeance belongs to you, HaShem. You avenge and give recompense. What can we do? Our hands are not strong enough and our arms are too short to save. HaShem, it is in your hand to afflict and it is in your hand to heal. If Haman were to rise up in this generation to trouble us, please HaShem, God of mercy, who has compassion on all mankind, and who has given his only son—Yeshua the Messiah—as a communal sacrifice on behalf of all who have been struck and afflicted by sin so that they may be healed, please have mercy on us. Remove the accuser, troubler, and enemy from us so that he may not overtake us.

OUR JOY AND OUR HOPE

Behold, we are joyful and merry on Purim. These sentiments are national and universal for each and every Jewish person. For this reason my hope continues to grow. My hope is that my Jewish brothers will open their eyes and see that HaShem has sent the remedy before he sent the affliction by sending us Yeshua the Messiah to be our ransom, righteousness, and holiness. He is grace, kindness, and truth, and our redemption is in him. In him Israel will return to being a people again, and HaShem will send the pillar of cloud to guide Israel by day and a pillar of fire by night. He will guard Israel from all pain and torment, for Israel will walk securely in the Light of the World.

Behold, we rejoice and send gifts to our neighbors. Sending gifts is a sign of brotherhood and love, and we are all brothers. One God created us, and he gave us one Torah, and all of us have one Shepherd who gave his life as an atonement on behalf of the flock he tends. Behold, our joy is as great as it was in ancient days during the harvest festival. However, our joy is entirely consecrated to HaShem. We reject frivolity and regard recklessness as shameful. Our joy is not fleshly, acquired through wine, rather it is a joy of the spirit for all the good things HaShem has bestowed upon us.

As we sit at the table to dine, we dine on HaShem's words, and we will tell our neighbors of the miracles and wonders that HaShem performed for his people Israel and for all who dwell on earth. He makes his sun to shine on the evil and good alike, and he causes the rains to fall on the righteous as well as the wicked. Through Yeshua the Messiah he grants life and kindness to all who desire righteousness and life. And it is not just to us Jews that he has shown signs of his kindness, but to all the peoples and nations who turn to him.

This is how we celebrate Purim, and this is the joy that it elicits within us. This holiday is also holy to HaShem, even if he did not directly command it in the Torah. The sages of the Mishnah and those who came after them made this holiday a regulation and celebrated it themselves. Our Master Yeshua told us to obey everything they teach us because they sit in the seat of Moses, and we obey the commands of our Master. We long for the day when our Jewish brothers will realize that they have the remedy in the blood of the Redeemer. We long for the day when they will not separate themselves into factions against their fellow Jews, but will sit with all of them and celebrate this familial holiday together. Then HaShem will have compassion on all his people Israel. Amen.

דִּבְרֵי שָׁלוֹם וֶאֱמֶת
WORDS OF PEACE AND TRUTH

(אסתר ט׳:ל׳) (Esther 9:30)

יהודה מתחנן   JUDAH PLEADS

א   I

הַמַּלְכָּה הָעֲדָנָה הַצְּרוּרָה בִּצְרוֹר־הַח
הָאָחוֹת הַיְקָרָה, שָׁם בִּשְׁלַוֹת נֶצַח!
הַבִּיטִי עַל עַמֵּךְ, הַשְׁקִיפִי נָא מִשָּׁמַיִם
עַל גּוֹי זֶה הַצִּלְתְּ מִכְּלִמַּת רֶצַח.

O gentle queen, who in the bundle of life is bound!
Beloved sister, who in eternal serenity resides!
Look upon your people; from heaven's heights gaze down;
Rescue this nation as murder reproaches and derides.

ב   II

עוֹדוֹ קוֹדֵר יִתְהַלֵּךְ, עוֹד יֶאֱנַח מָרָה
נַפְשׁוֹ עָלָיו תֶּאֱבָל, עוֹד יֻדְכֶּה יָשׁוּחַ
הַבּוֹגֵד עוֹדוֹ בּוֹגֵד, וַחֲמָתוֹ לֹא סָרָה
וִיהוּדָה יָדוֹד בְּאֵין אוֹנִים וָכֹחַ.

For in gloom walks he still, still with a bitter moan,
His soul languishes on, he is still beaten and bent;
The cheater still cheats, and his wrath has not flown,
And Judah is among the weak and the spent.

ג   III

יָדוֹד יַעַ בְּשִׁבְרוֹן מָתְנַיִם
מֵאֶרֶץ לְאֶרֶץ וּמִפֵּאָה לְפֵאָה
נִגְרָשׁ נִרְדָּף בַּחֲמַת אַפַּיִם
וּלְפָנָיו וּלְאַחֲרָיו יִקְרְאוּ „צֵאָה".

He wanders about with disjointed hips
From land to land, from corner to corner,
He is expelled, pursued, and with burning rage on
    their lips
They will call after him, "Get out of here, foreigner!"

ד   IV

הָאֲגָגִים לֹא מֵתוּ, עוֹד יִפְרְצוּ פֶּרֶץ
וְאֶת אַחֶיךָ יִשְׂטְמוּ מַשְׂטֵמָה נִמְרָצָה
יָמִירוּ כְבוֹדָם בְּקָלוֹן, יְתַעֲבוּם כְּשֶׁרֶץ
יְחָרְפוּם יְגַדְּפוּם גַּם יַרְבּוּ לָמוֹ נְאָצָה.

The Aggagites have not yet died, they still widen
    the breach,
Your brothers they loathe with a powerful rancor,
Exchanging glory for disgrace, despising them as insect,
    as leach,
Insulting and cursing, blaspheming with great fervor.

ה   V

קוּמִי הֲדַסָּה, שִׁפְכִי נָא דִמְעוֹתַיִךְ כַּמַּיִ
יָחֹן אֶת עַמּוֹ מַלְכֵּךְ הַגּוֹאֵל וּמוֹשִׁיעַ
שַׁאֲלִי רַחֲמִים עַל עַמֵּךְ זֶה אָהַבְתָּ
    שִׁבְעָתַיִם
יְחַלְּצֵהוּ מִמֵּצַר, וּמִידֵי פּוֹרְצֵי פֶּרֶץ יוֹשׁ

Arise Hadassah, pour out like water your tears,
That your King, Redeemer, Savior may pardon, may save;
Request mercy for your people whom you love seven
    times as dear,
And rescue your nation from the bottomless grave.

אסתר עונה   ESTHER RESPONDS

א   I

יְהוּדָה! עַמִּי! יוֹשֵׁב בְּסֵתֶר לִבָּתִי!
אַהֲבָתִי לָךְ עַזָּה גַם נֶאֱמָנָה.
יְגוֹנְךָ הוּא יְגוֹנִי, יִלְלָתְךָ יִלְלָתִי.
אֲהָהּ! כִּי פָנָה הוֹדְךָ גַּם זִיוְךָ פָּנָה.

Judah! My people! In my heart's secret chambers you
    reside!
My love for you is intense and true.
Your agony is mine, your cry is my cry,
How your majesty and splendor to naught are reduced.

ב   II

אַךְ מִקּוֹל יִלְלָתְךָ נִדְהַמְתִּי נִבְהַלְתִּי.
כִּי לָמָה זֶה מִמֵּצַר אֵלַי קָרָאתָ?
הֲלֹא כָמוֹךָ גַם אֲנִי בְּעָוֹן חוֹלָלְתִּי
הַאוּכַל אֲנִי כַפֵּר אִם לְמַלְכְּךָ חָטָאתָ?

The sound of your wailing has startled me, frightened me,
But why do you call me while in your dire strait?
Have not I—just as you—through crime desecrated
    equally,
Can I atone for your sin and your King's punishment
    abate?

ג   III

הִנֵּה גּוֹאֵל הֵקִים לָךְ זֶה רַבּוֹת בַּשָּׁנִים
אֶת בְּנוֹ יְחִידוֹ, אֶת הַמְנַחֵם יֵשׁוּעַ;
אוֹתוֹ עוֹדְךָ מְתָעֵב גַּם הַיּוֹם כְּלְפָנִים
תְּמָאֵן, תְּמָאֵס בָּאוֹר לַצַּדִּיקִים זָרוּעַ

The Redeemer has raised up for you so many years ago
The Comforter, Yeshua, his one and unique son;
Just as before so you still loathe him now,
You continue to refuse the light sown for the righteous
    ones.

ד   IV

מִבֵּית לֶחֶם עָלְתָה גֶּפֶן פּוֹרַחַת
גַּם הִבְשִׁילוּ אֶשְׁכְּלוֹתֶיהָ: „פִּדְיוֹן וָיֶשַׁע".
הִנֵּה דַם עֲנָבֶיהָ לְפִצְעֲךָ הַמִּרְקַחַת
יָהּ הֵכִינָהּ לְעַם־שָׁבֵי־פֶשַׁע.

From Bethlehem arose a blossoming vine,
Its clusters of ransom and salvation ripened, and it
    was pruned.
HaShem has prepared for those who repent of all their
    crimes
The blood of its grapes as healing balm to all their wounds.

ה   V

„בֹּאוּ אֵלַי כָּל נֹשְׂאֵי עָמָל וּתְלָאָה
וַאֲנִי אֶתֵּן לָכֶם מְנוּחַת־נֶפֶשׁ וּמַרְגּוֹעַ"
הַבְּשׂוֹרָה הַזֹּאת גַּם לָךְ יָצְאָה
אֵלֶיהָ תִּפְנֶה, לְקוֹלָהּ תִּשְׁמַע שָׁמוֹעַ.

"Come to me all who labor and bear trouble,
Complete rest for your souls shall I surely give."
This good news was issued for you, too, its value doubled,
Turn to it and listen closely to its voice and surely live!

אָז, יִשְׂרָאֵל, תִּוָּשַׁע תְּשׁוּעַת עוֹלָמִים
יֵחָפְרוּ וַיֵּבוֹשׁוּ נֶצַח כָּל אוֹיְבֶיךָ הָאֲגָגִים.

Thus shall you, Israel, be saved with salvation unending,
And your Aggagite foes shall be ever shamed for their
    dissenting.

THE EVENTS OF PASSOVER[464]

Volume I Issue 7, Nisan 5648 (1888) pgs. 103–112

I.

It was a night of vigil in the Jewish settlement of a small Austrian village, and joy abounded. The Jews in that village were sighing over the yoke of life—the yoke of Egypt as it were—that weighed heavily upon them. They labored to procure bread by the sweat of their brow, but there was no bread. Their anguished cries reached Heaven. Only during the festivals did they forget all their labors and set their hearts solely upon rejoicing, and on the night of vigil their joy increased beyond measure. They imagined arising like powerful giants and leaving Egypt en masse like military battalions as they once did so long ago, with the sea splitting before them—instantly becoming a free people, nevermore to toil and labor.

There was joy in the village mayor's house on this festival eve. A warm light emanated from every corner of the house, both lower and upper levels. In one of the upper rooms the members of the household gathered together to sit and listen to the Passover story. Israel Ben-Tzviel reclined, dressed in white, wearing an ornate head covering, while his

---

464 [According to Reverend William Daland—the editor of the Jewish Christian periodical entitled *The Peculiar People*—the following story is true, only the names of the characters have been changed. According to Daland, the figure of Eliakim is actually Lucky. See "A Translated Extract from the Hebrew Monthly 'Eduth l'Israel' (Witness unto Israel)," *The Peculiar People* 1 (1888–1889): 30–53.]

wife, sons, and daughters sat around the table. Even the young woman Hannah who taught Israel's daughters and Eliakim the teacher, who tutored his two sons, sat with them. Israel performed the full Passover Seder, going through the entire Passover Haggadah with the assistance of his children. Even Eliakim participated in the seder in ardent faith, sanctifying the day, washing his hands, and eating bitter herbs: everything written in the Haggadah.

Hannah alone did not participate in the ritual. She was like the third of the four sons in the Haggadah.[465] Her eyes wandered and darted back and forth as if to ask, "What is this?" From time to time, the family members laughed at her. Only Eliakim did not laugh, for he was engrossed in the seder, so much so that everyone was astonished.

On that night Eliakim appeared as if he himself had left Egypt with his dough on his shoulder. He read the words of the story with holy emotion, sometimes in a strong voice, sometimes in a soft voice, depending on the context of the portion. During the meal the events of the Israelite exodus from Egypt were on his tongue, recounting them as if he had seen the mighty acts that HaShem performed for Israel with his very own eyes. When he read aloud, "Next year in Jerusalem!" his heart erupted with excitement and he added, "amen and amen" with all his might.

His behavior that night surprised the members of the household. They also did not understand why he would occasionally reword the things written in the Haggadah. He added many embellishments here and there. In the section that begins with the words, "How much more so," he would add, "And he renewed his covenant through a sacrifice to atone for all our transgressions," and so on.

Yet neither Hannah's obliviousness nor Eliakim's strange enthusiasm detracted from the joy of that festive night. On the contrary, they heightened the joy. The members of the household teased and laughed at Hannah. They recounted to her how with a strong hand HaShem brought us out from Egypt, and for this reason we participate in this seder. They even taunted Eliakim a bit harshly, saying that even though he had suddenly turned into a great believer that evening his piety was

---

465 [The "simple" or clueless son.]

sure to vanish along with the night. This is how they amused themselves, and afterward the Passover seder was completed in accordance with its rules and regulations. Those reclining arose from their chairs and each went to his or her own room to embrace slumber and to delight in the night's sweet dreams.

II.

Slumber came sweetly for Yetta, the lady of the house. She was exhausted from her Passover preparations, but her joy surpassed all limits that night. She was the daughter of parents who came from noble families in Israel and Judah. In her father's house, Torah and nobility united together. Her mother, on whose lap she was reared, was a woman of valor who feared HaShem and observed all the Torah commands that apply to women. Yetta learned the ways of her mother.

When the time came for her to be spoken for, her father chose a candidate whom he deemed suitable and honorable who also came from a noble Israelite family. He, too, was raised in the laps of renowned Torah teachers. The early days of her marriage to Israel Ben-Tzviel were wonderful. HaShem blessed her with daughters and sons, and her husband followed in the ways of his father and observed the Torah and the commandments. He grew his *peyot*[466] long and he wore clothes that observant Jews wore in that country. He never studied the wisdom of the Gentiles, nor did he ever entertain it.

Then, abruptly, a different spirit came upon him. He changed his garments and wore clothing consistent with those Jews who rebelled against the Torah, and he walked in the ways of the Gentiles. He cut off his *peyot* and occasionally shaved his beard whenever he went to the capital city. If Yetta was not present with him in the room, he would forget to lay *tefillin* daily. He had his daughters educated by a Gentile tutor, and she taught them literature, languages, how to sing, play instruments, and dance. He forgot the words of Rabbi Eliezer who said that a woman's wisdom is in her spindle (b. *Yoma* 66b).

---

466 [Side locks.]

He also educated his sons in these evil ways. He handed them over to instructors and tutors who did not know the teachings of Rabbi Chiya or Rav, nor did they know the *Shulchan Aruch* or *Chayei Adam*. May I not be a gossiper or reveal secrets, but I will reveal that they did not even know the Holy Writings! He gave his sons to teachers such as these, and Yetta cried in secret day and night. She greatly feared that the hearts of her daughters and sons would turn away from the God of Israel. She pleaded with her husband to turn away from the evil path, for if he did not, she believed she would be cut off before her time had come. He did not listen to her, for he did not find a religious teacher whom he liked.

In those days, a man came from Germany to live in that area. That man's good reputation circulated throughout the whole region. He was a wise and educated man, well-versed in foreign languages and philosophy. He was also well-versed in the Hebrew language and Jewish literature. All those who were learned and knowledgeable in Jewish wisdom revered this man's name. Even his knowledge in mystical literature and Jewish mysticism surpassed all his contemporaries. Eliakim was his name.

Yet his ways were deemed strange, for even though Eliakim's value was great in the eyes of others, it was small in his. He was humble before everyone and spoke softly and tenderly. He had no properties or possessions, rather his fate was that of a poor man. His clothing attested to the fact that Eliakim never found wealth. Nevertheless, he constantly helped the poor by giving charity and showing kindness. There were, however, some who gossiped and slandered, saying he had come to lead the Israelites astray after the impurity of the Gentiles and other such things. But this man found favor in Israel Ben-Tzviel's eyes, and he brought him to live in his house and educate his sons.

From the time Eliakim began teaching in Yetta's house, a new spirit entered the hearts of her husband and children. Each day they began to cherish the treasures of our people more and more. Every evening, without fail, Israel would sit with Eliakim the teacher—along with the teacher's two pupils—and together they would study and discuss everything that was happening among the Jewish people, including controversies between one rabbi and another. Occasionally Yetta would offer her own thoughts about these controversies. Eliakim was careful not to embarrass or disgrace her, so he respected everything she said without dispute.

As time passed she realized that the evil rumors she heard about him were not true. Eliakim did not give his heart over to the impurity of the Gentiles as the gossipers had said. Rather he loved his people Israel with all his heart. Nevertheless, she was still afraid, for during the entire time that he lived in their house she never saw him perform a commandment like she had seen in her father's house or amongst the Jews of that region.

However, this night every fear left her, for she saw with her very own eyes that Eliakim was a faithful Jew. In addition, he turned her husband's and children's hearts back toward her. It delighted and comforted her to see her husband and children celebrating Passover, just as Israel had done in the first years of their marriage. Her joy was overwhelming and her slumber was sweet that night. Israel Ben-Tzviel was also overjoyed in seeing the raging tempest inside his wife's heart subside and pass. Now she was no longer distressed over him.

Yet sleep eluded Israel's sons and daughters. They were intelligent and inquisitive, and the question of, "Why was this night different from all other nights?" kept them wide awake. What happened to Eliakim their faithful teacher whose ways, up until now, were spiritual in nature? Today he had changed into one who obeys the letter of the Torah and not just the spirit.

Hannah also could not fall asleep. She tossed and turned on her bed like a door on its hinge. Countless questions rose up within her, for she was dumbfounded by what she saw. She was a Gentile. Her father and mother were registered Christians. Occasionally they would go to church on an important holiday, but they were not devoted to matters of faith or seeking truth. They were not familiar with the Scriptures, nor did they study them. Hannah also did not know these things.

When she was six years old, her father sent her to school where she learned to read, write, and do calculations, but she never learned anything of the Scriptures. Even when she was fourteen and went to high school, no one ever taught her these things. HaShem graced her with great talent and keen intellect; however, she did not know the true source of wisdom. She did not know why she went to the Roman Catholic church every year to perform the rituals. In reality she did not believe in anything, rather she went because it was customary to go.

She was ignorant of the ways of the Jews; she had never seen how they lived. She had only heard that they were exclusive and incredibly wealthy on account of charging 100 percent interest and other such things. She had also heard that the Jews killed the Son of God, and they were therefore evil. However, she did not delight in these rumors. When Israel Ben-Tzviel asked if she would come and tutor his daughters and two sons, she joyfully responded, "I will!" because she truly desired to see how the Jews lived.

She lived in the Ben-Tzviel household for about a year. She saw much; she learned much. One thing she learned was that the Israelites distinguished themselves from the Gentiles in what they ate and drank. When she saw that the new generation no longer distinguished themselves, she said to herself that the day was near when the Jews would intermingle with the other peoples of the earth and they would assimilate and become one family. She thought, "Not long from now the Jews will eat everything we eat and they too will become Christians."

Everything changed when Eliakim came to the Ben-Tzviel home. He brought a vibrant spirit with him. Even if people thought his words strange, his magical charisma never left him and he attracted the hearts of those around him. Hannah was unable to resist it. She would sit and listen to everything Eliakim said. Every day she came to respect him more.

She had never seen a man like him amongst the Gentiles she knew, nor even amongst the Jews. Nor did she know what he was. She asked herself, "If Eliakim is a Jew as he says, then why does he exalt the name of Jesus Christ in front of me and speak about him as if he were a faithful believer? I am ashamed, for I have never had such a faith! And if he is a believer in Christ, why does he say that he is a Jew? If he is truly a freethinker, if he has cast off the fetters of religion, why is he deceiving us for no reason? Could a righteous man such as he be so deceptive?" She did not expect to see Eliakim performing the "commandments of men" and other irrational ceremonies. Thus she tossed and turned to these thoughts until it was time to get out of bed.

III.

The night passed and a morning without clouds came. The dawn opened its eyelids and lavished the face of creation with its radiant light. Ben-Tzviel's sons, Joseph and Solomon, arose to enjoy the early morning along with their sisters. Sitting on the outer railing of the house, they talked about Eliakim their teacher, over whom they had puzzled all night long. Their sisters Batya and Penina also entered the discussion. While they talked, Hannah came out and joined them.

She told them she could not sleep the whole night because she could not figure out who or what Eliakim was. Joseph and Solomon said, "We cannot figure it out either, even though we are his pupils! He has revealed many mysteries to us, but he has shown you even greater respect lately, for you have found favor in his eyes. He speaks with you about the deepest of things, from the acts of creation to mystical subjects, from the wisdom of God to his love for mankind. He has not withheld anything from you. Why not ask him yourself? We would be most grateful to you, for we also long to know about him."

Hannah blushed at her students' words, and she answered them, "Indeed, I know that he has always been kind and truthful with me, but how can I summon the courage to ask him these personal and intimate questions?" Joseph, Solomon, Batya, and Penina were disappointed to hear this, as was Hannah herself, but they all had the idea to approach Eliakim together and ask him. The three girls had to wait, however, while Ben-Tzviel, Eliakim, and the two boys went to where the Jews of that village prayed the afternoon *minchah* prayers. Afterward they returned and retired to their respective rooms: Israel to rest and Eliakim and the boys to study Torah.

Eliakim was in the library when the door opened and all of his students, boys and girls, entered. The sudden audience startled Eliakim but he felt no apprehension, for he was prepared at all times to answer any question posed to him.

"We came to ask you some large questions," Hannah began wisely, since she was the designated spokesperson.

"Ask whatever you wish. I am more than happy to be of service to you as HaShem permits," replied Eliakim lovingly.

"But this time I want to ask you some personal questions."

"If my answers may be of some benefit to you, then I will reveal all. I will not hide anything."

"Then tell us, who and what are you? We have discussed this and thought about it, but we have been unable to figure it out. Your ways are too difficult for us to understand. What are you? Are you a Jew, a Gentile, or what? Do you follow the teaching of Moses or the teachings of the Gentiles, or are you a free thinker with no religion at all?"

Eliakim answered:

> Your question is a complicated one, my sister. Forgive me for speaking to you thus, but how can you ask if I am a Gentile?! Do you not know me, and do you not see that I live among my people, that I am a Hebrew and I fear the God of heaven? All my deeds attest to this. If evil people slander and whisper wicked things about me, saying that I have betrayed my people, they are lying. I love my people with a love that knows no bounds. The holy tongue that was spoken by Isaiah, Jeremiah, etc. is of the utmost value to me, and I guard the history of my people as I would the apple of my eye. Jewish blood flows through my veins.
>
> As to whether or not I observe the Torah of Moses, even if I explained it you would not understand. You are a Gentile and have not studied the ways of Scripture. You say to yourself that Christianity is the religion of the Gentiles, but you have not weighed this matter with knowledge and truth.
>
> It is true, many Gentiles have now turned to the Christian discipline since they have cast away their idols and have come to know that there is a God who judges the earth. In so doing they have been engrafted into the natural olive tree and have also become sons of Abraham according to the spirit. But the Torah never ceased being the Torah of Israel. The Messiah is the purpose of the Torah of Moses and Israel. Thus the Torah

of the messianic[467] faith is the same as the Torah of Judaism: it is not the teaching of the Gentiles.

Please bear with me as I explain this more thoroughly. The Torah of truth is but one Torah. It is the same Torah that HaShem, who is good, gave to his people Israel through Moses on the mountain amidst the fire. It was then that HaShem made an everlasting covenant with our forefathers. Yet he did not make it with our forefathers alone, but with those of us who are alive today. The covenant was made for me, for you, and for all humanity. But the Torah was first given to the children of Israel, for they are the natural branches of the holy tree.

All the other Gentiles were ignorant and exchanged the glory of God for images of men and creatures. So God gave them over to their impurities. Yet the time of compassion and grace has come to the Gentiles. About forty years before the destruction of the Temple, HaShem took pity on all mankind and sent his only son Yeshua the Messiah, the Son of God, in power and majesty. He gave him as a sacrifice to eradicate sin, atone for transgression, and to bring everlasting righteousness.

Through this sacrifice HaShem renewed his covenant with the people of Israel, and he opened to the rest of the nations the gate through which believers enter. The good news of God went out powerfully among the Gentiles, and he gave them the Holy Spirit, cleansing their hearts from sin. In this age a tremendous number of Gentiles believe in the good news, and great nations have attached themselves to that good news.

Even now my people Israel are obstinate and refuse to turn their hearts to the faith proclaimed according to the good news, and yet the first evangelists came from them! The good news of Messiah originated in Jerusalem, spreading

---

467 [Or Christian. Lucky sometimes uses the terms "messianic" and "Christian" synonymously.]

to Asia and Europe. Most of the first believers were Jews. In every generation thereafter HaShem has even opened the hearts of a few Israelites, and they believed in HaShem and his Messiah.

Even in this generation HaShem has been kind and gracious, opening the eyes of a small number of my people so that they would see the gleaming light of the good news of Messiah and be saved through faith. I, too, am one of those who were saved by HaShem's mercy. I believe that Yeshua, the Prince of Life, gave his life as an atonement even for me, and has given me a portion among the children of God.

Nevertheless, the Gentiles who believe in the good news do not possess some other teaching. Rather, they have received the same Torah of HaShem, which was revealed first to Israel through the veil of Moses and then later revealed when the Temple's veil was torn in two, from top to bottom, as the earth shook and the rocks split. So how can you say that I observe the teaching of the Gentiles? Their teaching comes from the Torah of Israel. Your eyes are sealed, my beloved sister, since you have not read the Scriptures nor studied the Torah of truth. You are like a blind woman groping the wall in the darkness, as are you Joseph, Solomon, Batya, and Penina, my dear students.

Hannah listened to all his words and responded:

Please forgive me, my instructor and teacher! Your words are true wisdom, but I cannot understand them. I would be very surprised if there was one in one thousand among your people who agreed with this path you have chosen for yourself. Where is the source from whence you derived these thoughts? I am too small to understand why you liken your people to the branches of a holy tree. And ... and ... what was that you said about the Temple curtain being torn from top to bottom? All your words are much too figurative and metaphoric for me.

Eliakim replied:

I know very well that my words are like those of a sealed book to you since you do not know the Scriptures. Indeed, how could you understand what I am saying? But I implore you to guard my words in your heart, for a day will come when a light from heaven will shine upon you, then you will understand all these things. If you listen to my counsel and if you are wise, you will devote yourself to study the Holy Writings in knowledge and understanding. Afterward you will be able to discern.

Hannah answered:

My heart truly thanks you. You have been very kind with me, teaching me wisdom and knowledge in humility on many occasions, including today. However, please bear with me if I continue to burden you with these questions that all the children asked. Why were you acting differently last night? Why was last night different from all other nights?

Eliakim answered and said:

Do not be astonished, my sister. It is true. This night is unique among all other nights of the year. There is none like it. The events that occurred on it were greater than anything that has ever occurred in all of human history. Many are the miracles that HaShem performed thereon. On this night HaShem showed grace and kindness to all the peoples, but most especially to the people of Israel. On this night the great nation of Israel was born. This has been a night of vigil for all Israelites throughout their generations because HaShem brought his people Israel out of Egypt with a strong hand, smiting the Egyptians and rescuing our entire household.

The Passover sacrifice was the first sign of our people. HaShem commanded that the whole community of Israel slaughter the unblemished lamb together, without breaking its bones, as a Passover to HaShem. From the day HaShem brought all the people out of Egypt, Judah became a nation and Israel a dominion. The Passover sacrifice is still a sign of our people, for Israel has still remained a nation even though dispersed and scattered throughout all the nations.

The day about which Zechariah prophesied will yet come, when HaShem will pour out upon the house of David and the inhabitants of Jerusalem a spirit of grace and supplication, and they will look to him whom they have pierced, and they will mourn for him as one mourns for an only son. Then they will celebrate the Passover sacrifice of the Lamb of God who bears all the transgression of the world and who was sacrificed by the entire community of Israel on this night without breaking any of his bones.

How beautiful is this image that HaShem has shown our people! HaShem revealed it to those who obey his word. This vision fills my heart with hope. Behold, the children of Israel are waking from their slumber and the light is shining on them. Who knows? Perhaps this year HaShem will uphold his word, which he spoke to the spirit, "Breathe on these who were slain and they shall live." HaShem will one day open the graves of my people and bring them to the land of Israel. The Son of David will be king over them and he will establish an eternal covenant of peace with them. Israel is the stake upon which the glory of all the nations of the earth hangs. If Israel's scattering brought a time of favor for all the inhabitants of the earth, then how much more so will their regathering be?

Thus, my sister, Passover is a wondrous night. The events that took place on it changed the course of history. Who knows what is yet to occur? But the heavens shall pass away and the earth shall vanish, yet the words of HaShem shall never disappear. He said that Israel shall live again. Therefore I await Israel's salvation in hope and silence.

Eliakim gripped the hearts of his listeners. They sat there with their eyes wide open, intently fixed on Eliakim. Afterward, the youngest son, Solomon, spoke up and said, "Hannah was right, your words are difficult! How will we be able to understand you? But if we have found favor with you, continue to deal kindly with us and show us what we must do in order to understand these lofty thoughts." Eliakim answered in sincere love:

> I have already shown you the way. Opened in front of you, Joseph and Solomon, are the books of the Torah and the prophets in Hebrew, along with the books of the evangelists and the apostles. Read them, either in Greek or Hebrew, and you will find all this goodness and your souls shall live. And I give this book to you, my sisters; take it. It contains all the books of the Torah, prophets, evangelists, and apostles together. Read it and discover the truth. My greatest hope is that your eyes would be opened and that you would see the precious light. May HaShem be with you.

With those words he handed each of the girls a book of the Scriptures translated into the common vernacular.[468] Afterward they went their separate ways, for the day had quickly turned to evening and it was time for services. Eliakim and his two students went to pray.

IV.

Some ten years passed, and the Ben-Tzviel family celebrated Passover nine times without Eliakim present. A scholarly conference in Switzerland required his attendance, and he never did return. He left the Ben-Tzviel house brokenhearted and the Ben-Tzviel children also wept. Everyone loved Eliakim intensely, but Eliakim's love of truth and wisdom did not permit him to remain in this village, so he left. Hannah, too, left after having celebrated only three Passovers in the Ben-Tzviel house.

Joseph and Solomon grew quickly. Joseph became mayor of the village and became powerful and wealthy. Solomon went to university and studied philosophy and science. Penina had been given in marriage

---

468 [Yiddish or German.]

and already had a son. Batya had already given birth to a son and a daughter by then. Yetta had left the valley of sorrows and passed away, ascending to heaven to delight in ethereal joys. However, Eliakim knew none of these things. He was like a stranger to his pupils. Why did he not write to them? Yet all his ways were strange, so why should they be surprised at his silence?

Throughout his journeys Eliakim arrived in a major city one day. He had heard that a righteous teacher of the Messianic faith named Benjamin lived there, so he went to see him. He was shocked to discover that Benjamin already knew of him, for he was originally from the region where Israel Ben-Tzviel lived. In fact, he was seventeen years old when Eliakim lived with the Ben-Tzviel family.

"This time I will hold onto you and not let you go!" Benjamin told Eliakim. "You shall not leave my house, for I am greatly indebted to you."

"How so?" asked Eliakim astonished.

"Do me the honor of staying here with me for a while, and I will show you what I mean," Benjamin replied.

A few moments later the door opened and Benjamin's wife entered the room. She stopped and stood at the threshold like a statue, marveling in astonishment. She composed herself and called out, "Eliakim my teacher!"

Eliakim answered her as if only ten months had passed since he had last seen her instead of ten years, "Why are you so surprised Hannah?"

"How could I not be?" she replied.

"Tell me everything that has happened to you since I left, for I am in your home and attentively listening," Eliakim said.

Hannah replied:

> The events of Passover did all this. The Passover of such and such year is still impressed in my memory and I will never forget it all the days of my life! It was then that the gate through which the righteous enter was opened to me. I began to try to understand the Scriptures, and I found the Way, the Truth, and the Life. God has greatly blessed me, for he has given me the honor of bringing others to his glorious footstool. My

husband Benjamin is one of them. I learned the "language of Canaan" [Hebrew] and I have never ceased studying it.

Eliakim listened intently. After she had finished he asked, "What ever happened to the Ben-Tzviel children?"

"Joseph, Solomon, Batya, and Penina have never forgotten that Passover," she replied, "and all their deeds bring blessing to the entire land."

"Oh, that Passover!" Eliakim cried out, full of emotion, "Now I know that the Word of HaShem does not return void, rather it accomplishes what it was sent to do. From now on I will be doubly encouraged, and if my heart ever weakens I shall remember the events of that Passover and I will be clothed in a new spirit."

Hannah and Benjamin rejoiced and swore that the "events of Passover" would be kept on the doorposts of their house all the days of their lives.

RABBI SHIMON BAR YOCHAI

Volume IV Issue 2, Nisan 5657 (1897) pgs. 11–16

The eighteenth day of the month of Iyyar, the month of brilliance (*ziv*), is a festive day for the little children of Israel: it is Lag Ba'Omer.[469] As I write about this holiday, many memories return to me from my childhood and I think on all the things that I did year after year. These recollections come before me now.

RASHBI'S WEDDING

Lag Ba'Omer is a great and important holiday to me; it was then, and it still is now. I grew up in the lap of a certain sect in Israel which, in this country, is called the sect of the Chasidim.[470] This sect follows after the Baal Shem Tov of Medzhybizh (also called Rabbi Yisroel ben Eliezer, or Besht) and his disciples. For those of us who belong to this sect, Lag Ba'Omer, the day that Rashbi died,[471] is a holiday. We also

---

469 The thirty-third day of the Counting of the Omer, leading to Shavuot. This day marks the end of the plague that afflicted and killed the disciples of Rabbi Akiva.

470 Chasidim believe in miracle-workers and follow them. They seek to guide those who do not follow miracle-working rabbis and who have even strayed from following HaShem, God forbid. Thus, since our sect is called *Chasidut* (piety), the assumption is that most of the nation has strayed from HaShem's paths.

471 Rashbi is the abbreviation for Rabbi Shimon bar Yochai. It is only a tradition that this is the day of his death; we did not receive this from Sinai, so it is not necessarily for certain.

call it "Rashbi's wedding," or *"Hillula*[472] *de-Rashbi."* It is a day of joy and celebration, for on this day Rashbi abandoned the valley of sorrows and ascended to be conjoined with eternal life, forever satiated with heavenly joys.

Every single year my fellow Chasidim and I would decorate our synagogue with candles and banners. We would put the banners in the synagogue windows and on them we would write in big letters, *"Hillula de-Rashbi."* This is how it has been for generations. My joy on this day was greater than any other because the memory of Rashbi is very holy to me. From my youth I followed those who were mighty in spirit amongst our people: Rabbi Chanina ben Dosa, Rabbi Chanina ben Tradyon, Rabbi Akiva, Rabbi Shimon bar Yochai, Rabbi Pinchas ben Yair, etc. However, I loved Rashbi much more than all the others, for I believed that he was the author of the *Zohar*,[473] and in my youth I was consumed with love for the *Zohar*, studying it day and night.

THE WAYS OF THE CHASID

When I was young there was nothing I craved more than to be with Rashbi. I poured out my heart before God on high, asking him to give me the strength and fortitude to live in a cave for thirteen years, eating only carob and dates[474] like Rashbi and his son.[475] He was one

---

472 The word *hillula* means a day of joy and celebration, a wedding day. This word is used in the Talmud (b.*Brachot* 6b; 31a; b.*Sanhedrin* 105a).

473 It is no longer certain if he actually wrote it. Many scholars argue that he did not. Those scholars provide some strong evidence that somebody else wrote this book using Rashbi's name. See the book *Ari Nohem* by Rabbi Yehudah Aryeh di Modena and the writings of Rabbi Abraham Geiger. Even the learned Messianic Jewish Kabbalistic scholar Raphael Biesenthal concurs and believes the writings reflect a later composition. However, I am inclined to believe that the author of the *Zohar* did not invent everything on his own, rather that he possessed hidden, unknown scrolls that were written in antiquity that were Rashbi's teachings. Instead of writing his own name he wrote Rashbi's, since he was transmitting his words. It is therefore our duty to read this book with a critical eye, differentiating between the old and the new within it, but not dismissing it outright.

474 [Some sources say it was twelve years.]

475 See *Genesis Rabbah*, Parashat VaYishlach, and *Esther Rabbah*.

of the Chasidim—men of faith—whose whole being was constantly engrossed in the service of the heart (prayer). All his ways were ways of modesty, self-control, perseverance, and piety,[476] and he always walked after HaShem with a pure heart.

While I was still a youth I drank from the waters of his well. His instruction was like some healing remedy or magic potion for my very being, and my soul was strengthened because of it. Therefore, even now, as we approach that day, that time of the year when we commemorate him,[477] we do not fast or refrain from eating, rather we dine well in memory of his soul during the Counting of the Omer.

Rabbi Shimon bar Yochai was one of the sages of Israel: he was a Tanna.[478] The Mishnah records his name 325 times,[479] and the times that he is mentioned in the tractates of Talmud are innumerable. However, the place of his birth, the occupations of his parents (and everything that happened to them), and the events of his early life have disappeared from our records. We are only told of his father's name: Yochai, which is a shortened form of the name Yochanan.[480]

We can reasonably assume that in the dawn of his youth Rashbi was a devoted disciple and a quick learner, for his righteous end testifies to a righteous beginning. Just as Scripture says, "Do not let this book

---

476 Keifa the apostle mentioned all of these attributes (*middot*) in his second letter (1:6).

477 We call this his yahrzeit, and many scholars say this was commemorated even in the Talmudic Period.

478 [A Jewish sage in the first century CE.]

479 Professor Emil Schürer, a wise teacher with true knowledge of God from Giessen, Germany, who wrote the book entitled *The History of the Jewish People in the Time of Jesus Christ*, came up with this number through his own calculation. We can trust it, because we cannot deny that the Germans are meticulous in everything they do.

480 This is not the only name that was shortened in those days. They shortened so many that we do not even know what some of the original, longer forms were before they were shortened.

of Torah ever depart from your lips,"[481] he never let it depart from his.[482] Even after he was married he no longer continued to pursue worldly vocations in order to support his own physical needs and those of his wife; rather, he chose the vocation of eternal life. In so doing, he studied in a yeshiva in Bnei Brak,[483] the city in which Rabbi Akiva taught his students who were hungry for the bread of Torah and thirsty for the Word of HaShem. Rashbi's wife agreed with his decision to do this. How did she make a living for herself the whole time her husband was learning in Bnei Brak? This information has also disappeared, so we have no clue.

The events of his life are obscured for us, covered over tightly, and completely shrouded. We know only a little bit here and there about them. We know that he remained in Bnei Brak for thirteen years. His neighbors praised him, and Rabbi Akiva, his rabbi, ordained him. Many disciples came to collect the dust from his feet.

In those days HaShem's burning wrath was still upon the land of Israel. Hadrian Caesar was dead, but his evil intentions still thrived.[484] When Rashbi protested the actions of the Romans (for he did not heed the counsel of Bava ben Buta, who lived during the time of Herod)[485] the Roman commissioners issued an evil decree concerning him, so he was forced to flee and hide in a cave somewhere on the outskirts

---

481 Joshua 1:8.

482 In b.*Brachot* 35b Rashbi asks what will become of the Torah if man plows during the plowing time, etc. All the commentators attempt to explain Rashbi's words here, for they are hard to understand and quite strange. However, it occurs to me that Rashbi meant this as a parable. If man devotes himself to his fields, vineyards, and his means of livelihood, what will become of the Torah? Indeed, every man is tasked with making a living for himself, yet he must do so without giving his heart over to it, just as Rabbi Yehudah bar Ilai says in this *daf* (Ilai is a shortened form of Elazar). And both of them—Rashbi and Rabbi Yehudah bar Ilai—are speaking the words of Yeshua the Messiah (see Matthew 6:33–34). Only Rashbi attempted to interpret this concept, but he did not do a very good job.

483 A city in the territories of Dan. See Joshua 19:45.

484 During Antoninus' reign they annulled all the wicked decrees of Hadrian, yet all the king's advisors never ceased to put guardians in place to ascertain the thoughts and intentions of the people.

485 See b.*Bava Batra* 3b.

surrounding the city of Meron. There he remained for thirteen years.[486] His son Elazar was with him in the cave, and they sustained themselves by eating carob and drinking water. They engrossed themselves in Torah study and prayer day and night.

HaShem showed him kindness by miraculously sustaining him through those thirteen years. Then a voice from heaven told him to leave the cave. When he returned to civilization he chose to bathe in the warm springs of Tiberias, and there he resided, teaching Torah to the masses. All record of the end of his life has disappeared, and we have a tradition that his tomb is in the city of Meron.[487] Rashbi indeed was a favorite subject of legend, and legend wove an intricate crown of flowers around his head, making him into a holy man of God, for HaShem did many wondrous things for and through him.

INFLUENCES OF YESHUA AND THE "MINIM"

It is not my intent to plumb the depths of the legends or critically assess their validity. I do not attempt to separate the actual history from the embellishments and hyperbole of the legends. That will be reserved for another time. However, this much may be ascertained from the legend: Rashbi was a pious, righteous man. His theology and practice attest to this. I actually believe that the spirit of the disciples of Yeshua our Master was in him.

The teachings of Yeshua and his apostles erupted all throughout the land during his time, and disciples were being made daily. Even the nations situated around the land of Israel had sons and daughters who were being brought into the assembly of Messiah. The more the Roman caesars afflicted the disciples, both men and women, the more they multiplied and the stronger they became. They paid no heed to the fury of their oppressors and persecutors, and they sacrificed their earthly lives for eternal life in the presence of our Master. The strong resolve that Rashbi saw in those disciples greatly inspired him.

---

486 b.*Shabbat* 33b; *Genesis Rabbah* 79, etc.

487 My intention here is not to provide all the events of Rashbi's life, rather I am commemorating him. Therefore, I have not attempted to recount everything, I have only given an overview of the most notable events.

Many in Israel believed in Yeshua, and those believers remained with the rest of their brothers. They did not separate themselves, even though their brothers rejected Yeshua and burdened and insulted them with the name *minim* (sectarians). These "*minim*" loved their people sevenfold, even after their people started calling them *minim*. They continued to pray for their brothers, following Yeshua the Messiah's example when he wept over Jerusalem.

In Rashbi's days the writings of the *minim* circulated throughout the camps of Israel. The holy Gospel of Matthew was well known in the community, and Rashbi surely would have read it. Thus, it should be no surprise to us that traces of the sayings of Yeshua the Messiah and King of the Jews can be found in his teachings. Rashbi said, "When you pray, do not make your prayer a fixed formula, rather appeal for mercy and grace";[488] "Recite prayer softly in a whisper";[489] "Solomon and a hundred like him will be annulled, but not one *yod* of yours will ever be annulled!"[490]

TEACHINGS OF THE TAX-PAYING KING

I will no longer weary you, dear reader. I will bring my words to an end. If it is HaShem's will, someday I will write down all Rashbi's sayings and interpret them through the light of Yeshua's teachings. But before I leave you I want to show you proof that Rashbi read the book of Matthew. In the Gemara it says:

> Rabbi Yochanan said in the name of Rabbi Shimon bar Yochai that a stolen lulav is invalid because it is a commandment fulfilled through a transgression. Rabbi Yochanan said in the name of Rabbi Shimon bar Yochai, "What does the verse 'I, HaShem, love justice and hate robbery with a burnt offering' (Isaiah 61:8) mean? It can be compared to a king

---

488 *Pirkei Avot* 2:18.

489 b.*Sotah* 32b.

490 *Leviticus Rabbah* 19:2. Rashbi chose to use the Hebrew letter *yod* in his interpretation because he knew the teachings of Yeshua, "Until heaven and earth pass away, not one *yod* will pass away from the Torah" (see Matthew 5:18).

of flesh and blood who went to the tollbooth and said to his servants, 'Give the tax to the tax collectors,' and they said to him, 'Does not all the tax money belong to you?' He said to them: 'All those who travel this way should learn from my example never to avoid paying the tax.' So too, the Holy One, blessed be he, says, 'I, HaShem, hate robbery with a burnt offering, and my children should learn from me and flee from robbery.'" (b.*Sukkah* 30ab)

Look! Everyone who has eyes can see and will understand, even at first glance, that this king is Yeshua our King and Savior. This King commanded Shimon Keifa to go to the sea, cast a fishhook in it, and pay the tax with the money he found inside the fish's mouth: the half-shekel that the collectors were requesting (Matthew 17:24–27). This parable of Rashbi is certain proof that Rashbi read these words in Matthew. He greatly enjoyed Yeshua's words when he said, "In order that we will not be an obstacle to them," and those words penetrated the heart of this pious man who engrossed himself in prayer.[491]

He repeated those words to his own disciples and passed them down to his disciple Yochanan, and Rabbi Yochanan always spoke them in the manner that Rashbi had taught him. Rashbi did not even introduce this citation from Isaiah 61:8 of his own accord. Instead, it was also a part of the original teaching passed down by Yeshua's disciples, for Matthew employed the interpretative method of comparing one passage to another seemingly unrelated passage in order to explain the first through the second.

MATTHEW'S INTERPRETATION

In recounting the incident of the half-shekel, Matthew attempted to explain what Yeshua had said just before, "The son of man will ultimately be handed over to men" (Matthew 17:22). In essence, Matthew was asking: why would the Messiah be a man of sorrows and pain, sick and wounded because of our crimes, and beaten because of our transgressions? Because HaShem loves justice. Human beings sinned

---

491 See *Sefer Iyun Tefillah* by Rabbi Abraham Krochmal.

and the mouth of HaShem commanded that a sacrifice be brought for that sin. His words shall not be overruled. Therefore, HaShem himself made the Messiah to be the offering.

Through the medium of a sign and miracle, Yeshua commanded that the half-shekel should be paid because the kings of the land do not take the tax from their children. If the Messiah had not been the offering, there would have been "robbery with the burnt offering" (Isaiah 61:8). If the Messiah had not handed himself over to be that offering, the burnt offering would have legally been considered stolen.[492] Why did Matthew fail to cite this passage in Isaiah? I find that astonishing. Perhaps it was edited out—whether intentionally or unintentionally—when translated into Greek.[493]

Matthew placed this event of the half-shekel in the seventeenth chapter, the chapter of the transfiguration—the chapter of the sukkah—for in my opinion when Moses and Elijah appeared on the mountain it was during Sukkot, and the Gemara cites the words of Rashbi in conjunction with Sukkot in Tractate Sukkah. The critical eye will immediately notice the thread that connects the book of Matthew with the words of Rashbi. This is my commemoration of Rabbi Shimon bar Yochai, and Lag Ba'Omer is the day we remember him.

---

492 This entire chapter of Isaiah (51) is about the Messiah. Thus, when Yeshua was called up to the Torah on Shabbat as the *maftir* for Parashat Nitzavim (Deuteronomy 29:9–30:20), he read the *haftarah* in Isaiah 60, reading the entire chapter, then saying, "Today this passage has been fulfilled." Not one person rebuked him, saying, "This prophecy is not about the Messiah!" All the many commentators in Israel confirm and affirm that this is about the Messiah. Only Rashi and Radak deviated from this consensus.

493 I am of the opinion that the book of Matthew is a translation from Hebrew. I also think that a Jewish man whose native tongue was Hebrew but was a Greek scholar translated it. In the time of Rashbi the book would have still been in Hebrew.

SHAVUOT

BY A FAITHFUL CELEBRANT

Volume 4 Issue 1, Sivan 5650 (1890): 9–12

The sixth day of this month (Sivan), which is the fiftieth day of the Counting of the Omer, is a holiday for us. It is the second of three holidays that are called "pilgrimage festivals." On this day, when we were still in our own land, we ascended to the place HaShem chose for his name to dwell and all our males would appear before HaShem. We would rejoice along with our sons, daughters, manservants, maidservants, the Levite who dwelled in our gates, the stranger, the orphan, and the widow in our midst.

This day is a holy convocation. We must not do any form of work on it, for it is sanctified and dedicated to the worship of the heart (prayer), the study of Torah, joy, and delight. This holiday is also a reminder that we were once slaves to Pharaoh in Egypt.[494] Therefore, just like Passover and the Festival of Unleavened Bread, this holiday is also called, "The Festival of Liberty" (*Chag HaDror*), the festival of redemption from slavery in Egypt. Our sages call it, "The Conclusion of Passover" (*Atzeret Pesach*),[495] or just "The Conclusion" (*Atzeret*).[496] This

---

494 See Deuteronomy 16:12: "And remember that you were slaves in Egypt."

495 *Song of Songs Rabbah* 38.

496 y.*Rosh HaShanah* 1:2; y.*Chagigah* 2:4; Josephus, *Antiquities of the Jews* 3:252–254/x.6.

means that this holiday marks the end of Passover, the last day of the Festival of Unleavened Bread, as well as the end of the harvest season that began when the priesthood indicated "the day after the Sabbath," which is the second day of Passover.[497]

If we were to call this holiday, "The Beginning of the Festival of Liberty," we would be grasping the true meaning of this holiday and not missing the mark. This holiday, in its very essence, calls out to us and says, "Look at how numerous the mercies of HaShem are! He has brought the children of Israel out of Egypt and shattered the burdensome yoke that weighed them down. He led them upright to the land that he swore to give to their forefathers. He made a covenant with them and gave them the early and late rains in their proper time, abundant produce, and he blessed their harvest. His kindness has been with them every day. Indeed he is your Father, Redeemer, and Comforter."

THE FIRST OF THE FRUITS OF ISRAEL

In our present day, all Jews call this holiday "Shavuot," the name that was established in the Torah.[498] The Gentiles, who do not speak Hebrew, call it "Pentecost."[499] This is a very pleasant holiday for us, for through it Israel's suffering has been eased and his fate has improved. This holiday is the offspring of the month of Sivan, a child of the

---

497 People disagreed on this topic. See y.*Menachot* 10:3, b.*Menachot* 68b, and y.*Chagigah* 2:4. The Pharisees interpreted the word "Sabbath" to mean "festival," thus the "day after the Sabbath," or the second day of Passover, is the day that comes after Passover. The halachah agrees with the Pharisees. However, the Karaites, Samaritans, Sadducees, and Boethusians interpreted the word "Sabbath" to mean "Saturday," i.e., "the fixed Sabbath." Because of this they brought their two sheaves on Sunday, the first day of the week. We, on the other hand, act in accordance with the teachings of the Pharisees.

498 Deuteronomy 16:10.

499 In Greek, the word *Pentecost* means "fifty days" or "the fiftieth day." Thus it is called "The Festival of the Fiftieth Day." Even Josephus calls it this in *Jewish Wars* 2:39–44/iii.1, and it appears in Acts 2:1. However, Professor Franz Delitzsch of blessed memory translated it into Hebrew as Shavuot in his New Testament translation. Even in English they use the name Pentecost, and other languages, such as German, have derived their own variations of this word. Yet it is better to call it by its true Hebrew name "Shavuot." But what can we do? Even our own people in this present day speak every language *except* Hebrew.

month of elation and joy. Flowers, lily blossoms, and roses adorn it all around. Meadows are dressed in the wool of their sheep and valleys are wrapped in linen; hills are girded with elation and everything rejoices. The verdant fields are filled with goats, sheep, and livestock, and the land overflows with milk and honey.

How could we not rejoice and exult as well? How beautiful is our custom of eating milk and cream products during this holiday, for it is good to enjoy the fullness of HaShem's gifts that come from the land instead of eating the flesh of animals and fowl. It is also our custom to adorn our houses and synagogues with flowers and blossoms that give a pleasing scent to all who enter[500] and to set up thick tree branches in the synagogues and delight in their beauty and splendor.

This holiday is the remembrance of the history of our people, the remembrance of our forefathers and their way of life. In Israel this holiday used to be called the "Day of First Fruits" and "The Festival of the Harvest."[501] They cooked the crops of the field, and the whole land was filled with produce. Our fathers brought the first of every fruit of the land to the place where HaShem had chosen to dwell. How beautiful that sight must have been!

Today, because of the sin of our people, we live in exile, far away from our land, and we have no produce of the field or the vine to bring to the Temple. We have no plow and we have no harvest, we do not go up to Jerusalem to present ourselves before HaShem, and we do not bring the first of our crop or the harvest with which HaShem has blessed us.

However, our forefathers dwelt in the land beneath their own vineyards and fig trees. The work of their fields was their form of worship, and the yield they produced from their trade was consecrated to HaShem. If HaShem blessed them with the fruit of the womb, they sanctified it before HaShem, and if HaShem blessed them with abundant produce from their fields, they brought the first of all their fruits to the holy place

---

500 We find evidence for this even in Scripture. HaShem commanded the children of Israel not to allow their flocks to graze at the base of the mountain (Exodus 34:3), which teaches us that the mountain was covered in grass and all sorts of greenery.

501 See Deuteronomy 16:9 and Numbers 28:26. In Exodus 23:16 it is called the Festival of the Harvest.

and gave the gifts of thanksgiving to the priest who would offer it on HaShem's altar. Before HaShem they would proclaim:

> Our father was merely a wandering Aramean, but you, Compassionate Father, have shown your kindness and you have saved us through signs and wonders, and you have given us a land flowing with milk and honey. So now we bring to you the first fruits of our crops that you have given us. Look down at us from your holy abode and bless your people Israel and the land that you gave us as you promised our forefathers.[502]

HOW LOVELY ARE THE STEPS OF ISRAEL

How beautiful it must have been to see all the myriads of people coming up to the Holy City with full baskets in hand blessing HaShem! During the Second Temple Era, it was impossible to count the number of people in Jerusalem on this holiday,[503] for the Jews gathered there from every corner of the known world. Concerning them our sages of blessed memory say (b.*Sukkah* 49b), "How lovely are the steps of Israel when they go up to celebrate the pilgrimage festival."

In those days a miracle would occur in Israel every time they went to worship HaShem. When they were standing in prayer they were pressed together so tightly that one could not even slide his hand in between two people. However, when they were prostrated there was a large space between each person, about a full body length.[504] This was one of the many miracles that would occur in the Temple. Whoever is truly an Israelite cannot refrain from rejoicing when reminiscing over those beautiful days.

---

502 [Deuteronomy 26:5–10.]

503 See Josephus, *Antiquities of the Jews* 14:337–341/xiii.4 and *Jewish Wars* 2:39–44/iii.1.

504 *Avot de-Rabbi Natan* 35 and b.*Yoma* 21a.

THE BIRTH OF THE WORLD AND THE DECALOGUE

We have received the tradition from our sages that on this day the Torah was given on Mount Sinai, so in our prayers we call this holiday "the time when the Torah was given." The holiness of this day comes from the holiness of the Torah. Is there any treasure more highly valued? Gold and precious stones could not equal its worth.

We celebrate the Festival of the Torah on the sixth day of this month. HaShem brought us out of Egypt in order to give us his Torah of truth and implant spiritual and physical everlasting life within us. He brought us out from Egyptian servitude in order to sanctify us to serve him. Therefore, this holiday is indeed the conclusion to Passover, for on this day HaShem concluded his act of redemption and sealed it with the seal of the Living God.[505] Thus the joy of the holiday is greater than all the other joyful Jewish holidays.

This is the day that the world was born, the day that we stood before Mount Sinai as the mountain was enveloped in smoke with a dense cloud covering it. We heard the sound of thunder and the blasts of the shofar. Moses spoke and God answered him from within the fire, and HaShem spoke with him face to face. Everything that dwelled on earth became completely still. The bird did not screech, the ox did not plow, the fowl did not fly, even the heavenly *ofanayim*[506] stood still; the

---

505   Liberal Jewish teachers in Germany criticized this interpretation. According to them, this tradition is uncertain. The rabbis were divided on this topic (b.*Rosh HaShanah* 6b) whether the Torah was given on the morning of the sixth day of the month or the morning of the seventh. According to m.*Rosh HaShanah* 6:2 the giving of the Torah could have happened on the fifth day. The author of *Magen Avraham* discusses this, and also in *Sifrei* to Deuteronomy 16:10 the question is asked if this holiday is celebrated during the harvest. Therefore, the teachers in Germany thought that this idea of celebrating the giving of the Torah on Shavuot was a recent innovation and not practiced by our forefathers in the land of Israel—rather, that this idea was birthed sometime in the third century. However, they are mistaken. Everything that happened on this holiday testifies faithfully that HaShem chose this day as a holy day, thus we can trust that on this day the Torah was also given. Halachah agrees with this. On the sixth day of the month HaShem descended upon Mount Sinai and spoke the Ten Commandments.

506   [Spinning "wheels" as mentioned in Ezekiel 1:16 and on, Daniel 7:9, and which are considered to be angelic beings in Judaism.]

seraphim did not cry out "holy," and the sea did not stir or move. All of creation halted. The entire universe fell silent while the Most High spoke the words, "I am HaShem your God."[507]

This is the day that HaShem became King over us and we swore to be his servants and treasured people. On this day we called out, "We will do and we will obey." How could this day not become extremely holy in our eyes?

Thus, on this day, in the morning, we will sing praise for all your kindness, for on this day HaShem clothed us in majesty and splendor,[508] and we were like those about to be married,[509] and on this day he raised us up and we were alive before him.[510] On this morning we give thanks to HaShem our God and we sing the Ten Commandments to him with a ten stringed harp,[511] for this day is great to our Master.

THE GREAT REDEMPTION AND THE SPIRIT

On this day HaShem poured out his Holy Spirit on the whole assembly of the Messiah in Jerusalem and gave them wonders in heaven above and signs on earth below. We call this day "the time when the Holy Spirit was given to his assembly." This day is the conclusion to Passover, the festival of the great redemption that HaShem gave to all the peoples and to all flesh, and it shall be called "The Festival of the Redemption of Humanity from Slavery to Sin."

It was HaShem's will to renew his covenant through the sacrifice of the Messiah on the eve of Passover and to make a covenant with all the other nations of the earth. He brought his work to a completion

---

507 See *Exodus Rabbah* 29.

508 *Exodus Rabbah* 18. When Israel accepted the Torah they were clothed in majesty and splendor.

509 See *Song of Songs Rabbah*. This day was like a wedding, thus the children of Israel were like the bride.

510 See *Genesis Rabbah* to Parashat Vayera. It is written, "On the third day he will raise us up and we will live before him, etc. (Hosea 6:2). On the third day after the giving of the Torah, as it is written: 'And on the third day...' (Exodus 19:16)."

511 *Yalkut Shimoni* to Psalm 33 speaks of the harp in the Temple as having ten strings instead of seven in the days to come.

by sending the Holy Spirit to be with his assembly and to lead them to wellsprings of truth, righteousness, and virtue.

Imagine for yourself, my brother and reader, what this experience was like, with seven weeks having passed and the fiftieth day before us, all the disciples of Messiah congregated together in one place, in Jerusalem, engrossed in prayer. The words that our Master spoke to us when he was ascending to heaven are engraved before us as if with an iron stylus, saying, "You will receive power when the Holy Spirit rests upon you, and you will be my witnesses in Jerusalem and all of Judea and to all the ends of the earth.[512] For I will send the Spirit of Truth to you, and he will comfort you, and the God of all truth will comfort you."[513]

And now we pray profusely before HaShem our Father to keep his word and comfort us. Imagine a voice suddenly comes from heaven with a loud noise, and tongues of fire descend from heaven and all of us are filled with the Holy Spirit and we are speaking different languages, yet everyone hears the words in our own language. How great is our happiness! We can see that the One who hears prayers has heard our petitions and prayers, and he gave us his Holy Spirit.

CONCLUSION TO REDEMPTION

This day is a remembrance of all these acts of HaShem. On this day HaShem completed his work of redemption in that he gave the Messiah and sealed these works with the Spirit of Truth. Therefore, this holy day rises above all the other holidays. Every disciple of our Master, the Righteous Messiah, the Messiah of the Living God, will rejoice in this holiday along with all his household. This is a holiday to our Master.

This holiday causes hope to swell up within our hearts and we say:

> HaShem our God, and God of our forefathers, who redeemed us from slavery in Egypt and made us his covenanted people when he made a covenant with us on Mount Sinai; HaShem our God, who later renewed his covenant through the sacrifice of the Messiah and wrote his Torah upon our hearts,

---

512 Acts 1:8.
513 John 16:7, 12.

will never forsake his people that he chose, and he will never abandon us. On this morning when the Torah was given to Israel, when the Holy Spirit was given to his assembly, he will raise up his entire people Israel and we will live before him. With a pure heart we will worship him, and we will be a people who fears HaShem and truly thinks on his name.

NOTICE THE DIFFERENCE

Volume I Issue 1, Tishrei 5648 (1888) pgs. 7–8

The first day of Parashat Va-Etchanan—the first day of the month of July—fell on the Ninth of Av, a day of sorrow and fasting for all our Jewish brothers in the Diaspora. But if you are willing to open your eyes, look at what happened in the camp of Israel. Even though the fast day fell on the first day of the week (Sunday), when there is no commerce or work done in these lands in which we live (due to the government's laws), our Jewish brothers still did not observe the day of their mourning. Many of them did not go to the synagogues to pray, and many of the synagogues were closed and locked, as if it were just another day of the week.

Most of the Jews whom we encountered that day were eating, drinking, and enjoying themselves as if their land was not lying desolate and as if their cities were inhabited. Even the few of them who gathered together to utter laments—the Russian and the Polish Jews—did not offer the aroma of their prayers with sincerity. The words they spoke did not come from their hearts, and they did not feel sorrow over the breached walls of Jerusalem. They only spoke rote words they had learned in accordance with the prescribed ordinances of men. There are no differences between the customs of the Jews of our lands and the Jews of Poland, except the throwing of thorns and thistles at each other on the Ninth of Av.[514] Nevertheless, these Polish Jews boast that they are real Jews; they and no one else.

For all those who believe in Yeshua the Messiah, the first day of Parashat Re'eh (August 14) was a day for remembering the Messiah's lament over Jerusalem. Who could have heard the words proclaimed by the priests and yet failed to mourn over Jerusalem and her destruction? Words of sorrow, which the preachers proclaimed from their podiums, made their way into every heart and stomach, filling every person with grief and pain for the people of HaShem, the people of Israel—the people who once experienced wonders, yet now have no cure for their ailments.

Nevertheless, our Jewish brothers look contemptuously upon all those who believe in Yeshua and consider those believers to be their enemies. They degrade us as well, we who are also Israelites who issued from the founts of Judah, and rob us of the name "faithful Jew."

Not long ago, while I was traveling, I was sitting on a train with two other Jewish men. We began to converse, and they asked me what I was. I said, "I am a Jew, I am a Hebrew, and I fear the God of heaven,[515] but I believe that Yeshua, the one who was born in Bethlehem and who was pierced because of our crimes on Mount Moriah, is the faithful Messiah of whom the prophets prophesied." The two men became very angry and said, "If you believe in Yeshua, why do you call yourself a Jew?" and other such things.

Despite all of this, not one of them worries over the fate of our people. They make a laughingstock of Jerusalem and her settlements when they say, "Why do we even have Jerusalem? It is much better for us to live here, eating off the fat of the Gentiles!" We whom are driven away from receiving our portion in our Jewish heritage and whom they label as "apostates," we set our hearts, day and night, on Jerusalem and its treasured status. He who has eyes to see, look! He who has ears to hear, listen!

In all our prayers we mention Jerusalem, and everyone who reads the prayer of Rabbi Yechiel Even-Tzohar (Lichtenstein) the Chasid with

---

514 [A Polish Jewish custom on the Ninth of Av.]

515 [Jonah 1:9.]

any sort of intent will weep with us over the fate of Jerusalem. They will pray as we do, even though they have distanced themselves from us. This is the prayer:

> O LORD, in accordance with all your acts of righteousness, let your anger and wrath turn away from your city Jerusalem, your holy mountain.[516] Our Father, our King, lift a banner to the peoples to return Israel to its pasture.[517] Gather us together from the four corners of the earth to our land,[518] and plant us within its borders on the mountain of our inheritance.[519] Bring us to Zion, your city, with singing and to Jerusalem, your holy city, with eternal joy. Build it in your compassion and let it remain perched and inhabited in its place.[520] Establish your Holy Temple in it and gladden us in your House of Prayer.[521] Return your Dwelling Presence to Zion, your city, and send us Yeshua our Messiah a second time.[522] Let him reign upon the throne of David in Jerusalem, your holy city. Lift up the horn of the salvations of your people Israel in the house of David your servant—salvation from our enemies and from the hand of all who hate us, just as you have spoken through your prophets.[523] O LORD, hear! O LORD, forgive! O LORD, listen and act! Do not delay, for your own sake, our God, for your name is called upon your city and upon your people.[524] Hurry, HaShem, to help us![525] Ransom your people Israel from all its iniquities[526] and from

---

516 [Daniel 9:16.]

517 [Jeremiah 50:19.]

518 [Isaiah 11:12.]

519 [Exodus 15:17.]

520 [Zechariah 14:10.]

521 [Isaiah 56:7.]

522 Acts 3:20.

523 [Luke 1:69–71.]

524 [Daniel 9:19.]

525 [Psalm 38:23(22).]

526 [Psalm 130:8.]

all its troubles,[527] for the time to be gracious has come, for the appointed time has come.[528] Amen.

This is the prayer of a so-called "protestor" who has also been labeled as an "apostate." Now, dearest readers, if you have read these words, then please open your eyes and notice the difference between the two. Decide for yourself who is the faithful Jew with a heart continually devoted to his people. Is it we, the so-called "protestors," or is it those who presume to bear the name "Jew" but do not?[529]

---

527 [Psalm 25:22.]

528 [Psalm 102:13 (14).]

529 [Cf. Revelation 2:9. Lucky is not suggesting that his critics are not actually Jewish, rather he is employing apostolic language to state that they are not behaving as proper Jews should.]

LAMENTATIONS

Volume V Issue 3, Av 5650 (1890) pgs. 72-76

D uring the evening on the eighth of the month of Av, the fifth month from the anniversary of the exodus from Egypt, people take off their shoes after the cantor calls out *"Barchu."*[530] They also withdraw the curtain in the ark that contains the Torah scrolls, and after the evening prayers they read the book of Lamentations while sobbing and wailing, sitting on the floor, and no one says a blessing over the reading. Therefore, forgive me, dearest reader, for asking you to take a look at this book with me in order to see its good qualities and to understand why it is incumbent upon us to read it. Let us look at a few things.

THE BIBLICAL ORDER

First of all, where is it located in the Tanach? The Masoretes[531] placed it after the book of Ruth in the five *megillot.*[532] However, Martin Luther's

---

530 [A command to the congregation to bless HaShem. This word is a call to worship that introduces synagogue liturgical prayer. In this particular instance, it introduces the evening (*ma'ariv*) prayers.]

531 [Jewish scholars between the sixth and tenth centuries CE who preserved the Hebrew biblical (Masoretic) text and decided which books were canon and in which order they appear.]

532 [The five *megillot* (scrolls) are: Song of Songs, Ruth, Lamentations, Ecclesiastes, and Esther. These books appear in this order in the Hebrew Bible.]

translation places it after Jeremiah, and it is the same in Hieronymus'[533] [Vulgate] translation and in the Septuagint. Our ancient predecessors also placed it there. Thus, we can confidently assume that Josephus and the ancient leaders of the Messiah's assembly also placed it there. The talmudic sages placed it after Song of Songs, but that was merely the rabbinic opinion. Had not the Masoretes gathered these *megillot* and arranged the order as they did, we would also be compelled to place it after the book of Jeremiah.

A BOOK OF LAMENTS

Second, why was this book considered canon and added to the Holy Writings? Why was it prescribed reading on the ninth of the fifth month, the Ninth of Av? What is the meaning of this book's name? The rabbis called it *Kinnot* (Laments), and many refer to it by this name. The Septuagint, along with the ancient leaders of Messiah's assembly who lived in Greek-speaking areas called it the Book of Laments (i.e., Lamentations), or in Greek: Θρῆνοι *(Threnoy)*. The Romans called it *Lamentationes*. Many called it by the name given to it in Greek or Latin. However, its name in Hebrew, as the Midrash and even Jewish people call it today, is *Eichah*.[534]

In Hieronymus' translation he prefaces the book by saying that this is a book of Jeremiah's laments over Jerusalem when a foreign enemy destroyed Jerusalem and the Israelites went into exile. The book of laments was added to the Holy Writings because it contains the remembrance of the destruction that came upon Jerusalem and her Temple—the House of Splendor, the Holy House—to which there was nothing that could be compared among all the edifices of the peoples. Likewise, the book is a remembrance of Israel, the holy people, a people unlike any other people. The Septuagint also writes something similar to Hieronymus at the beginning of this book.

---

533 [Also known as St. Jerome.]

534 [*Eichah* comes from the word *eich* (אֵיךְ), meaning "how," but one might understand it to mean "alas," or even perhaps as an exclamatory word indicating utter woe, grief, and bewilderment.]

WRATH FROM THE SOURCE OF COMPASSION

In addition to these remembrances, the book intends to show us that there is a God who judges the earth. HaShem is that judge. Yet his actions are acts of kindness and compassion. Even in his anger he remembers his mercy, and his acts of anger come from the source of that mercy. Therefore, HaShem did not end us, for he takes no desire in the death of the "dead man," rather he desires that he should repent from his evil ways and live.

The blows that HaShem has delivered to us are the refining and smelting fires that make us like pure silver. Thus the fire of affliction cannot extinguish the fire of hope in our hearts. The heart that continues to hope, even amidst all its troubles, is a faithful witness to the fact that HaShem brings calamity upon us only in order to benefit us afterward.

How good and how pleasant is this book! It tells us that HaShem's hand is always with us! If our hearts are tormented, aching, or wounded, we should read this book. In all days of mourning and grief we must read and recount it, and it will be like balm and perfume for us.[535]

On the ninth of this month we all mourn over Zion and Jerusalem. What Jewish heart is not troubled on this day? What Jewish heart is not deeply stirred, like raging waters, when we remember how HaShem cast the glory of Judah and Israel from heaven to the ground? Therefore it is our duty to read from this book. In it we see that HaShem our God and Father was concerned about us. In it we see both his firm hand and his abundant mercy. We see the affliction that he brought upon us and the hope that he poured out into our hearts. We see the comfort by which he wants to comfort us.

THE YOKE OF ZION'S CRIMES

In the first elegy, Zion stands as a starving widow before us, weeping and wailing over her difficult days and the bitter lot that has befallen her. The lamenter speaks as if he were Zion, and she pours out her

---

535 According to halachah, it is forbidden to read the Tanach, the Mishnah, the Gemara, and to study halachah and other Jewish literature when in mourning. It is, however, permissible to read Job, Lamentations, and the depressing things in Jeremiah. See Rambam's "Laws of Mourning" 5:1.

embittered heart before us, despairs over her sins, and requests all her listeners to comfort her. She prays that God on high send her help, rescue her, and avenge her from her enemies.

In the first seven verses of the elegy, the lamenter describes the former splendor of Zion and her utter defeat. In the next seven verses, the lamenter awakens Zion to her sins, "Jerusalem has greatly sinned … therefore she has become an unclean thing,"[536] and she responds by saying, "The yoke of my crimes is bound tightly in his hand."[537] From verse 15 to 22, Zion admits that the judgment that has come against her is merited, and she confesses that her rebellion brought all these evil things upon her. In verse 22 she calls out to HaShem and asks him to deal with those who hate Zion in the same manner that he has punished her for her crimes.

After he recounts Zion's defeat, he proclaims, "Jerusalem greatly sinned … she has become an unclean thing, etc.," then he puts the words in her mouth: "The yoke of my crimes is bound tightly." She continues to speak until the end of the chapter, saying, "You have brought the day that you threatened." This is said in relation to verse 22.

Yet there is another way to parcel up this first elegy into two different sections. Up until verse 12 the lamenter speaks about Zion. In verse 12, Zion herself comes and speaks before us. For eleven verses we hear the lamenter, and for the remaining eleven verses Zion pleads her case. However, there is no section break, per se, in this chapter; we must infer one based on context within this elegy.

HASHEM LAYS SIEGE

In the second elegy, the lamenter awakens an utterance over Israel, over the people, over the daughter of Zion, yet not Zion herself. In the first elegy he mourns over the kingdom; in the second, he raises his broken cries for the children of the kingdom. When the children of the kingdom committed crimes, their Father reproached them. But they

---

536 [Lamentations 1:8.]
537 [Ibid., 1:14.]

rebelled and did not heed their Father's reproach, therefore their Father banished them from his sight and took their kingdom from them.

This second elegy describes HaShem to us as a mighty king who himself went up to Jerusalem in order to wreak havoc upon her and fight against her. He did not merely send out his generals to war against her; he himself waged war. He himself did these things, and he himself carried out a slaughter on the battlefield. HaShem has laid waste without pity,[538] he has demolished in his wrath,[539] he has destroyed and broken her bars,[540] and so on. The lamenter depicts all these scenes for us as a masterful artist with his stylus. He shows us everything that happened to the inhabitants of Zion in the days of siege.

He also tells us something that we have never heard before in all of human history—women ate the fruit of their own wombs; they devoured their newborn babies![541] He calls upon the inhabitants of the city to pour out their words [of supplication] before HaShem,[542] for he both wounds and bandages; the same hands that deal crushing blows also work healing. He hears prayers and is quick to be compassionate.

Throughout the entire elegy, the lamenter speaks to the daughter of Zion. We do not know if he is actually the speaker, or if he is quoting someone else. Perhaps it is the city of Zion speaking. She proclaims all these words to her daughter, "the daughter of Zion," and afterward turns to HaShem and says, "Look, HaShem, and take notice!"[543] Queen Zion says, "Those whom I bore and raised my enemy has consumed."[544] However, this is not the place to elaborate on this.

THE MIDPOINT OF REPENTANCE

The third elegy is the midpoint of all five of these elegies. In it, one man laments about all the evil that has happened to him, "I am the

---

538 Ibid., 2:2.
539 Ibid.
540 Ibid., 2:9.
541 Ibid., 2:20.
542 Ibid., 2:18–19.
543 Ibid., 2:20.
544 Ibid., 2:22.

man who has seen affliction by the rod of his wrath[545] ... upon no one but me does he bring down his hand repeatedly, all day long[546] ... for he has made me the target of his arrows."[547] In this manner the man lamented.

Amidst the troubles and the evils that the Most High brought upon him, he sees the tender mercies of HaShem and trusts in him, for the mercies of HaShem are never ending. They are new every morning. Thus, he puts his hope in him, and thus he sits alone silently, hoping in the goodness and salvation of HaShem. HaShem does not desire to oppress the oppressed. Rather, he desires and wishes only to turn them toward life. About what can a living human being complain? Should man not suffer for his sins? There is nothing else to do but return to HaShem. All the things that befell him inspired him toward repentance, but afterward he prays that HaShem would enact vengeance on his adversaries and contend with those who hate him.

A FINAL CRY OF RETURN

In the fourth and fifth elegies the lamenter repeatedly reiterates the same laments that he spoke in the first and second elegies. He laments over the evils that befell the good, righteous, and generous people in Israel. The fourth elegy informs us that, had it not been for the sins of Zion's worthless prophets and the transgressions of her bloodthirsty priests, HaShem would not have poured out all his wrath. As he speaks all the thoughts rushing into his mind, he feels enraged and proclaims to Edom, "The cup shall also pass to you!"[548] And to Zion he says, "Your transgression has been expiated."[549]

In the fifth elegy he calls out a prayer, "HaShem, remember what has befallen us,[550] for evil has occurred to us at home and evil has

---

545 Ibid., 3:1.

546 Ibid., 3:3.

547 Ibid., 3:12.

548 Ibid., 4:21.

549 Ibid., 4:22.

550 Ibid., 5:1.

occurred to us abroad. Why have you forgotten us forever?"[551] When the lamenter concluded all his words, he cried out, "Return us to you HaShem and let us return!"[552]

Who knows how many other elegies he lamented? All the others have been lost, only these five remain for us. Therefore, they were added to the Holy Writings, for that is what they are. They will avail us if, when we read them, we allow them to elicit our sympathy.

JEREMIAH THE LAMENTER

When was this book written? Most importantly, who is the author? There are myriads of answers to this last question. Tradition tells us that Jeremiah was the author of this book. This tradition has been passed down orally. There are those who call these laments and wailings the "Songs of Jeremiah." Our rabbis say, "Jeremiah wrote the book that bears his name, 1 and 2 Kings, and Lamentations."[553] I have already cited Hieronymus' words and mentioned the Septuagint, both of which attribute the book to Jeremiah.

The Aramaic translation called "*Peshitta*" also cites Jeremiah as the author. The Targum[554] we have for Lamentations begins with the words, "Jeremiah, prophet and high priest." The church leaders in the third century also said that Jeremiah was the author. Perhaps the works of Josephus also confirm the matter. In *Antiquities of the Jews* (10:74–80/v.1), Josephus says that Jeremiah wrote lamentations over Josiah and so on.[555]

LITERARY COMPARISON

Critical scholars of our present century claim that other authors wrote this book. However, they have not sufficiently proven their case to us,

---

551 Ibid., 5:20.

552 Ibid., 5:21.

553 b.*Bava Batra* 15a.

554 [Aramaic translation of the Scriptures. Usually referring to Targum Jonathan in particular.]

555 [Josephus, *Antiquities* 10:74–80/v.1; cf. 2 Chronicles 35:25.]

and there are yet other scholars, equally as educated as they, who hold to the traditional opinion. The strongest indication that Jeremiah wrote the book is that both the book of Jeremiah and Lamentations were written in the same style and spirit. The language and the concepts in both books bear the same attributes.

A bereaved heart and mournful soul speak in both. The things that happened to the man who saw affliction by the rod of HaShem's wrath are the things that happened to Jeremiah. For instance, the man who saw affliction laments, "My enemies have ensnared me like a bird for no reason; they have ended my life in a pit, etc."[556] Who else was in a pit but Jeremiah? Jeremiah 38:6 tells us that his enemies placed him in a pit.

In this book the lamenter proclaims multiple times that Zion's defeat came by way of her sins. In his book, Jeremiah proclaims, "For you ask yourself, 'Why have all these things happened to me?' It is because of your great iniquity that your skirts have been lifted up and your limbs have been exposed."[557] He also proclaims in the name of HaShem, "And I will also lift your skirts over your face and your shame will be seen."[558] There are many other similar passages.

The lamenter complains about the worthless prophets and their shallow, insubstantial prophecies, and he complains about the iniquitous and sinful priests whose hands are covered in the blood of the righteous. Jeremiah cries out, "The priests never asked, 'Where is HaShem?' The shepherds committed crimes against me and the prophets prophesied by Baal![559] The prophets prophesied falsely and the priests acted accordingly.[560] The prophets prophesied falsely in my name," etc.[561]

The lamenter weeps over the fact that all of Zion's neighbors have betrayed her.[562] Jerusalem called out to her lovers but they deceived her. Concerning this Jeremiah also cries out and proclaims, "What

---

556 Lamentations 3:52–53.

557 Jeremiah 13:22.

558 Ibid., 13:26.

559 Ibid., 2:8.

560 Ibid., 5:31.

561 Ibid., 14:14.

562 Lamentations 1:2.

good is it for you to go to Egypt?[563] How much you cheapen yourself by changing your course! You shall be shamed by Egypt, just as you were shamed by Assyria.[564] You will also come away from it with your hands on your head.[565] All your lovers who once strengthened you and gave you confidence will no longer come to dote on you."

COMPOSED OUT OF DESTRUCTION

If Jeremiah is indeed the lamenter and the author of Lamentations, then this book was written after Nebuchadnezzar captured the city. It must have been written during the time when Nebuzaradan, chief of the guards, came and burned down the House of our God and all the houses in Jerusalem, tearing down the walls that surrounded her.[566] The lamenter says:

> Jerusalem weeps at night because all her lovers have betrayed her and have become her enemies.[567] Zion's roads are in mourning, empty of festival pilgrims; all her gates have been deserted, her priests groan, her maidens have been afflicted, and it is utterly bitter for her.[568] Even her children are left desolate, because the enemy prevailed.[569] Her priests and her elders have perished in the city,[570] for HaShem has ended festival and Sabbath in Zion.[571] The elders of Zion have sat on the ground and strewn dust on their heads.[572] Therefore she must arise at the beginning of the watch and pour out her heart like water,[573] for the sacred gems have been spilled

---

563 Jeremiah 2:18.

564 Ibid., 2:36.

565 Ibid., 2:37. A gesture symbolizing utter grief.

566 Ibid., 52:12–14.

567 Lamentations 1:2.

568 Ibid., 1:4.

569 Ibid., 1:16.

570 Ibid., 1:19.

571 Ibid., 2:6.

572 Ibid., 2:10.

573 Ibid., 2:19.

out at every street corner.[574] Those who were raised in purple embrace refuse heaps.[575] Even the steps of the children of Israel were monitored, and they could not go about in the streets.[576] They have tormented women in Zion, maidens in the cities of Judah.[577] The elders have left the gates and the young men have left their music.[578]

All these things would seem to indicate that the destruction is complete and the siege is over. According to the lamenter, the people search for bread and have bartered their treasured possessions in order to preserve their lives.[579] The priests and the elders perished in the city as they searched for food,[580] Zion's infants lie faint on every street corner, and women eat the fruit of their own wombs.[581] The tongue of the suckling child cleaves to its palate out of thirst; infants ask for bread, yet not one morsel is given them.[582] Those who were slain by the sword are better off than those slain by hunger. The very hands of compassionate women cooked their own children.[583]

The lamenter is speaking of the days of siege here. However, the lamenter says, "Her gates have sunken to the ground, he has destroyed and broken her bars; her king and officials are exiled among the nations, and there is no Torah."[584] He also says, "The breath of our nostrils—the messiah[585] of HaShem—was captured in their traps; it was in his shadow that we thought we would live among the nations."[586] He also says, "The foe has laid hands on everything that is precious to

---

574 Ibid., 4:1.

575 Ibid., 4:5.

576 Ibid., 4:18.

577 Ibid., 5:11.

578 Ibid., 5:14.

579 Ibid., 1:11.

580 Ibid., 1:19.

581 Ibid., 2:19–20.

582 Ibid., 4:4.

583 Ibid., 4:9–10.

584 Ibid., 2:9.

585 [The Hebrew word here is *mashiach*. Most translations read "anointed."]

586 Lamentations 4:20.

her, for she has seen that nations have invaded her sanctuary.[587] Then HaShem rejected his altar, reviled his Sanctuary, handing over the walls of its citadels to the enemy,[588] and priest and prophet are killed in the Sanctuary of HaShem."[589]

The reader could decide that the lamenter is speaking these things during the days of destruction, during the time when the inhabitants of Jerusalem were going into exile and the wicked enemy was striking down everything holy. The third lament, however, makes it difficult for us to judge the correct time period that it was written. Even if he had written this book long after Israel went into exile, it still does not account for the encouraging and positive tenor of his words.

Therefore, I believe that Jeremiah began to write these laments prior to the arrival of Nebuzaradan but was unable to finish them. In fact, he wrote lamentation after lamentation, filling many books. Finally, after a very long time, Jeremiah finished his laments and compiled all of them into only one book: this book. This is my opinion.

And you, delightful reader, forgive me if I have prolonged this explanation. I still have much to say about this book. However, for your sake, I will stop here and wish you peace from the Prince of Peace, the breath of our nostrils—the Messiah of HaShem—in whose shadow we will live among the nations.

---

587 Ibid., 1:10.

588 Ibid., 2:7.

589 Ibid., 2:20.

CLEAR EVIDENCE

THAT THE MESSIAH SON OF DAVID
IS ALSO THE SON OF GOD

Volume II Issue 7, Tishrei 5650 (1890) pgs. 7–9

Let us imagine that we live in a time when Jews dwelt securely on their own land, still holding fast to the covenant that their God had made with them; a time when they possessed all the advantages of belonging to their nation and participating in their religion. A time when all the nations of the earth were ignorant, serving idols, unaware of the one true God. Let us pretend that I am a Gentile, belonging to one of these ignorant, wretched nations, and that one of you Jews, in your compassion upon this ignorant wretch, attempted to convince me to leave my idolatry and cleave to the knowledge of the true God.

Let us continue to imagine that I discovered that I wanted to believe your counsel, but only if you could prove to me that truth resided with you and that I was walking in error. If you could, then I would favorably receive your call to ascend to Jerusalem with you for one of the great festivals, just as all Israelite men gather to the holy city to worship HaShem in his holy Sanctuary. On this pilgrimage my eyes would behold how the Jews flock to one central location, turning their faces toward Zion, for she is their final destination. I would watch as the feet of those masses of people brought them closer to Jerusalem, and how they would all congregate in that holy place upon their arrival.

IS THIS YOUR GOD?

Longing to see how the Jews worship their God, I would lift up my eyes and see a massive and splendorous edifice. The Jews fall down onto the ground before it when they see it, as if they were worshiping it.

I would ask my beloved companion, "What are you all doing here?"

He would answer me, saying, "Here, in this place, we congregate to worship God, the Creator of heaven and earth."

And I, in my innocence, would continue to ask, "So where is your God? Is he the amazing and splendorous thing that I behold standing before me? For I notice that everyone kneels before it as if they were worshiping it. Is this your God?"

Perhaps my friend would laugh at my lack of understanding and say, "No my friend, this is not our God."

And I would hastily respond to him, "If so, then why do you worship and pray to it?"

He would answer, "We do not worship it nor do we pray to it. What we are doing, rather, is worshiping and praying *in front of it.*"

"Why do this if it is not your God?"

"This entity at which we are looking is merely a structure. We do not pray to nor plead to the structure. This is the Sanctuary of the Living God. He desired to reside in it, and we pray in the direction of his dwelling place within the Sanctuary. We kneel and bow down in that direction."

CAN HE BE RESTRICTED?

Now I, in my astonishment over this, would exclaim belligerently, "So then can he be restricted? What are you telling me? Can it be that the god you have decided is omnipresent—in heaven and on earth—can be contained within the walls of this building? Is not the whole world his kingdom?"

Even though my fellow would respond and say that God can be in every place and also dwell physically in this Sanctuary, I would nevertheless maintain that I absolutely could not understand this. For if God can be found in every place *while* he is in the Sanctuary, then why is there any need to leave your houses or residences in order to come here from long distances and worship him? Is it not preferable to worship God where you live?

Even though my fellow would continue to explain that truly all God's creatures can worship him—and do worship him—in every place, he desired to bestow upon every child of Israel the advantage of ascending to appear before him in Jerusalem—the place in which he chose to dwell and reveal his glory in actuality. Nevertheless, it would be difficult for my heart to understand.

My misunderstandings would most likely keep me from accepting this honorable faith. Doubts would continue to persist in my heart. And after the burning of the holy Sanctuary, I might ridicule you by asking, "Now what do you think has become of the God of Israel? Was he in the Sanctuary when it was engulfed in flames?" You would say that God is a spirit and that the burning of the Sanctuary could not harm him. And I counter that, if God really resided within this House, his divine power should have been able to extinguish the fire that Nebuchadnezzar ignited that destroyed his Temple.

Undoubtedly you would respond that indeed he had the ability to do so if he desired, but he allowed this to happen because of your transgressions, and that because Israel violated his Torah, even the House that bears his name would be burned down. While you were giving me this explanation you would surely tell me that even though this Sanctuary has been destroyed as a result of your transgressions, you nevertheless believe it will be rebuilt and reestablished in honor and majesty, surpassing that of the first, and that there will yet again be a dwelling place for the Living God.

THE APOSTLE'S LESSON

And now, honorable people! This is what the apostle says:

> Allow me to describe another matter to you in speaking of the similarities between the Sanctuary and the Messiah. Behold, you believe that God, who is omnipresent, can make the Sanctuary in Jerusalem his abode, and that he will not become the Sanctuary and the Sanctuary will not become God. The Sanctuary remains what it always was—a build-

ing, a work of human hands. And God will remain as he always was—without change or variation. Yet he made this Sanctuary his physical abode. You worship him continually in it, even though he is present in everything and rules the whole universe.

In a similar way we also believe that the God of Israel, who resided in the Sanctuary while the old covenant was in effect, wanted to reveal himself and make for himself a Sanctuary for when the new covenant took effect. The difference is that instead of choosing a sanctuary in the form of an edifice, he wanted to reveal himself in the bodily form of a man, and he made the human nature of the Messiah (his body, soul, and spirit) his dwelling place.

God will not become man and man will not become God. The qualities of God will not change and become like man's, and man's qualities will not change and become like God's. No, the humanity of the everlasting Messiah will be what it was from the very beginning, just as God will also remain what he was: without change or variation. The only difference is that the Messiah will be become the divine Sanctuary and the chosen resting place and, without ceasing to be present in every place, it is *in him* that God desires to dwell, receive worship, and rule over the entire universe:

When, because of Israel's transgressions, God allowed the Sanctuary to be destroyed and burned, so too, he allowed the sanctuary of his body to be destroyed because of the transgressions of *all* mankind. And just as the Israelites believe this Sanctuary—this building—will be rebuilt and that there will yet again be a Temple for God, so too, in accordance with the words of his prophets, the God of Israel raised up the body of the Messiah from the dead on the third day. He not only did that, but he also gave that body greater honor and majesty than before. He gave it eternal life, so that it

will never see destruction, because he desired to make it
his dwelling place yet again, nevermore to separate from it.

This is how the apostle describes the similarities between the Sanctuary and the Messiah. His words made a good impression, for he used the foundations of the old covenant to shed light on the foundations of the new. He was happy because he knew that the revelation of God in his Temple in Jerusalem was a precious and astounding model of his revelation in flesh. It is confirmation that Yeshua of Nazareth is truly the Son of God.

PROCLAIMED TO US ALL ALONG

And now we shall continue to prove that this lesson in the divinity of the Messiah—or, what we mean to say, that Yeshua of Nazareth is the Son of God—is not a fictitious thing contrived by man, nor is it a new teaching invented by Christians or Messianic Jews. Rather it is something that is holy and true, revealed to us in the Holy Writings. Thus we say that this has been proclaimed to us all along through the signs and wonders written of in the Tanach, and then, using those writings, we proved that the lesson of the new covenant on this matter is in full agreement with that of the old.

מִי? הוּא!
WHO? HIM!

מִי יַעֲלֶה לָּנוּ הַשָּׁמְיִם?
הֲלֹא תֵדְעוּ מִי יָרַד אַרְצָה מֵהָאָב
וְשָׁם מֵעֲלֵי הַר־שְׁפָיִם
עָלָה שְׁחָקִים עַל כַּנְפֵי־עָב
עַל כֵּס־שַׁדַּי לִימִין אֱלֹהִים
הוּא יוֹשֵׁב בָּרֹאשׁ, כַּאֲשֶׁר שְׁמַעְתֶּם
וְלְאֵבָרָיו קוֹרֵא הָרֹאשׁ מִגְּבוֹהִים
„בַּאֲשֶׁר אֲנִי, שָׁם תִּהְיוּ גַם אַתֶּם."

Who among us to the heavens may ascend?
You know who descended from the Father's heights,
And there on the barren mount where they stand
On the wings of a cloud he ascended the skies;
Upon the throne of Shaddai, positioned at God's right
He sits as the head, just as you know,
And the head calls to all his limbs from on high
"Where I am, there shall you be also."